LIVING *the* WORD

Scripture Reflections and Commentaries
for Sundays and Holy Days

Dianne Bergant, C.S.A., and
Rev. James A. Wallace, C.Ss.R

NOVEMBER 28, 2010 THROUGH NOVEMBER 20, 2011   YEAR A

LIVING *the* WORD

**Scripture Reflections and Commentaries
for Sundays and Holy Days**

Vol. 26   November 28, 2010–November 20, 2011

Published annually

Individual copy: $14.95
(2-9 copies: $10.95 per copy;
10-24 copies: $9.95 per copy;
25-99 copies: $8.95 per copy;
100 or more copies: $6.95 per copy)

Editors: Michael E. Novak and Alan J. Hommerding
Copy and Production Editor: Marcia T. Lucey
Typesetter: Tejal Patel
Cover Design: Jane Pitz and Tejal Patel
Director of Publications: Mary Beth Kunde-Anderson

In accordance with c. 827, with the material having been found free from any doctrinal or moral error, permission to publish is granted on August 4, 2010, by the Very Reverend John F. Canary, Vicar General of the Archdiocese of Chicago.

Copyright © 2010 by World Library Publications,
the music and liturgy division of J. S. Paluch Company, Inc.
3708 River Road, Suite 400, Franklin Park, IL 60131-2158
800 566-6150 • fax 888 957-3291
wlpcs@jspaluch.com • www.wlpmusic.com
All rights reserved.

Printed in the United States of America
WLP 006772 • (ISSN) 1079-4670 • (ISBN) 978-1-58459-493-2

Our liturgy presumes that those who gather for Eucharist, as members of the body of Christ, are already familiar with the word that they hear proclaimed every Sunday. *Living the Word* is designed to assist individuals, homilists, catechumens, candidates, discussion groups, religious education classes, and similar gatherings to deepen that familiarity with the Sunday scriptures.

Inside this book you will find the readings for each Sunday, holy day, and major celebration from November 2010 through November 2011, Year A of the liturgical cycle. Each day's readings are preceded by a brief passage intended to suggest a focus or approach to consider while reading these particular scriptures. The readings are followed by a commentary that provides a context for understanding them, making use of biblical scholarship and the Church's longstanding traditions. Then a reflection is offered that expands upon the initial focus and incorporates the fuller understanding from the commentary section. The discussion questions and suggestions for responses that follow are provided as helps to move from reflection to action, since the word of God always invites us to respond not only with our hearts but with our hands and lives as well.

When reflecting on the scriptures in a group setting or individually, it is best to do so in the context of prayer. Users of this book are encouraged to create an atmosphere that will foster prayerful reflection: in a quiet space, perhaps with lit candle and simple seasonal decoration (incense or soft music may also be appropriate), begin with a prayer and reading of the scriptures aloud for that day, even if you are alone. In a group, encourage members to focus on one word or idea that especially strikes them. Continue with each reading the same way, perhaps taking time to share these ideas with one another.

After you have sat quietly with the readings, ask yourself how they have changed you, enlightened you, moved you. Move on to the commentary, reflection, and response. Allow the discussion questions to shape your conversation, and try the "response" on for size. Will you rise to its challenge? Does it give you an idea of something to try in your own life? Share your ideas with someone else, even if you have been preparing alone.

Once you have spent a suitable time in reflection or discussion, you may wish to make a prayerful response to the readings by means of a song or a blessing of someone or something. Pray spontaneously as you think about the texts' meaning for you, or invite people in the group to offer prayers informally.

Finally, challenge yourself, or each other in your group, to take action this week based on your understanding of the readings. You may propose your own prayer for help to undertake this mission or simply stand in a circle and pray the Lord's Prayer. If you are in a group, offer one another a sign of peace before departing. If alone, surprise someone with a sign of peace, either in person, by making a phone call, or offering a simple prayer.

As you repeat this pattern over time, your prayerful reflection can deepen your appreciation of God's word and enable you to live it more fully every day.

Table of Contents

Prayers Before Reading Scripture

Lord Jesus,
we give you praise.
Speak to us as we read your word,
and send your Spirit into our hearts.
Guide us today and each day in your service,
for you are our way, our truth, our life.
Lord Jesus, we love you:
keep us in your love for ever and ever. Amen!

or

Blessed are you, Lord God,
king of all creation:
you have taught us by your word.
Open our hearts to your Spirit,
and lead us on the paths of Christ your Son.
All praise and glory be yours for ever. Amen!

or

Lord, open our hearts:
let your Spirit speak to us
as we read your word. Amen!

or

Lord Jesus,
to whom shall we go?
You have the words of eternal life.

Speak, Lord,
your servants are listening:
here we are, Lord,
ready to do your will. Amen!

Prayers After Reading Scripture

Blessed are you, Lord God,
maker of heaven and earth,
ruler of the universe:
you have sent your Holy Spirit
to teach your truth to your holy people.
We praise you for letting us read your word today.

Grant that we may continue to think and pray
over the words we have read,
and to share your thoughts with others
throughout this day.

Loving God, we praise you
and thank you in Jesus' name. Amen!

or

God of all graciousness, we thank you
for speaking to us today
through your holy word. Amen!

The liturgical seasons of Advent and Christmas present us with a very challenging scenario of the reign of God. With a few exceptions, the first readings come from Isaiah—the Advent readings from First Isaiah, the Christmas readings from Second and Third Isaiah. This prophetic book is known for its focus on the reign of God that will transform the minds and hearts of women and men. This is the year when the Gospel according to Matthew takes center stage in our liturgical reflection. It, too, calls our attention to the reign of God, and its second major focus is the person of Jesus as the one who inaugurates this reign. The second readings for these two seasons tell us what it is like to live in that reign. Looking briefly at the readings of these two seasons, we might say that Advent looks forward to the glorious transformation of God's reign and Christmas rejoices in the day of its dawning.

Mary plays an important role in both Advent and Christmas. In the Gospel readings she is presented as a role model for those who would participate in the reign of God. In the scene of the Annunciation (proclaimed on the solemnity of the Immaculate Conception), she is portrayed as a willing participant in God's plan even though she does not understand it (Luke 1:26–38). On the solemnity of the Blessed Virgin Mary, the Mother of God (January 1), we see her in contemplative reflection on the role that her son will play in establishing the reign of God (Luke 2:16–21). She welcomes those of another faith who come in search of her son (Epiphany, Matthew 2:1–12), and she becomes a refugee in order to save his life (Holy Family, Matthew 2:13–15, 19–23).

The readings of these seasons also exemplify God's loving concern for those who are on the margins of society. Advent's pictures of a future reign of peace and harmony are really promises of restoration. The prophetic words were spoken to people who had been crushed by political collapse or economic hardship. Only such people would look forward to some form of transformation. The wondrous events described in the Christmas Gospels were participated in or witnessed by a young betrothed girl who lived in a patriarchal society, poor shepherds who were often despised by the more respectable members of society, and foreigners who, despite their abilities and possessions, were led astray by those in power. The reign of God will only be accepted by those who are open to the newness of God.

Advent and Christmas are not merely seasons for children. They are seasons for those who, like children, are dependent on the goodness of others, namely God. They look toward a better life, not because people are successful and secure, but because they are loved. They promise the greatest gift of all, the generosity of God in the person of Jesus.

November 28, 2010

FIRST SUNDAY OF ADVENT

Today's Focus: Something's Coming

The season of Advent/Christmas, indeed, the entire liturgical year, opens with a poetic description of the reign of God, a reign of peace for which we all yearn. This Sunday also contains a caution to be prepared for its coming, because we do not really know when that day will dawn.

FIRST READING
Isaiah 2:1–5

This is what Isaiah, son of Amoz,
saw concerning Judah and Jerusalem.
   In days to come,
the mountain of the LORD's house
   shall be established as the highest mountain
   and raised above the hills.
All nations shall stream toward it;
   many peoples shall come and say:
"Come, let us climb the LORD's mountain,
   to the house of the God of Jacob,
that he may instruct us in his ways,
   and we may walk in his paths."
For from Zion shall go forth instruction,
   and the word of the LORD from Jerusalem.
He shall judge between the nations,
   and impose terms on many peoples.
They shall beat their swords into plowshares
   and their spears into pruning hooks;
one nation shall not raise the sword against another,
   nor shall they train for war again.
O house of Jacob, come,
   let us walk in the light of the LORD!

PSALM RESPONSE
Psalm 122:1

Let us go rejoicing to the house of the Lord.

SECOND READING
Romans 13: 11–14

Brothers and sisters: You know the time; it is the hour now for you to awake from sleep. For our salvation is nearer now than when we first believed; the night is advanced, the day is at hand. Let us then throw off the works of darkness and put on the armor of light; let us conduct ourselves properly as in the day, not in orgies and drunkenness, not in promiscuity and lust, not in rivalry and jealousy. But put on the Lord Jesus Christ, and make no provision for the desires of the flesh.

GOSPEL
Matthew 24: 37–44

Jesus said to his disciples: "As it was in the days of Noah, so it will be at the coming of the Son of Man. In those days before the flood, they were eating and drinking, marrying and giving in marriage, up to the day that Noah entered the ark. They did not know until the flood came and carried them all away. So will it be also at the coming of the Son of Man. Two men will be out in the field; one will be taken, and one will be left. Two women will be grinding at the mill; one will be taken, and one will be left. Therefore, stay awake! For you do not know on which day your Lord will come. Be sure of this: if the master of the house had known the hour of night when the thief was coming, he would have stayed awake and not let his house be broken into. So too, you also must be prepared, for at an hour you do not expect, the Son of Man will come."

❖ Understanding the Word

The first reading contains a vision of universal peace and an invitation to participate in that peace through faithfulness to God's word. The image of the reign of God found in the reading from Isaiah is of a city, not known for its political prominence or military might, but revered as the dwelling place of God. This is a vision of the future reign of God, of an eschatological age of complete faithfulness to God and the peace and harmony among people that will flow from it.

Paul, too, speaks about the reign of God, but from a different perspective. He tells the Roman Christians that they are living in a decisive moment, the *kairós*, the period of transition from the age of sin to the long-awaited age of fulfillment. Paul employs several images to characterize this division of time. He says that this age is like slumber, or night and darkness, while the age to come is like wakefulness, or day and light. He urges the Christians to wake from sleep and to live in faithfulness. The apparent incongruity between these two ages exemplifies the paradox that we sometimes hear, "already but not yet." It is a way of acknowledging that the age of fulfillment, the reign of God, has already dawned, but it has not yet been brought to completion in our lives.

Jesus also speaks about this transition from one age to the next. The question he addresses is not whether this time will come, but when it will come. Like a good teacher he uses examples to make his point. The people at the time of Noah were oblivious to the danger that faced them and so they were not ready. The same was true in the analogies he uses of the men and women, and the parable of the householder, all of whom blindly go about their daily lives. The moral of the story? Be prepared!

9

The musical *West Side Story* was revived in New York City recently. The first song is "Something's Coming." Tony, a young man, senses something wonderful approaching but he does not know what. That very night he will meet Maria and fall in love. On the cusp of this new world opening up before him, he sings about his heightened sense of anticipation that something miraculous is about to happen, and it's just out of his reach.

It is that kind of excitement that today's readings are meant to evoke in us. There is something wonderful coming in our future—something no eye has seen or ear heard, something that God has ready for those who love God. But have we stopped looking forward to "something coming"? Have we given up on the hope that something new is coming, that a miracle is due, and at any moment, possible?

Jesus calls to us across the centuries in Matthew's Gospel, at a moment when he is about to enter Jerusalem to die. He calls on us to live in hope that at any moment God's rule can be experienced, that the peace that only God can give will touch our lives and suddenly settle on our hearts and minds.

How can we prepare for this sudden coming of God's presence? Try to live consciously aware of what we proclaim every week in the liturgy: Christ has died, Christ has risen, Christ will come again.

✣ *Consider/Discuss*

- When was the last time you looked forward to something in a way that made you feel fully alive, alert, and awake?
- Do you believe that the day is coming when God will reign, bringing all nations to live in peace and harmony?

✣ *Responding to the Word*

We pray every week: "Thy kingdom come, thy will be done on earth as it is in heaven." Pray it daily as if for the first time. Ask God to allow the kingdom to come to your family, to your workplace, in your neighborhood, among the people of your city, country, and world.

December 5, 2010

SECOND SUNDAY OF ADVENT

Today's Focus: Visions and Prophecies

Today the biblical authors sketch models for us as we embark on our journey to eschatological fulfillment. Isaiah depicts the righteous messianic king; Paul provides us with a glimpse of Jesus who ministers to all; and Matthew describes John the Baptist, the prophet who prepared for the advent of Christ.

FIRST READING
Isaiah 11:1–10

On that day, a shoot shall sprout from the stump of Jesse,
and from his roots a bud shall blossom.
The spirit of the Lord shall rest upon him:
a spirit of wisdom and of understanding,
a spirit of counsel and of strength,
a spirit of knowledge and of fear of the LORD,
and his delight shall be the fear of the LORD.
Not by appearance shall he judge,
nor by hearsay shall he decide,
but he shall judge the poor with justice,
and decide aright for the land's afflicted.
He shall strike the ruthless with the rod of his mouth,
and with the breath of his lips he shall slay the wicked.
Justice shall be the band around his waist,
and faithfulness a belt upon his hips.
Then the wolf shall be a guest of the lamb,
and the leopard shall lie down with the kid;
the calf and the young lion shall browse together,
with a little child to guide them.
The cow and the bear shall be neighbors,
together their young shall rest;
the lion shall eat hay like the ox.
The baby shall play by the cobra's den,
and the child lay his hand on the adder's lair.
There shall be no harm or ruin on all my holy mountain;
for the earth shall be filled with knowledge of the LORD,
as water covers the sea.
On that day, the root of Jesse,
set up as a signal for the nations,
the Gentiles shall seek out,
for his dwelling shall be glorious.

PSALM RESPONSE
Psalm 72:7

Justice shall flourish in his time, and fullness of peace forever.

SECOND READING
Romans 15: 4–9

Brothers and sisters: Whatever was written previously was written for our instruction, that by endurance and by the encouragement of the Scriptures we might have hope. May the God of endurance and encouragement grant you to think in harmony with one another, in keeping with Christ Jesus, that with one accord you may with one voice glorify the God and Father of our Lord Jesus Christ.

Welcome one another, then, as Christ welcomed you, for the glory of God. For I say that Christ became a minister of the circumcised to show God's truthfulness, to confirm the promises to the patriarchs, but so that the Gentiles might glorify God for his mercy.

As it is written:
Therefore, I will praise you among the Gentiles
and sing praises to your name.

GOSPEL
Matthew 3: 1–12

John the Baptist appeared, preaching in the desert of Judea and saying, "Repent, for the kingdom of heaven is at hand!" It was of him that the prophet Isaiah had spoken when he said:
A voice of one crying out in the desert,
Prepare the way of the Lord,
make straight his paths.

John wore clothing made of camel's hair and had a leather belt around his waist. His food was locusts and wild honey. At that time Jerusalem, all Judea, and the whole region around the Jordan were going out to him and were being baptized by him in the Jordan River as they acknowledged their sins.

When he saw many of the Pharisees and Sadducees coming to his baptism, he said to them, "You brood of vipers! Who warned you to flee from the coming wrath? Produce good fruit as evidence of your repentance. And do not presume to say to yourselves, 'We have Abraham as our father.' For I tell you, God can raise up children to Abraham from these stones. Even now the ax lies at the root of the trees. Therefore every tree that does not bear good fruit will be cut down and thrown into the fire. I am baptizing you with water, for repentance, but the one who is coming after me is mightier than I. I am not worthy to carry his sandals. He will baptize you with the Holy Spirit and fire. His winnowing fan is in his hand. He will clear his threshing floor and gather his wheat into his barn, but the chaff he will burn with unquenchable fire."

❖ *Understanding the Word*

Isaiah wrote of a time when the monarchy had been conquered and there seemed to be no hope for a future king. Yet out of this "stump" a new ruler would emerge. The image of his "peaceable kingdom" recalls the primal paradise of Eden (see Genesis 2), where the animals did not follow their predatory instincts, and natural enemies lived in harmony with each other. In this new reign, all creation will be either transformed or recreated. This vision is not a return to the past, but one of future peace and fulfillment.

Paul bases his teaching of universal salvation for all on God's original promise that Abram and his descendants would be a source of blessing for others (see Genesis 12:2; 22:18). Paul argues that it was in fulfillment of this promise that the Gentiles have been brought into the family of God through the love of Christ. In his prayer for the community, he asks for three different expressions of unity: "to think in harmony," to be in "one accord," and to glorify God in "one voice" (Romans 15:5–6). This unity in no way obliterates the differences between Jew and Gentile; it is a unity in diversity.

John's baptism was neither the kind that proselytes to Judaism underwent, nor the repeated ritual cleansing that the Essene community of Qumran practiced. It was a devotional rite with eschatological significance, administered to Jews, accompanied by their acknowledgment of sinfulness and a resolve to live an ethical life. John admits his subordinate role when compared with Jesus. He, John, is the voice that announces the coming of another. The winnowing of which he speaks refers to the separation of those who respond to John's call to repentance from those who do not. John does not act as judge; the one who is to come will do the judging. In other words, the time of the Messiah will be a time of both redemption and judgment.

❖ Reflecting on the Word

Last year I went to a Christmas concert to help get myself into the Christmas spirit. The concert was moving along at a comfortable and comforting pace, enjoyable but nothing out of the ordinary, when suddenly the choir came out and sang a piece that moved me to tears. I searched the program and found its name and composer: *The Dream Isaiah Saw* by Glenn Rudolph, text by Thomas Troeger. I went home and found it online, a youth choir performing it.

Its refrain brought together the passage of Isaiah we heard today and the event that we will celebrate in a few weeks. It does this very simply with several variations for the final line: "Little child whose bed is straw, /take new lodgings in my heart. /Bring the dream Isaiah saw: /a) life redeemed from fang and claw. /b) justice purifying law. /c) knowledge, wisdom, worship, awe."

Advent is a season that sets before us visionaries and prophets like Isaiah, the missionary Paul, and the herald John. Each offers us a vision of things coming together. For Isaiah, it is all creation—animal and human; for Paul, it is Jews and Gentiles; for John it is the One who is coming to gather the wheat into his barn, God's harvest, those baptized in the Spirit.

We are brought together each Sunday to think, live, and sing in harmony to the gracious God who has come to us in Jesus Christ, the One who came filled with the spirit of the Lord, to draw us more deeply into the life so generously offered by God.

- Does the dream of Isaiah with its pairing of opposites offer hope in our own day, when there is so much division in the world, in government, and even in the Church?
- What would arouse John the Baptist's wrath today? What in our lives can be considered as worthy wheat and as chaff to be swept up and tossed into the fire?

✢ Responding to the Word

We pray this season that we may come to "think in harmony with one another, in keeping with Christ Jesus, that with one accord [we] may with one voice glorify the God and Father of our Lord Jesus Christ" (Romans 15:5–6).

December 8, 2010

THE IMMACULATE CONCEPTION OF THE BLESSED VIRGIN MARY

Today's Focus: God's Grace Draws Us Closer

Mary was not chosen because she was righteous; she was made righteous by being chosen. She is the first example of how we are all made holy by the blood of Jesus.

FIRST READING
Genesis 3: 9–15, 20

After the man, Adam, had eaten of the tree, the LORD God called to the man and asked him, "Where are you?" He answered, "I heard you in the garden; but I was afraid, because I was naked, so I hid myself." Then he asked, "Who told you that you were naked? You have eaten, then, from the tree of which I had forbidden you to eat!" The man replied, "The woman whom you put here with me—she gave me fruit from the tree, and so I ate it." The LORD God then asked the woman, "Why did you do such a thing?" The woman answered, "The serpent tricked me into it, so I ate it."

Then the LORD God said to the serpent:
"Because you have done this,
    you shall be banned from all the animals
    and from all the wild creatures;
on your belly shall you crawl,
    and dirt shall you eat
    all the days of your life.
I will put enmity between you and the woman,
    and between your offspring and hers;
he will strike at your head,
    while you strike at his heel."
The man called his wife Eve, because she became the mother of all the living.

PSALM RESPONSE
Psalm 98:1a

Sing to the Lord a new song, for he has done marvelous deeds.

SECOND READING
Ephesians 1: 3–6, 11–12

Brothers and sisters: Blessed be the God and Father of our Lord Jesus Christ, who has blessed us in Christ with every spiritual blessing in the heavens, as he chose us in him, before the foundation of the world, to be holy and without blemish before him. In love he destined us for adoption to himself through Jesus Christ, in accord with the favor of his will, for the praise of the glory of his grace that he granted us in the beloved.

In him we were also chosen, destined in accord with the purpose of the One who accomplishes all things according to the intention of his will, so that we might exist for the praise of his glory, we who first hoped in Christ.

15

GOSPEL
Luke 1:26–38
The angel Gabriel was sent from God to a town of Galilee called Nazareth, to a virgin betrothed to a man named Joseph, of the house of David, and the virgin's name was Mary. And coming to her, he said, "Hail, full of grace! The Lord is with you." But she was greatly troubled at what was said and pondered what sort of greeting this might be. Then the angel said to her, "Do not be afraid, Mary, for you have found favor with God. Behold, you will conceive in your womb and bear a son, and you shall name him Jesus. He will be great and will be called Son of the Most High, and the Lord God will give him the throne of David his father, and he will rule over the house of Jacob forever, and of his kingdom there will be no end." But Mary said to the angel, "How can this be, since I have no relations with a man?" And the angel said to her in reply, "The Holy Spirit will come upon you, and the power of the Most High will overshadow you. Therefore the child to be born will be called holy, the Son of God. And behold, Elizabeth, your relative, has also conceived a son in her old age, and this is the sixth month for her who was called barren; for nothing will be impossible for God." Mary said, "Behold, I am the handmaid of the Lord. May it be done to me according to your word." Then the angel departed from her.

❖ *Understanding the Word*

The first reading was probably chosen for this feast because the traditional depiction of Mary as the Immaculate Conception has her foot on the head of the serpent. Actually, the text has "he will strike at your head" (Genesis 3:15), not she. However, the meaning of the passage continues to be important. Since there is no mention of a "fall" from grace, it is best to think of this story simply as an account of sin. After the sin, the woman and man are naked (spiritually exposed), and they refuse to take responsibility for their fault. Each blames another. The final words state that throughout their lives, human beings will have to battle temptation.

Paul insists that salvation in Christ was not an afterthought, but was in God's plan from the beginning. Furthermore, believers are not chosen because they were holy and blameless, but that they might be made holy and blameless. In other words, salvation is the cause, not the consequence, of righteousness. Paul further states that we were destined for adoption through Christ, so we have been redeemed by his blood. Our redemption exacted a ransom, and that ransom was the shedding of Christ's blood. All this was done so that God's plan finally would be brought to fulfillment, the plan to bring all things together in Christ.

According to the passage from Matthew's Gospel, the conception of Jesus took place within the broader picture of God's plan of salvation. The angel's words are both reassuring and perplexing. Mary, a virgin, will bear a son whose name indicates the role that he will play in God's plan (Jesus means "God saves"). Her response does not question that all of this will happen according to God's plan, but she wonders how it will happen. She is also a model of openness and receptivity, regardless of the apparent impossibility of what is being asked. The reading shows that the expectations of the past are now being fulfilled.

I remember a young mother saying to me on Mother's Day, "I hope you're not going to preach to us about Mary. She makes us all feel so guilty. She never yelled or got angry. She was just perfect."

The Immaculate Conception is often seen as a feast that puts Mary at a distance from us, since she was "free from all taint of sin." But this feast is really a feast that should bring her closer.

God's presence to and love for Mary surrounded and touched her life from its beginning. This was done because of the unique role she would play in God's plan of salvation for all. Mary's role was necessary to bring to fulfillment God's desire that all be saved. So, her being graced in a unique way does not distance her from us, but places her even more at the heart of the human family.

As the Letter to the Ephesians reminds us today, God chose us in Christ before the foundation of the world "to be holy and without blemish before him" (Ephesians 1:4). God "destined us for adoption" and destined us to exist "for the praise of the glory of his grace" (Ephesians 1:5, 6). We all are destined to be drawn closer to God and each other through God's grace.

Mary's gracious response to God is a model of what God desires from each of us singly and as a community: our saying "Yes" to God's plan, so that the world can know and love and serve the living God revealed in Jesus.

❖❖ *Consider/Discuss*

- Do I think of Mary as one removed from or uniquely close to the community of believers?
- Do you see yourself as having been chosen in Christ before the foundation of the world to be holy?

❖❖ *Responding to the Word*

Today we can praise God for revealing to us that what was done for Mary is a sign of God's will for all of us, that we know ourselves as chosen by God and as existing to praise the glory of God's grace. We ask Mary to lead us more deeply into the mystery of the God who is Father, Son, and Holy Spirit.

December 12, 2010

THIRD SUNDAY OF ADVENT

Today's Focus: The Promise of Joy

Today is Gaudete Sunday, the midpoint in Advent, a time for rejoicing. As we move further into the season, we come to realize that being invited into the reign of God is the reason for our rejoicing.

FIRST READING
Isaiah 35: 1–6a, 10

The desert and the parched land will exult;
    the steppe will rejoice and bloom.
They will bloom with abundant flowers,
    and rejoice with joyful song.
The glory of Lebanon will be given to them,
    the splendor of Carmel and Sharon;
they will see the glory of the LORD,
    the splendor of our God.
Strengthen the hands that are feeble,
    make firm the knees that are weak,
say to those whose hearts are frightened:
    Be strong, fear not!
Here is your God,
    he comes with vindication;
with divine recompense
    he comes to save you.
Then will the eyes of the blind be opened,
    the ears of the deaf be cleared;
then will the lame leap like a stag,
    then the tongue of the mute will sing.
Those whom the LORD has ransomed will return
    and enter Zion singing,
    crowned with everlasting joy;
they will meet with joy and gladness,
    sorrow and mourning will flee.

PSALM RESPONSE
Isaiah 35:4

Lord, come and save us.

SECOND READING
James 5:7–10

Be patient, brothers and sisters, until the coming of the Lord. See how the farmer waits for the precious fruit of the earth, being patient with it until it receives the early and the late rains. You too must be patient. Make your hearts firm, because the coming of the Lord is at hand. Do not complain, brothers and sisters, about one another, that you may not be judged. Behold, the Judge is standing before the gates. Take as an example of hardship and patience, brothers and sisters, the prophets who spoke in the name of the Lord.

GOSPEL
Matthew 11:
2–11
When John the Baptist heard in prison of the works of the Christ, he sent his disciples to Jesus with this question, "Are you the one who is to come, or should we look for another?" Jesus said to them in reply, "Go and tell John what you hear and see: the blind regain their sight, the lame walk, lepers are cleansed, the deaf hear, the dead are raised, and the poor have the good news proclaimed to them. And blessed is the one who takes no offense at me."

As they were going off, Jesus began to speak to the crowds about John, "What did you go out to the desert to see? A reed swayed by the wind? Then what did you go out to see? Someone dressed in fine clothing? Those who wear fine clothing are in royal palaces. Then why did you go out? To see a prophet? Yes, I tell you, and more than a prophet. This is the one about whom it is written:

> *Behold, I am sending my messenger ahead of you;*
> *he will prepare your way before you.'*

Amen, I say to you, among those born of women there has been none greater than John the Baptist; yet the least in the kingdom of heaven is greater than he."

❖ Understanding the Word

Isaiah depicts two ways in which the renewal promised by God is manifested: the barren wilderness filled with new life, and the healing of those suffering some physical malady. In a world that believes that God created everything in proper order, imperfection of any kind is often perceived as a consequence of sin. This explains why healing was seen as restoration to that proper order. Such restoration was a sign of the transformation that only God can effect. It was a testimony to God's presence in the world and to God's victory over evil. God had reestablished the original order of creation, and all life began again to flourish.

Patience is the controlling theme in the second reading. *Parousía*, which means "coming" or "presence," became a technical term for the future coming of Christ to inaugurate the definitive manifestation of God's eternal dominion. Because the exact time of this advent was unknown, patience would be necessary until that day of fulfillment dawned. The example of the farmer waiting for the crop to grow and mature highlights some important aspects of this patient waiting. Believers are told to take the prophets as their models in bearing the hardships of life and in waiting patiently for the coming of the Lord.

In his response to the questions of the Baptist's followers, Jesus links his own wondrous deeds with the prophets' allusions to visions of fulfillment. Healings of the needy were all signs of the dawning of the eschatological age. They were also indications of the type of messiah that Jesus would be. Those who were expecting a political or military leader who would free them from Roman domination or a priest who would bring them together as a cultic community would be disappointed with Jesus. Jesus then states that regardless of how insignificant his followers might be, as citizens of the reign of heaven they enjoyed a privilege that John did not know.

Joy is different from happiness. Happiness is a transient experience, but joy has more depth to it, more lasting roots. It can be independent of what is going on around us. In John's Gospel, the night before he died, Jesus says to his disciples that he wants his joy to be in them and their joy to be complete (John 15:11). And Paul writes to the Thessalonians: "Rejoice always" (2 Thessalonians 5:16).

Today's readings invite us to think about what brings us joy. Isaiah offers images of a world that will blossom or bloom, flowering into fullness. The prophet gives us wonderful images of dry, parched land suddenly breaking into a colorful display of new and abundant life.

This fullness also results from something being restored that had been lost or that was missing from the start: sight, hearing, being able to sing and leap with joy, health of body and spirit. Such fullness comes from God. It is gift, pure and simple.

God wants us to have this fullness of life, to be sure. It will come with the coming of the Lord. In the meantime, we are to wait patiently, not complaining, but with hearts marked by certitude. We have assurance in that we have already been welcomed into the kingdom at our baptism. The rest is only a matter of time. In speaking of John as more than a prophet, Jesus concludes by saying, "Yet the least in the kingdom of heaven is greater than he" (Matthew 11:11).

✤ Consider/Discuss

- What makes you happy? What makes you joyful? Is there a difference?
- How is God asking you to be patient at the present time?

✤ Responding to the Word

We can ask God to give us that joy that the world cannot give, a joy that is found rooted in our faith in God, in our trusting that the God who raised Jesus up will also bring us to fullness of life.

December 19, 2010

FOURTH SUNDAY OF ADVENT

Today's Focus: Living a Dream

We are on the threshold of the eschatological age of fulfillment. Today's readings tell us that faith is required for us to step over that threshold. Before us are set two figures, two examples of human response to the call to faith: Ahaz, who failed the test, and Joseph, who, despite his quandary, was a paragon of faith.

FIRST READING
Isaiah 7:10–14

The LORD spoke to Ahaz, saying: Ask for a sign from the LORD, your God; let it be deep as the netherworld, or high as the sky! But Ahaz answered, "I will not ask! I will not tempt the LORD!" Then Isaiah said: Listen, O house of David! Is it not enough for you to weary people, must you also weary my God? Therefore the LORD himself will give you this sign: the virgin shall conceive, and bear a son, and shall name him Emmanuel.

PSALM RESPONSE
Psalm 24:7c, 10b

Let the Lord enter; he is king of glory.

SECOND READING
Romans 1:1–7

Paul, a slave of Christ Jesus, called to be an apostle and set apart for the gospel of God, which he promised previously through his prophets in the holy Scriptures, the gospel about his Son, descended from David according to the flesh, but established as Son of God in power according to the Spirit of holiness through resurrection from the dead, Jesus Christ our Lord. Through him we have received the grace of apostleship, to bring about the obedience of faith, for the sake of his name, among all the Gentiles, among whom are you also, who are called to belong to Jesus Christ; to all the beloved of God in Rome, called to be holy. Grace to you and peace from God our Father and the Lord Jesus Christ.

GOSPEL
Matthew 1: 18–24
This is how the birth of Jesus Christ came about. When his mother Mary was betrothed to Joseph, but before they lived together, she was found with child through the Holy Spirit. Joseph her husband, since he was a righteous man, yet unwilling to expose her to shame, decided to divorce her quietly. Such was his intention when, behold, the angel of the Lord appeared to him in a dream and said, "Joseph, son of David, do not be afraid to take Mary your wife into your home. For it is through the Holy Spirit that this child has been conceived in her. She will bear a son and you are to name him Jesus, because he will save his people from their sins." All this took place to fulfill what the Lord had said through the prophet:

Behold, the virgin shall conceive and bear a son,
and they shall name him Emmanuel,
which means "God is with us."

When Joseph awoke, he did as the angel of the Lord had commanded him and took his wife into his home.

❖ Understanding the Word

Isaiah tells Ahaz to ask for a sign that will confirm earlier promises made to the Davidic dynasty of which he was the present heir. Feigning humility, he refuses. The prophet then promises an *emmanuel*, which means "God with us." Since every king was considered a sign of God's presence with the people, this prophecy could have had any king in mind. It probably refers to Ahaz's yet-to-be-born son. However, the people's disappointment with the monarchy soon gave the prophecy more importance. At issue here is the fulfillment of God's promise to be present with the people, regardless of the situations in which they find themselves.

By stating that Jesus was a descendant of David, Paul attributes to him all of the promises and blessings ascribed to the person of David and to the dynasty that he had established. As a descendant of David, Jesus is a member of the people of Israel and placed squarely within the fold of human society. Paul maintains that the Gentiles (in Rome) are beloved of God, called to be holy people. The lines of initiative and responsibility are clear. God called Paul and set him apart for the ministry of the gospel. Paul is sent to the Gentiles to set them apart for God as well.

Several features of the angel's message found in the Gospel call for serious consideration. First, the Holy Spirit is probably not a reference to Trinitarian theology but to the power of God that will be experienced at the time of eschatological fulfillment. Second, the child's name, "Jesus" is the Greek form of the Hebrew, which means "YHWH is salvation." Third, a solemn formula of fulfillment is proclaimed: "[T]o fulfill what the Lord had said through the prophet" (Matthew 1:22). Fourth, the child is given a second name, Emmanuel, God with us. These two titles identify Jesus as the saving power of God and the presence of God in the midst of the people.

22

The Bible offers us a rich variety of men and women who qualify as heroes, warriors, prophets, and wise men and women. And every so often it places before us a dreamer. Jacob had the first big dream, with that ladder connecting heaven and earth, bearing ascending and descending angels.

His son Joseph started off with dreams that put himself at the center, much to his brothers' chagrin, but later he saved himself by interpreting the dreams of others, including Pharaoh. However, the most important dreamer of all was Joseph, spouse of Mary and foster father to Jesus.

Joseph was asked to live out his dream. "[D]o not be afraid to take Mary your wife into your home. For it is through the Holy Spirit that this child has been conceived in her," he was told in a dream (Matthew 1:20). And not only that, he was to name the child Jesus, which means "God saves." What all this cost him we don't know. All we hear is that when he awoke from the dream, he did what had been asked and took Mary into his home.

That wasn't the end of the dreams. "Joseph, take the mother and child into Egypt—Herod is trying to kill him." "Joseph, take the mother and child out of Egypt—Herod is dead." And Joseph did. Maybe once you begin to live God's dream it gets easier.

God's dream is that we live in the world as God's adopted and saved children, working to bring God's peace and justice, mercy and forgiveness into our world wherever they are needed.

❖❖ Consider/Discuss

- What do you think God's dream is for our world today?
- Do you know Jesus as Emmanuel (God with us)?

❖❖ Responding to the Word

We ask God to continue to save us in our own day from all that would lead us away from God. We ask God to continue to help us to know Jesus as Emmanuel, God with us, so that our faith may be rooted in the wisdom and power of God.

December 25, 2010

THE NATIVITY OF THE LORD
CHRISTMAS MASS DURING THE DAY

Today's Focus: God's Last Word

There is progression of depth in the readings chosen for Christmas. At midnight, the birth in history is proclaimed. At dawn, the initiative of God's gift is declared and the baptized community's joyful gratitude is announced. In this third celebration, we meditate on the true identity of Christ and on our own new way of life in the Word made flesh.

FIRST
READING
Isaiah 52:7-10

How beautiful upon the mountains
    are the feet of him who brings glad tidings,
announcing peace, bearing good news,
    announcing salvation, and saying to Zion,
    "Your God is King!"

Hark! Your sentinels raise a cry,
    together they shout for joy,
for they see directly, before their eyes,
    the LORD restoring Zion.
Break out together in song,
    O ruins of Jerusalem!
For the LORD comforts his people,
    he redeems Jerusalem.
The LORD has bared his holy arm
    in the sight of all the nations;
all the ends of the earth will behold
    the salvation of our God.

PSALM
RESPONSE
Psalm 98:3c

All the ends of the earth have seen the saving power of God.

SECOND
READING
Hebrews 1:1-6

Brothers and sisters: In times past, God spoke in partial and various ways to our ancestors through the prophets; in these last days, he has spoken to us through the Son, whom he made heir of all things and through whom he created the universe, who is the refulgence of his glory, the very imprint of his being, and who sustains all things by his mighty word. When he had accomplished purification from sins, he took his seat at the right hand of the Majesty on high, as far superior to the angels as the name he has inherited is more excellent than theirs.

For to which of the angels did God ever say:
>   *You are my son; this day I have begotten you?*
Or again:
>   *I will be a father to him, and he shall be a son to me?*
And again, when he leads the firstborn into the world, he says:
>   *Let all the angels of God worship him.*

In the shorter form of the reading, the passages in brackets are omitted.

GOSPEL
John 1:1-18
or 1:1-5, 9-14

In the beginning was the Word,
>   and the Word was with God,
>   and the Word was God.
He was in the beginning with God.
All things came to be through him,
>   and without him nothing came to be.

What came to be through him was life,
>   and this life was the light of the human race;
the light shines in the darkness,
>   and the darkness has not overcome it.

[A man named John was sent from God. He came for testimony, to testify to the light, so that all might believe through him. He was not the light, but came to testify to the light.] The true light, which enlightens everyone, was coming into the world.

He was in the world,
>   and the world came to be through him,
>   but the world did not know him.
He came to what was his own,
>   but his own people did not accept him.

But to those who did accept him he gave power to become children of God, to those who believe in his name, who were born not by natural generation nor by human choice nor by a man's decision but of God.

And the Word became flesh
>   and made his dwelling among us,
>   and we saw his glory,
>   the glory as of the Father's only Son,
>   full of grace and truth.

[John testified to him and cried out, saying, "This was he of whom I said, 'The one who is coming after me ranks ahead of me because he existed before me.' " From his fullness we have all received, grace in place of grace, because while the law was given through Moses, grace and truth came through Jesus Christ. No one has ever seen God. The only Son, God, who is at the Father's side, has revealed him.]

The proclamation of good news from Isaiah is dramatically portrayed in several ways. It begins with a sketch of a messenger running swiftly over the mountains with the message of peace and salvation. The people to whom the messenger runs have been desolate for so long, waiting for a ray of hope. The messenger announces that God has won victory and the people can now begin anew. Then the very ruins of the city are called on to break forth in song. Peace is no longer a hoped-for dream, nor is salvation only a promise for the future. They are now accomplished facts for which to rejoice.

The confessional hymn celebrated in the reading from Hebrews proclaims that Christ is the agent of revelation, creation, and salvation. It begins with a comparison of the ways that God communicates with humankind. In the past, God spoke to the ancestors through the prophets; in the present, God speaks a definitive word to the believers through God's own Son. Since this Son is also the Wisdom of God, it stands to reason that he would be superior even to the angels. As the agent of salvation, he sits enthroned in the place of greatest honor, at the right hand of God.

The Gospel of John begins with one of the most profound statements about Jesus found in the entire New Testament. Its lofty Christology is comparable to that found in the reading from Hebrews. Both characterize Christ as preexistent and as an agent in the creation of the world. However, the Word of God, who is also the holiness of God and the wisdom of God, now dwells in the midst of humankind. While the Word is the true light that comes into the world, John is merely the witness who testifies to the authenticity and superiority of this light. Women and men have been transformed by the love that first prompted God's revelation and Christ's incarnation.

❖ *Reflecting on the Word*

A recent movie called *The Messenger* tells the story of two soldiers on duty to inform next of kin about the death of a loved one in the wars in Iraq and Afghanistan. It poignantly portrays not only the grief that this word brings to families and loved ones but also the sorrow of those who have to deliver it.

Today's readings remind us that both those who deliver and those who receive the word of God about Jesus are entrusted with something that is lifegiving. Isaiah's messenger carries word of a birth that brings joy, hope, and song, so much so that the very feet that deliver this message are declared blessed. It is not difficult to see why this reading was chosen for Christmas.

God's own Son is the message sent to us in the fullness of time. While God is portrayed as One who turned to words from the very beginning of creation—"Let there be light"—and while God continued to speak to Abraham, Moses, and the prophets, this speech was partial and fragmentary, often seeming more like a bad connection on the receiving end for all it was listened to.

But in Jesus the Word became flesh and took up residence among us, truly one of us and truly God. The magnificent concerto that is the Prologue of John rings out in three movements, proclaiming the Word present at Creation as the Word enfleshed in Jesus of Nazareth, and finally as the Word that continues to be born in us who by baptism have received a share in his fullness.

✤ Consider/Discuss

- What does calling Jesus the Word of God tell me about God?
- How does accepting Jesus as God's Word have an impact on my/our lives?

✤ Responding to the Word

We pray that we might first hear the Word that is Jesus, then that we might understand this Word, and finally that we might live out of our understanding. We pray that this Word may so imprint itself on our minds and hearts and souls that when we speak, others hear the spirit of Jesus singing its love song to the world.

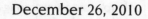

December 26, 2010

THE HOLY FAMILY
OF JESUS, MARY, AND JOSEPH

Today's Focus: Becoming a Holy Family

Today's readings highlight the relational character of family life. Sirach points to some dynamics of family living and responsibility as exercised in the ancient world. Paul directs our attention to the manner of relational living required of us as members of the family of God. The Gospel narrative shows us a family following the directives of God.

FIRST READING
Sirach 3:2–7, 12–14

God sets a father in honor over his children;
  a mother's authority he confirms over her sons.
Whoever honors his father atones for sins,
  and preserves himself from them.
When he prays, he is heard;
  he stores up riches who reveres his mother.
Whoever honors his father is gladdened by children,
  and, when he prays, is heard.
Whoever reveres his father will live a long life;
  he who obeys his father brings comfort to his mother.

My son, take care of your father when he is old;
  grieve him not as long as he lives.
Even if his mind fail, be considerate of him;
  revile him not all the days of his life;
kindness to a father will not be forgotten,
  firmly planted against the debt of your sins
  —a house raised in justice to you.

PSALM RESPONSE
Psalm 128:1

Blessed are those who fear the Lord and walk in his ways.

In the shorter form of the reading, the passage in brackets is omitted.

SECOND READING
*Colossians 3: 12–21
or 3:12–17*

Brothers and sisters: Put on, as God's chosen ones, holy and beloved, heartfelt compassion, kindness, humility, gentleness, and patience, bearing with one another and forgiving one another, if one has a grievance against another; as the Lord has forgiven you, so must you also do. And over all these put on love, that is, the bond of perfection. And let the peace of Christ control your hearts, the peace into which you were also called in one body. And be thankful. Let the word of Christ dwell in you richly, as in all wisdom you teach and admonish one another, singing psalms, hymns, and spiritual songs with gratitude in your hearts to God. And whatever you do, in word or in deed, do everything in the name of the Lord Jesus, giving thanks to God the Father through him.

[Wives, be subordinate to your husbands, as is proper in the Lord. Husbands, love your wives, and avoid any bitterness toward them. Children, obey your parents in everything, for this is pleasing to the Lord. Fathers, do not provoke your children, so they may not become discouraged.]

GOSPEL
Matthew 2:
13–15, 19–23

When the magi had departed, behold, the angel of the Lord appeared to Joseph in a dream and said, "Rise, take the child and his mother, flee to Egypt, and stay there until I tell you. Herod is going to search for the child to destroy him." Joseph rose and took the child and his mother by night and departed for Egypt. He stayed there until the death of Herod, that what the Lord had said through the prophet might be fulfilled,

Out of Egypt I called my son.

When Herod had died, behold, the angel of the Lord appeared in a dream to Joseph in Egypt and said, "Rise, take the child and his mother and go to the land of Israel, for those who sought the child's life are dead." He rose, took the child and his mother, and went to the land of Israel. But when he heard that Archelaus was ruling over Judea in place of his father Herod, he was afraid to go back there. And because he had been warned in a dream, he departed for the region of Galilee. He went and dwelt in a town called Nazareth, so that what had been spoken through the prophets might be fulfilled,

He shall be called a Nazorean.

❖ *Understanding the Word*

The reading from Sirach is instruction about family life, identifying the kind of living that results in family harmony. As wisdom instruction, Sirach lists the blessings that follow such a way of life. The child who respects and obeys both father and mother is promised life itself, remission of sins, riches, the blessing of children, and the answer to prayer. The entire teaching about respect for parents takes on a completely different perspective when we remember that it is addressed to an adult offspring, not a youth.

Paul's exhortation to virtuous living is introduced with the stated rationale for such a manner of life. Because Christians are God's chosen, holy and beloved, they should act accordingly. The virtues themselves are all relational, directed toward others, requiring unselfish sensitivity. While the author still insists that wives must be subject to their husbands, he instructs the husbands to act toward their wives with love and thoughtfulness. Children are still told to obey their parents, but fathers are advised to be moderate in the training of their children lest discipline become oppressive. This means that in Christ, the relationships between man and woman and child have been radically altered.

29

The Gospel reading consists of two discrete narratives, the flight to Egypt and the return. They contain many echoes of the Exodus tradition. The family's flight into Egypt, precipitated by the hatred of Herod, recalls Joseph's escape to that same land because of the hatred of his brothers. Both the Holy Family and the family of Jacob/Israel remained in Egypt until the death of a ruler persuaded them to return to their land of origin. Just as Israel's return resulted in its being shaped into the "people of God," so Jesus returns to his homeland, there eventually to establish the reign of God. This reading emphasizes the early Christians' belief that the active presence of God directed the events in the life of Jesus.

❖ Reflecting on the Word

Today's Gospel story reveals that God's Son was born into a dangerous world. From the beginning those in power saw the child as a threat. Herod was a ruthless king. Because Joseph listened to his dream, the child was saved from Herod's murderous rage. The parents of Jesus played a crucial role in God's plan from the beginning.

The Christmas season is traditionally a time for families getting together and enjoying each other's company. But this doesn't always happen because divisions occur even within families. Today's feast invites us to reflect on what holds a family together and what loosens and even destroys the family bond. How does the mystery of the Incarnation, of Christ being born in us in our own day, enter into the dynamics of family life? The first two readings provide a focus on the family.

While Sirach focuses on the honor and respect that children owe their parents, Colossians also urges fathers—and mothers—not to discourage their children. And the relationship between husbands and wives is to be marked by mutual love and respect. The call for wives to be "subordinate" is an unfortunate choice of words, given today's reality of spousal abuse.

At the heart of the mystery of the Incarnation is that all our relationships should bring the presence of Christ to the world. We do this when we put on the virtues of compassion, humility, gentleness, patience, forgiveness, and, above all, love. When these are found in family life, then Christ once again is born in our family.

❖ Consider/Discuss

- Do you think that the Holy Family was a perfect family?
- What makes for a holy family in our day?

❖ Responding to the Word

We can pray for all families in our world, families of blood and families of choice. We pray for the family of nations, especially where division has resulted in hatred and violence. We pray for the virtues that will draw us closer together in the Church so the world may see us clearly as part of God's family.

January 1, 2011

THE BLESSED VIRGIN MARY, THE MOTHER OF GOD

Today's Focus: A New Year's Blessing

New Year's Day places Mary, model of the Church, before us, inviting us to seek her intercession with her Son to create a place within our hearts where Christ can dwell. The change that begins within can then flow outward into our world and make global peace a reality.

FIRST READING
Numbers 6: 22–27

The LORD said to Moses: "Speak to Aaron and his sons and tell them: This is how you shall bless the Israelites. Say to them:
    The LORD bless you and keep you!
    The LORD let his face shine upon you, and be gracious to you!
    The LORD look upon you kindly and give you peace!
So shall they invoke my name upon the Israelites, and I will bless them."

PSALM RESPONSE
Psalm 67:2a

May God bless us in his mercy.

SECOND READING
Galatians 4:4–7

Brothers and sisters: When the fullness of time had come, God sent his Son, born of a woman, born under the law, to ransom those under the law, so that we might receive adoption as sons. As proof that you are sons, God sent the Spirit of his Son into our hearts, crying out, "Abba, Father!" So you are no longer a slave but a son, and if a son then also an heir, through God.

GOSPEL
Luke 2:16–21

The shepherds went in haste to Bethlehem and found Mary and Joseph, and the infant lying in the manger. When they saw this, they made known the message that had been told them about this child. All who heard it were amazed by what had been told them by the shepherds. And Mary kept all these things, reflecting on them in her heart. Then the shepherds returned, glorifying and praising God for all they had heard and seen, just as it had been told to them.

When eight days were completed for his circumcision, he was named Jesus, the name given him by the angel before he was conceived in the womb.

The blessing found in today's Numbers reading may be one of the oldest pieces of poetry in the Bible. Although it is the priests who ultimately bless the people, it is Moses who receives the blessing from God and who delivers it to Aaron and his sons. The blessing itself is quite crisp and direct. Each line invokes a personal action from God: to bless with good fortune and to keep from harm; to look favorably toward and to be gracious to; to look upon and to grant peace. Actually, all the petitions ask for the same reality, namely, the blessings that make life worth living. Peace is the fundamental characteristic of Jewish blessing, the condition of absolute well being.

According to Paul, the goal of Christ's mission was the transformation of the Galatians from slaves under the law to adopted children of God. He uses a social custom of the day to illustrate the contrast between servitude under the law and freedom in Christ. An heir too young to claim inheritance was appointed a legal guardian until he came of age. Paul compares the believers to underage minors who, until "the fullness of time had come," could not claim what might be rightfully theirs (Galatians 4:4). The law acted as legal guardian. All of this changes with the coming of Christ. Christians are no longer minors bound to the tutelage of the law.

The Gospel is essentially the same as that of the Christmas Mass at Dawn. However, this passage also speaks of the circumcision and the naming of Jesus. This slight addition shifts the focus of the passage from the shepherds to the child and his parents. As observant Jews, Mary and Joseph fulfilled all of the prescriptions of the law, seeing that the child was circumcised as custom dictated. Just as the angel had foretold, the child is named Jesus, which means savior. Now almost everything that the angel had announced has come to pass.

❖ Reflecting on the Word

We return once again to Bethlehem, accompanying the shepherds, to see the One announced by the angel as the Savior of the world. With them, we stand before the mother and contemplate the child wrapped in swaddling clothes and laid in a manger because there was no room in the inn. We are told that "Mary kept all these things, reflecting on them in her heart" (Luke 2:19).

Mary invites us to ponder in our hearts the mystery of her Son Jesus, truly God and truly human. He came for us and for our salvation, and so we ask him to banish any darkness from our hearts and to send us out to bring his light into the world.

The light that Christ brings is the blessing of God's peace, all that makes life full, and transforms the world into a place that cherishes and preserves, rather than neglecting and destroying life. Christ's gift of blessing is to let us know the Father and the Father's plan: that all be one, united as family, able to recognize in each other the dignity of God's adopted children, alive with the life of grace, destined to share in divinity.

Christ's blessing calls us to grow into maturity, keeping God's law of love, just as Jesus himself grew up, living a life that brought the law to its fulfillment. We don't do this on our own, as the name given to the child reminds us: Jesus, which means "God saves."

❖ Consider/Discuss

- What blessing do you ask from God for the coming year, for yourself, for your loved ones, for your country, for the world?
- Jesus came to save, to bring God's salvation. What do you need to be saved from?

❖ Responding to the Word

We pray that God will bless us with peace, with fullness of life, by drawing us ever more deeply into the life of the Trinity. We ask that the Holy Spirit will come upon us and transform us more completely into people the world can recognize as adopted children of God.

January 2, 2011

THE EPIPHANY OF THE LORD

Today's Focus: Arise and Shine Like a Star

This feast is the star on top of the liturgical Christmas tree, the crowning feast of our yearly celebration of the Incarnation, proclaiming that God became truly human in Jesus to bring salvation to all men and women of every nation. Christ continues to be revealed to those willing to journey.

FIRST READING
Isaiah 60:1–6

Rise up in splendor, Jerusalem! Your light has come,
the glory of the Lord shines upon you.
See, darkness covers the earth,
and thick clouds cover the peoples;
but upon you the LORD shines,
and over you appears his glory.
Nations shall walk by your light,
and kings by your shining radiance.
Raise your eyes and look about;
they all gather and come to you:
your sons come from afar,
and your daughters in the arms of their nurses.

Then you shall be radiant at what you see,
your heart shall throb and overflow,
for the riches of the sea shall be emptied out before you,
the wealth of nations shall be brought to you.
Caravans of camels shall fill you,
dromedaries from Midian and Ephah;
all from Sheba shall come
bearing gold and frankincense,
and proclaiming the praises of the LORD.

PSALM RESPONSE
Psalm 72:11

Lord, every nation on earth will adore you.

SECOND READING
Ephesians 3: 2–3a, 5–6

Brothers and sisters: You have heard of the stewardship of God's grace that was given to me for your benefit, namely, that the mystery was made known to me by revelation. It was not made known to people in other generations as it has now been revealed to his holy apostles and prophets by the Spirit: that the Gentiles are coheirs, members of the same body, and copartners in the promise in Christ Jesus through the gospel.

GOSPEL
Matthew 2: 1–12

When Jesus was born in Bethlehem of Judea, in the days of King Herod, behold, magi from the east arrived in Jerusalem, saying, "Where is the newborn king of the Jews? We saw his star at its rising and have come to do him homage." When King Herod heard this, he was greatly troubled, and all Jerusalem with him. Assembling all the chief priests and the scribes of the people, he inquired of them where the Christ was to be born. They said to him, "In Bethlehem of Judea, for thus it has been written through the prophet:

And you, Bethlehem, land of Judah,
  are by no means least among the rulers of Judah;
since from you shall come a ruler,
  who is to shepherd my people Israel."

Then Herod called the magi secretly and ascertained from them the time of the star's appearance. He sent them to Bethlehem and said, "Go and search diligently for the child. When you have found him, bring me word, that I too may go and do him homage." After their audience with the king they set out. And behold, the star that they had seen at its rising preceded them, until it came and stopped over the place where the child was.

They were overjoyed at seeing the star, and on entering the house they saw the child with Mary his mother. They prostrated themselves and did him homage. Then they opened their treasures and offered him gifts of gold, frankincense, and myrrh. And having been warned in a dream not to return to Herod, they departed for their country by another way.

❖ Understanding the Word

The reading from Isaiah opens with a twofold summons addressed to the city of Jerusalem: Arise! Shine! Although it had been downtrodden and enshrouded in darkness, it is now called out of this desperate state. The illumination into which it emerges is not merely the light of a new day, a new era of peace and prosperity. It is the very light of God. Its dispersed inhabitants return; its destroyed reputation is restored; and its despoiled prosperity is reconstituted. This is not a promise to be fulfilled in the future; Jerusalem's salvation is an accomplished fact. It is happening before its very eyes.

The primary message to the Ephesians, that in Christ the Gentiles are co-heirs, co-members, and co-partners with the Jews, had been revealed to Paul by God. Since what qualifies one as an heir is life in the Spirit of Christ and not natural generation into a particular national group, there is no obstacle in the path of Gentile incorporation. The body to which all belong is the body of Christ, not the bloodline of Abraham. The promise at the heart of gospel preaching is the promise of universal salvation through Christ.

As we near the end of the Christmas season we read another popular Christmas story: the Three Kings or Three Wise Men. Actually, they were astrologers, men who studied the heavenly bodies and sought to discover the meaning of human life on earth. These anonymous men come out of obscurity and they return to obscurity. All we know about them is that they were not Israelite, and this is the whole point of the story. It illustrates that people of good will, regardless of their ethnic or religious background, are responsive to the revelation of God. The openness of these astrologers brought them to the child, and they did not go away disappointed. This child draws Jew and Gentile alike.

❖ Reflecting on the Word

They were men in love with the lights of night—astrologers, star-gazers, mean-ing-makers tuned in to the signs in the heavens, as Matthew tells it. A strange star moving across the sky led them into Israel. Arriving in Jerusalem, they asked where the newborn king of the Jews was, so they could offer homage.

Herod was less than delighted, indeed "greatly troubled, and all Jerusalem with him," at hearing of a new king on the block (Matthew 2:3). But he assembled the chief priests and the scribes, who remembered that the prophet Micah had proclaimed that the Messiah would be born in Bethlehem.

So they set out again, with Herod's duplicitous request whispered into their ears. The star reappeared and led them to the house where the child and his mother were. Falling down in worship, they offered gifts, and went back home. End of story—as we like to remember it.

Of course, that is not the end. Receiving no word, Herod is enraged and orders the death of all children under the age of two. Joseph, Mary, and the child flee to Egypt. Power does not welcome competition, even in the form of a child.

But God wills all people to know salvation. Jesus came to draw all into the reign of God and to empower them to live the God-life that is the Father's gift. The darkness of evil continues to threaten but it will not overcome as long as there are those who seek the light, follow it, and allow it to lead them to the child.

❖ Consider/Discuss

- When has the light that is Christ come into your darkness?
- How are you being called to arise and shine like a star, leading others to Christ?

❖ Responding to the Word

We pray that the light of God's love, shown to us in Jesus Christ and placed within us with the gift of faith, may lead others to this same faith. We also pray that we may continue our own journey into the mystery of God and find Christ waiting for us at journey's end.

January 9, 2011

THE BAPTISM OF THE LORD

Today's Focus: Born to Serve

This Christological feast is the celebration of Jesus as the anointed servant of God. It brings to a close the Christmas season, the season that reveals who God is for us and who we are to be for others in Christ.

FIRST READING
Isaiah 42:1–4, 6–7

Thus says the LORD:
Here is my servant whom I uphold,
    my chosen one with whom I am pleased,
upon whom I have put my spirit;
    he shall bring forth justice to the nations,
not crying out, not shouting,
    not making his voice heard in the street.
A bruised reed he shall not break,
    and a smoldering wick he shall not quench,
until he establishes justice on the earth;
    the coastlands will wait for his teaching.

I, the LORD, have called you for the victory of justice,
    I have grasped you by the hand;
I formed you, and set you
    as a covenant of the people,
    a light for the nations,
to open the eyes of the blind,
    to bring out prisoners from confinement,
    and from the dungeon, those who live in darkness.

PSALM RESPONSE
Psalm 29:11b

The Lord will bless his people with peace.

SECOND READING
Acts 10:34–38

Peter proceeded to speak to those gathered in the house of Cornelius, saying: "In truth, I see that God shows no partiality. Rather, in every nation whoever fears him and acts uprightly is acceptable to him. You know the word that he sent to the Israelites as he proclaimed peace through Jesus Christ, who is Lord of all, what has happened all over Judea, beginning in Galilee after the baptism that John preached, how God anointed Jesus of Nazareth with the Holy Spirit and power. He went about doing good and healing all those oppressed by the devil, for God was with him."

Jesus came from Galilee to John at the Jordan to be baptized by him. John tried to prevent him, saying, "I need to be baptized by you, and yet you are coming to me?" Jesus said to him in reply, "Allow it now, for thus it is fitting for us to fulfill all righteousness." Then he allowed him. After Jesus was baptized, he came up from the water and behold, the heavens were opened for him, and he saw the Spirit of God descending like a dove and coming upon him. And a voice came from the heavens, saying, "This is my beloved Son, with whom I am well pleased."

✤ Understanding the Word

The reading from Isaiah is the first of four passages traditionally known as the "servant songs." Most significant in this description of the servant is his endowment with God's own spirit. Earlier Israelite leaders—the judges, kings, and prophets—were thought to have been seized by the spirit, thus empowering them to act within the community in some unique fashion. The servant will exercise justice, but not the harsh, exacting kind. Instead, it will be gentle and understanding, willing to wait for the establishment of God's universal rule. This justice will not compound the distress of an already suffering people. Rather, it will be a source of consolation.

Acts of the Apostles describes a scene that took place in the house of Cornelius, a newly converted Roman centurion. Normally, an observant Jew like Peter would not enter the home of a Gentile. The first words of his discourse ("I see that God shows no partiality") indicate that he was not always open to association with Gentiles as he is now (Acts 10:34). It was a newly gained insight about God that changed his view of those who did not have Jewish ancestry. Peter came to see that God shows no partiality, and Christ is Lord of all. The message of peace given initially to Israel now includes the Gentiles as well.

The Gospel reading opens with a statement about Jesus' leaving the familiarity and security of his home in Galilee and journeying to the Jordan River where John was baptizing. There is no description of the actual baptism, but we do have an account of what happened afterwards: the heavens opened and the Spirit of God descended. The Trinitarian scene is completed with the voice from heaven identifying Jesus as "Son." The words spoken combine an allusion to the "servant of the Lord" (see Isaiah 42:1) and the enthronement of the messianic king. He will accomplish this as "servant of the Lord."

A favorite plot is the rags-to-riches story, the adversity-to-triumph story, the weakling-who-becomes-strong story. It touches on our hope for personal transformation, for a change for the better. We find it in fairy tales like *Cinderella*, in novels like *David Copperfield*, and in movies like *Star Wars*.

This is not, however, the plot we get in the Jesus story. Jesus, who starts out in Bethlehem wrapped in swaddling clothes and lying in a manger, then grows up not to become the Messiah that Israel had hoped for—the strong warrior king who would restore the nation of Israel to the glory it had under King David. Instead, he grows up to become one who suffers for our sakes, who empties himself, who considers himself a servant—and calls on all who follow him to do the same.

On this final Sunday of the Christmas season, the Church celebrates the baptism of Jesus, an event that identifies him as the servant described by Isaiah, who comes in gentleness, breaking no bruised reed, quenching no smoldering wick. No shouting, no crying out, no making his voice heard in the streets. Rather, he will open eyes and hearts, release from confinement, and deliver from the dungeon's darkness.

The agenda was fairly simple, as Peter points out when preaching in the house of the Roman centurion Cornelius: Jesus went about doing good and healing all those oppressed by the devil. He came not to be served but to serve. And this is what he asks of us.

❖   *Consider/Discuss*

- Why do we end the Christmas season with the celebration of Jesus' baptism?
- Do you think of your baptism as committing you to a life of service?

❖   *Responding to the Word*

At our baptism, we became God's adopted sons and daughters. We pray to God as beloved sons and daughters, asking that God will be "well pleased" with us, and that God will direct us in the way of serving the needs of others so that we may "do good" and bring healing to a wounded world.

This period of Ordinary Time is really an interlude between seasons. Christmas is behind us and in a few weeks we will be entering the season of Lent. However, this in no way means that Ordinary Time is insignificant, the low period between two important highs. On the contrary, most of our life is "ordinary time," and lest we become complacent or even bored with it, we need direction that will help us live that life to the fullest. The liturgical readings for this section of Ordinary Time do this for us. They invite us to look at the teaching of Jesus and the subsequent teaching of Paul.

The story of the ministry of Jesus begins on the Second Sunday of Ordinary Time with John's account of Jesus' baptism. The Gospels for the Sundays that follow trace Jesus' ministry through the Gospel of Matthew. Although time and again we might catch a glimpse of the future, a hint of what lies ahead for Jesus and for those who are his disciples, during this interim period we hear excerpts from the "sermon on the mount."

Jesus' instruction is meant to show his listeners what it means to live in the reign of God, a reign that does not conform to the selfish and manipulative standards that so often rule human life and society. He calls us first to renounce our own sinfulness (Third Sunday) and then to accept the values found in the Beatitudes (Fourth Sunday). He challenges us to be our best selves (Fifth Sunday), to do more than simply obey the rules (Sixth Sunday). In fact, he asks us to do what might seem impossible; he asks us to love our enemies (Seventh Sunday). Being a disciple of Jesus, entering into the reign of God demands undivided commitment (Eighth Sunday). The only way to be genuinely successful at it is to be grounded in him (Ninth Sunday).

The first readings for this period of Ordinary Time were selected from various books of the First or Old Testament. While they are all somehow related to the basic theology of ancient Israel, which is covenant, they were chosen as Lectionary readings because they provide grounding for the Gospel reading.

The readings from Paul's First Letter to the Corinthians show us a religious leader who continues to be concerned about the faith and religious practices of his congregation even after he has left them. We see him encouraging them to be faithful, agonizing over their weaknesses, reproving them for their offenses. Paul is trying to shape them into true disciples of Christ, faithful members of the reign of God. Like Jesus before him, he is not willing to give up.

January 16, 2011

SECOND SUNDAY IN ORDINARY TIME

Today's Focus: God's Agenda: Our Holiness

The readings for today focus on discipleship. The Baptist directs the crowds to Jesus. He is the one whom they should follow. Paul boasts of his own apostleship. The sketch of the servant of the Lord becomes the lens through which we view discipleship these first Sundays of Ordinary Time.

FIRST READING
Isaiah 49:3, 5–6

The LORD said to me: You are my servant,
    Israel, through whom I show my glory.
Now the LORD has spoken
    who formed me as his servant from the womb,
that Jacob may be brought back to him
    and Israel gathered to him;
and I am made glorious in the sight of the LORD,
    and my God is now my strength!
It is too little, the LORD says, for you to be my servant,
    to raise up the tribes of Jacob,
    and restore the survivors of Israel;
I will make you a light to the nations,
    that my salvation may reach to the ends of the earth.

PSALM RESPONSE
Psalm 40:8a, 9a

Here am I, Lord; I come to do your will.

SECOND READING
1 Corinthians 1:1–3

Paul, called to be an apostle of Christ Jesus by the will of God, and Sosthenes our brother, to the church of God that is in Corinth, to you who have been sanctified in Christ Jesus, called to be holy, with all those everywhere who call upon the name of our Lord Jesus Christ, their Lord and ours. Grace to you and peace from God our Father and the Lord Jesus Christ.

GOSPEL
John 1:29–34

John the Baptist saw Jesus coming toward him and said, "Behold, the Lamb of God, who takes away the sin of the world. He is the one of whom I said, 'A man is coming after me who ranks ahead of me because he existed before me.' I did not know him, but the reason why I came baptizing with water was that he might be made known to Israel." John testified further, saying, "I saw the Spirit come down like a dove from heaven and remain upon him. I did not know him, but the one who sent me to baptize with water told me, 'On whomever you see the Spirit come down and remain, he is the one who will baptize with the Holy Spirit.' Now I have seen and testified that he is the Son of God."

The first reading is taken from the second "servant song" of Isaiah. The servant has been called to bring the people back to God. However, this mission has been expanded to include all people. This servant is to be a light to all the nations. It is noteworthy that a people struggling with its own survival because of its defeat by a more powerful nation should envision its God as concerned with the salvation of all, presumably even the nation at whose hands it suffered. Yet this is precisely what "light to the nations" suggests.

Paul begins his letter to the Corinthians by identifying himself as an apostle, one sent by another with a commission. He was called to be an apostle; he did not volunteer. Therefore, as an apostle, it is the authority of Christ that he exercises. He maintains that all of this transpired because it was God's will. In a very real sense, this official greeting is really a proclamation of faith on Paul's part. Just as he had been called to be an apostle, so the members of the Corinthian church had been called to be holy.

The scene portrayed in today's Gospel reading is familiar to many of us. It includes the report of the baptism of Jesus and the Baptist's identification of Jesus as Lamb of God. John did not know Jesus. He only recognized him through divine revelation. John then contrasts the person of Jesus and himself, as well as the efficacy of their respective baptisms. Jesus may have come after John, but he ranks far above him. And their baptisms are very different. John baptized with water. Jesus will baptize with the Holy Spirit, the same Spirit John saw descend on Jesus at the time of his baptism. This led John to testify to his belief in Jesus as the Son of God. These comparisons and this testimony point to Jesus as Son of God.

✦ Reflecting on the Word

To be a disciple of Jesus Christ means to learn from him. He is the teacher, we the students; he is the master, we his servants. But what is it we are to learn? One important title for Jesus is the Lamb of God who has come to serve by taking away our sin. He serves by leading us to participate in the holiness of God. We are to do the same for others.

Jesus came to understand his own calling by reading and praying the book of the prophet Isaiah, especially the four poems found there called the Servant Songs. Today we hear part of the second song in which the servant professes how he was formed as servant from the womb, not only to bring back Israel to God, but to be a light to the nations, so God's "salvation may reach to the ends of the earth" (Isaiah 49:6).

Those who serve Jesus as disciples are to join in this work of bringing God's salvation to the world. Paul recognizes this in his greeting to the Corinthians, noting his call to be an apostle of Christ, one sent by God to the church at Corinth, which has been made holy in Christ and called to be holy. Paul is sent not only to them, but to "all those everywhere who call on the name of our Lord Jesus Christ" (1 Corinthians 1:2).

God's will is our holiness. By responding to the call to know Jesus as the Lamb of God, we accept the invitation to participate in this holiness and become the vehicle for inviting others to dwell there.

❖ Consider/Discuss

- Do you believe that you are called to holiness? What does this mean? How do you respond to this call?
- Does your call to be a disciple lead you to pray for the world to grow in holiness?

❖ Responding to the Word

When at Mass, we call on Jesus several times as the Lamb of God—at the beginning in the Gloria and twice in preparation for Communion. Pray for our world this day to recognize Jesus as the Lamb of God who takes away the sin of the world.

January 23, 2011

THIRD SUNDAY IN ORDINARY TIME

Today's Focus: Living in the Light

Discipleship is not something that we take upon ourselves. We are called to it. If we are to be faithful disciples of Christ, we too must leave behind our inclination to take sides, to pit one religious position against another, to dismiss as disloyal or narrow-minded those who understand our common faith quite differently than we do.

FIRST READING
Isaiah 8:23 — 9:3

First the LORD degraded the land of Zebulun and the land of Naphtali; but in the end he has glorified the seaward road, the land west of the Jordan, the District of the Gentiles.

Anguish has taken wing, dispelled is darkness:
   for there is no gloom where but now there was distress.
The people who walked in darkness
   have seen a great light;
upon those who dwelt in the land of gloom
   a light has shone.
You have brought them abundant joy
   and great rejoicing,
as they rejoice before you as at the harvest,
   as people make merry when dividing spoils.
For the yoke that burdened them,
   the pole on their shoulder,
and the rod of their taskmaster
   you have smashed, as on the day of Midian.

PSALM RESPONSE
Psalm 27:1a

The Lord is my light and my salvation.

SECOND READING
1 Corinthians 1: 10–13, 17

I urge you, brothers and sisters, in the name of our Lord Jesus Christ, that all of you agree in what you say, and that there be no divisions among you, but that you be united in the same mind and in the same purpose. For it has been reported to me about you, my brothers and sisters, by Chloe's people, that there are rivalries among you. I mean that each of you is saying, "I belong to Paul," or "I belong to Apollos," or "I belong to Cephas," or "I belong to Christ." Is Christ divided? Was Paul crucified for you? Or were you baptized in the name of Paul? For Christ did not send me to baptize but to preach the gospel, and not with the wisdom of human eloquence, so that the cross of Christ might not be emptied of its meaning.

GOSPEL
Matthew 4:
12–23
or 4:12–17

When Jesus heard that John had been arrested, he withdrew to Galilee. He left Nazareth and went to live in Capernaum by the sea, in the region of Zebulun and Naphtali, that what had been said through Isaiah the prophet might be fulfilled:

Land of Zebulun and land of Naphtali,
the way to the sea, beyond the Jordan,
Galilee of the Gentiles,
the people who sit in darkness have seen a great light,
on those dwelling in a land overshadowed by death
light has arisen.

From that time on, Jesus began to preach and say, "Repent, for the kingdom of heaven is at hand."

[As he was walking by the Sea of Galilee, he saw two brothers, Simon who is called Peter, and his brother Andrew, casting a net into the sea; they were fishermen. He said to them, "Come after me, and I will make you fishers of men." At once they left their nets and followed him. He walked along from there and saw two other brothers, James, the son of Zebedee, and his brother John. They were in a boat, with their father Zebedee, mending their nets. He called them, and immediately they left their boat and their father and followed him.

He went around all of Galilee, teaching in their synagogues, proclaiming the gospel of the kingdom, and curing every disease and illness among the people.]

❖❖ *Understanding the Word*

Isaiah speaks about the reversal of the fortunes of Israel; the former times of hardship are contrasted with the present experience of salvation. The nation had been overrun by foreigners, but now that the land has been returned to Israel, the hardships that accompanied defeat and occupation have been lifted and the darkness is dispelled. The darkness included social disintegration, political collapse, and religious devastation. The reversal of fortunes is characterized by light. Salvation came when God dispelled the darkness and burst upon the land with the brightness of shining light. Truly the fortunes have been reversed, and the saving grace of God has taken over the world.

The Corinthian church was rife with bickering and pettiness. The natural differences that existed in the group had degenerated into rivalry. If left unchecked this rivalry could develop into serious divisions, even schism. In his appeal for unity, Paul addresses the Corinthians as brothers (and sisters), indicating that he considers them as companion members of the Christian community. Groups within the community claimed allegiance to various individuals. Paul insists that since Christ cannot be divided, neither the teachings nor the personal characteristics of religious leaders can be allowed to rival their allegiance to Christ.

John's imprisonment signaled both the end of his ministry and the beginning of Jesus' ministry. It was not Jesus' intent to pick up where John left off. Although he preached the same repentance as did the Baptist, he did it in fulfillment of the prophecies rather than in anticipation of a future event as John did. His first move was to call some followers. Two sets of brothers—Simon and Andrew, James and John—were called away from their occupation. It should be noted that these men were called; they did not initiate their own discipleship, as followers of rabbis normally did. The reign of God had come. The newly called disciples were witnesses of its appearance.

✤ Reflecting on the Word

During this annual week of praying for Christian Unity, it may be either consoling or disheartening to realize that from the beginning there were divisions in the church. In Paul's day, the bickering arose in Corinth over rival loyalties: "I belong to Paul . . . to Peter . . . to Apollos . . . to Christ." Paul tries to put an end to this from the start, asking the various factions, "Is Christ divided? Was Paul crucified for you? Or were you baptized in the name of Paul?" (1 Corithians 1:13).

Today's readings remind us that the darkness of division, whether among nations, churches, or families, is not part of the kingdom of heaven. Diversity, yes; division, no. The light that Christ came and continues to bring is the light that allows us to look into the face of our brother and sister and see the face of God.

Jesus came into Galilee preaching the good news of the coming of God's rule, proclaiming that God's loving presence was here even now: "Repent, for the kingdom of heaven is at hand" (Matthew 4:17). There is an urgency here, a call to repent, change, seek, and accept God's rule in our lives. This call is as urgent for us today as it was then. As nations continue to build up arsenals of nuclear weapons, there is an unparalleled possibility of devastation on a global level.

Jesus continues to seek others to join him in preaching this gospel message. A divided community is a counter-sign, not serving to bring about the kingdom. The death of Christ was to heal such divisions. When we settle for division, we "empty the cross of Christ of its meaning."

✤ Consider/Discuss

- Do I hear Jesus' call to repent as if it is spoken to me?
- Have I made peace with division in my life where there could be unity?

Turn to Psalm 27 (today's responsorial psalm) and use it for meditation. Today's short response can also serve as a mantra during the coming week: "The Lord is my light and my salvation." We pray that the Lord deliver us from any division that threatens the body of Christ and that we live in the light and be a light for others.

January 30, 2011

FOURTH SUNDAY IN ORDINARY TIME

Today's Focus: Getting into the Kingdom

As disciples, we are called to learn about the kingdom of heaven and to live in a way that will bring us there. A profile of those who are promised a dwelling place there is given in today's Gospel. Paul gives yet another listing. Living there later depends on how we are living here now.

FIRST
READING
Zephaniah 2:3;
3:12–13

Seek the LORD, all you humble of the earth,
    who have observed his law;
seek justice, seek humility;
    perhaps you may be sheltered
    on the day of the LORD's anger.

But I will leave as a remnant in your midst
    a people humble and lowly,
who shall take refuge in the name of the LORD:
    the remnant of Israel.
They shall do no wrong
    and speak no lies;
nor shall there be found in their mouths
    a deceitful tongue;
they shall pasture and couch their flocks
    with none to disturb them.

PSALM
RESPONSE
Matthew 5:3

Blessed are the poor in spirit; the kingdom of heaven is theirs!

SECOND
READING
1 Corinthians 1:
26–31

Consider your own calling, brothers and sisters. Not many of you were wise by human standards, not many were powerful, not many were of noble birth. Rather, God chose the foolish of the world to shame the wise, and God chose the weak of the world to shame the strong, and God chose the lowly and despised of the world, those who count for nothing, to reduce to nothing those who are something, so that no human being might boast before God. It is due to him that you are in Christ Jesus, who became for us wisdom from God, as well as righteousness, sanctification, and redemption, so that, as it is written, "Whoever boasts, should boast in the Lord."

GOSPEL
Matthew 5:
1–12a

When Jesus saw the crowds, he went up the mountain, and after he had sat down, his disciples came to him. He began to teach them, saying:

"Blessed are the poor in spirit,
for theirs is the kingdom of heaven.
Blessed are they who mourn,
for they will be comforted.
Blessed are the meek,
for they will inherit the land.
Blessed are they who hunger and thirst for righteousness,
for they will be satisfied.
Blessed are the merciful,
for they will be shown mercy.
Blessed are the clean of heart,
for they will see God.
Blessed are the peacemakers,
for they will be called children of God.
Blessed are they who are persecuted for the sake
of righteousness,
for theirs is the kingdom of heaven.
Blessed are you when they insult you and persecute you
and utter every kind of evil against you falsely because of me.
Rejoice and be glad, for your reward will be great in heaven."

✢ *Understanding the Word*

Zephaniah addresses the people with a threefold exhortation: Seek the Lord! Seek righteousness! Seek humility! Israel is told to seek the Lord after having violated the covenant; to seek righteousness after having turned to sin; to seek humility after having acted arrogantly. The second part of the reading provides a very different picture. This section is an oracle of salvation, loving words of God that offer assurance and hope. The path of righteousness followed by the remnant will be the consequence of their deliverance, not its cause. The blessings are not rewards for their fidelity. Rather, every good that comes to them is a gift from God.

Paul reminds the Corinthians that, judged by the standards of society, they are really nobodies. They have little about which they can boast. According to Paul, God chooses the nobodies of the world in order to shame those who think they are somebodies. Those who lack honor in the eyes of the world are highly honored by God by being chosen, while those whom the world honors are shamed by being overlooked by God. God acts this way so that no one can boast of her or his own accomplishments. Since every good thing is received because of Christ, "Whoever boasts, should boast in the Lord" (1 Corinthians 1:31).

The sermon on the mount was directed to Jesus' close followers, not to the broader crowds. While his teachings are all in some way directed toward the establishment of the reign of God, the type of behavior or values that he advocates here is frequently the opposite of that espoused by society at large. This fact offers us a way to understand the challenges set before us in the Beatitudes.

49

One way to interpret them is to look first at the blessings promised. We may see that the behavior that Jesus is advocating is at odds with what society claims will guarantee the blessing that we seek.

❖ Reflecting on the Word

Billy Collins' poem "The Afterlife" proposes that when we die, we will all go to the place where we always expected to go. And so, some will end up in the light, others before a judge; some will be singing in the choir, others seated around a food-filled table. He concludes somewhat wistfully, saying that the rest will just end up in their coffins, wishing they could return to do things they never did.

Matthew's Gospel has a lot to say about the kingdom of heaven, beginning with the Beatitudes, which can be thought of as "Be-Attitudes," ways of being in the world now that will get you into the world yet to come. They are not the usual rungs on the ladder to success that call for calculation, competition, and caring little for anyone other than oneself.

Being poor in spirit, mourning, being meek, hungering and thirsting for justice (God's, not the usual brand meted out in our world), showing mercy, being clean of heart, making peace, and putting up with persecution—this can sound like an eight-step program for being losers in the world.

But to those who chose to walk these ways, Jesus declares, "Blessed are they," and promises that "theirs is the kingdom of heaven" (Matthew 5:10). Or, as Paul puts it, God chooses the nobodies to work on, with, and through. It's enough to make you search out another kingdom. Only there you might not end up being blessed, just wishing you could return to do things you never did—but should have.

❖ Consider/Discuss

- What is your notion of the kingdom of heaven?
- To which of the groups Jesus names do you feel most akin? Which are least related to your life?
- Which quality do you hear Jesus inviting you to take up?

❖ Responding to the Word

We pray that we may become seekers of the kingdom of heaven now and learn the wisdom of God that was embodied in Jesus, a wisdom that will bring us to share in the "righteousness, sanctification, and redemption" that are to be found by living in Christ (1 Corinthians 1:30).

February 6, 2011

FIFTH SUNDAY IN ORDINARY TIME

Today's Focus: A Little Salt, a Little Light, a Lotta Difference

The Sermon on the Mount continues with two images that Jesus offers to disciples who choose to live as his followers. The community is to function as salt and light, bringing savor and illumination to a world that can be bland in its responsiveness to human need and blind to its gifts given for the sake of others.

FIRST READING
Isaiah 58:7–10

Thus says the LORD:
　Share your bread with the hungry,
　　shelter the oppressed and the homeless;
　clothe the naked when you see them,
　　and do not turn your back on your own.
　Then your light shall break forth like the dawn,
　　and your wound shall quickly be healed;
　your vindication shall go before you,
　　and the glory of the LORD shall be your rear guard.
　Then you shall call, and the LORD will answer,
　　you shall cry for help, and he will say: Here I am!
　If you remove from your midst
　　oppression, false accusation and malicious speech;
　if you bestow your bread on the hungry
　　and satisfy the afflicted;
　then light shall rise for you in the darkness,
　　and the gloom shall become for you like midday.

PSALM RESPONSE
Psalm 112:4a

The just man is a light in darkness to the upright.

SECOND READING
1 Corinthians 2:1–5

When I came to you, brothers and sisters, proclaiming the mystery of God, I did not come with sublimity of words or of wisdom. For I resolved to know nothing while I was with you except Jesus Christ, and him crucified. I came to you in weakness and fear and much trembling, and my message and my proclamation were not with persuasive words of wisdom, but with a demonstration of Spirit and power, so that your faith might rest not on human wisdom but on the power of God.

GOSPEL
Matthew 5:13–16

Jesus said to his disciples: "You are the salt of the earth. But if salt loses its taste, with what can it be seasoned? It is no longer good for anything but to be thrown out and trampled underfoot. You are the light of the world. A city set on a mountain cannot be hidden. Nor do they light a lamp and then put it under a bushel basket; it is set on a lampstand, where it gives light to all in the house. Just so, your light must shine before others, that they may see your good deeds and glorify your heavenly Father."

✢ Understanding the Word

Today's passage from Isaiah maps out the kind of behavior required if one is to enjoy the blessing of the covenant. It proclaims ethical mandates, not religious practices. Communion with God is dependent upon the fulfillment of social responsibility. The blessing that follows such a life is frequently described as some form of light. Light can be a symbol of deliverance, of prosperity, of truth, or of God's favor. It is associated with life and all of the good things that come with it. Because its meaning here is not explicitly stated, the reference to life can include all of the richness of the symbol.

Paul reminds the Corinthians of their lowly status in society. This lowliness enabled the power and glory of God to shine forth unimpeded through them. He applies this to his own manner of ministry. He insists that there is nothing extraordinary about him, but that will not hamper the spread of the gospel. Quite the contrary; Paul's ministerial approach was humble and unassuming because he did not want his manner of delivery to get in the way of the dynamism of the gospel. He wanted the faith of the community to be grounded in God and not in the cleverness of a preacher.

Jesus employs two metaphors to characterize the essence of discipleship. First, salt is both essential for life itself and valuable for preserving, seasoning, and purifying food. Its value is in its effect on something else. Applied to disciples, they too are valuable to the extent that they influence others. Second, the disciples are a light that shines forth in the darkness of ignorance or faithlessness, like a city on a mountain or a lamp on a stand in a house. They enlighten others not by words but by their manner of living, a manner of living that declares to the world that the reign of God has indeed been established in their midst, and the age of fulfillment has dawned.

One of the most common advertising strategies is showing what you can look like after you purchase a certain product or follow a particular program: a more pleasing shape, greater muscle definition, blemish-free skin, silkier hair, and so on. Jesus today offers two images to his disciples, salt and light, indicating what they can be if they follow his teachings. In both instances the benefits go to others.

Salt was important in Jesus' time for preserving meat and for bringing out the taste of food. Its usefulness depends on its interacting with something else. When it doesn't interact, it is useless. So, too, if a follower does not live in the world as a child of the kingdom, the world will be bland.

And not only that, but also blind, unable to glimpse God's presence here and now. The disciples must show themselves to the world as followers of Jesus, rooted like him in the law and the prophets. With so much darkness due to hatred, cruelty, and greed, the disciple who shares bread with the hungry, helps shelter the homeless, clothes the naked, and does not live indifferent to the needs of others, will truly be salt and light.

In the coming weeks, we will continue to hear the Sermon on the Mount, a compilation of teachings that Matthew has collected to give us the program we are to follow so that the world may catch a glimpse now and again of the reign of God.

❖❖ *Consider/Discuss*

- Do you see ways in which you can bring savor and light to the world?
- Do you recognize that Jesus is calling the church as a community of believers to dispel the darkness and gloom?

❖❖ *Responding to the Word*

Pray that God will help you to recognize the gifts given to you and your community for the good of others. We also ask God to give us the humility not to feel threatened by the gifts of others, but to rejoice in them and encourage their use.

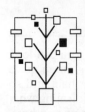

February 13, 2011

SIXTH SUNDAY IN ORDINARY TIME

Today's Focus: Blessed Are They Who Walk in the Law of the Lord

Jesus speaks today as a teacher, stressing that he has not come to abolish the law or the prophets but to complete their teaching. He contrasts his teaching with that of the scribes and Pharisees, calling on his followers to let their holiness surpass theirs. His bottom line must become ours.

FIRST READING
Sirach 15:15–20

If you choose you can keep the commandments,
    they will save you;
    if you trust in God, you too shall live;
he has set before you fire and water;
    to whichever you choose, stretch forth your hand.
Before man are life and death, good and evil,
    whichever he chooses shall be given him.
Immense is the wisdom of the Lord;
    he is mighty in power, and all-seeing.
The eyes of God are on those who fear him;
    he understands man's every deed.
No one does he command to act unjustly,
    to none does he give license to sin.

PSALM RESPONSE
Psalm 119:1b

Blessed are they who follow the law of the Lord!

SECOND READING
1 Corinthians 2:6–10

Brothers and sisters: We speak a wisdom to those who are mature, not a wisdom of this age, nor of the rulers of this age who are passing away. Rather, we speak God's wisdom, mysterious, hidden, which God predetermined before the ages for our glory, and which none of the rulers of this age knew; for, if they had known it, they would not have crucified the Lord of glory. But as it is written:

What eye has not seen, and ear has not heard,
    and what has not entered the human heart,
what God has prepared for those who love him,
    this God has revealed to us through the Spirit.

For the Spirit scrutinizes everything, even the depths of God.

In the shorter form of the reading, the passages in brackets are omitted.

GOSPEL
Matthew 5:17–
37 or 5:20–22a,
27–28, 33–34a,
37

Jesus said to his disciples: ["Do not think that I have come to abolish the law or the prophets. I have come not to abolish but to fulfill. Amen, I say to you, until heaven and earth pass away, not the smallest letter or the smallest part of a letter will pass from the law, until all things have taken place. Therefore, whoever breaks one of the least of these commandments and teaches others to do so will be called least in the kingdom of heaven. But whoever obeys and teaches these commandments will be called greatest in the kingdom of heaven.] I tell you, unless your righteousness surpasses that of the scribes and Pharisees, you will not enter the kingdom of heaven.

"You have heard that it was said to your ancestors,
You shall not kill; and whoever kills will be liable to judgment.
But I say to you, whoever is angry with his brother will be liable to judgment; [and whoever says to brother, 'Raqa,' will be answerable to the Sanhedrin; and whoever says, 'You fool,' will be liable to fiery Gehenna. Therefore, if you bring your gift to the altar, and there recall that your brother has anything against you, leave your gift there at the altar, go first and be reconciled with your brother, and then come and offer your gift. Settle with your opponent quickly while on the way to court. Otherwise your opponent will hand you over to the judge, and the judge will hand you over to the guard, and you will be thrown into prison. Amen, I say to you, you will not be released until you have paid the last penny.]

"You have heard that it was said,
You shall not commit adultery.
But I say to you, everyone who looks at a woman with lust has already committed adultery with her in his heart. [If your right eye causes you to sin, tear it out and throw it away. It is better for you to lose one of your members than to have your whole body thrown into Gehenna. And if your right hand causes you to sin, cut it off and throw it away. It is better for you to lose one of your members than to have your whole body go into Gehenna.

"It was also said,
Whoever divorces his wife must give her a bill of divorce.
But I say to you, whoever divorces his wife—unless the marriage is unlawful—causes her to commit adultery, and whoever marries a divorced woman commits adultery.]

"Again you have heard that it was said to your ancestors,
Do not take a false oath,
but make good to the Lord all that you vow.

But I say to you, do not swear at all; [not by heaven, for it is God's throne; nor by the earth, for it is his footstool; nor by Jerusalem, for it is the city of the great King. Do not swear by your head, for you cannot make a single hair white or black.] Let your 'Yes' mean 'Yes,'and your 'No' mean 'No.' Anything more is from the evil one."

❖ Understanding the Word

The legitimacy of the instruction from Sirach is grounded in the theology of retribution, which maintains that wise or righteous living will result in happiness or blessing, and foolish or depraved living will meet with misfortune or punishment. Today's reading addresses human freedom and human choice. The eyes of God look on the righteous with pleasure, just as the righteous look to God in fidelity. Although it is God's desire that all will live in conformity to the order established, God has predestined no one to sin or to blessedness. All have been given freedom of choice. It is up to us to use it wisely.

Paul contrasts the wisdom of the gospel with the wisdom of this age. The plan of God was hidden in the past, but is clearly revealed in the present. The mature are those who have entered into the dying and rising of Christ by accepting the wisdom of the gospel. Everything hinges on the essential mystery of the death and resurrection of Christ. Paul maintains that if the rulers of this world had known that the glory of God resided in the man Jesus, they would not have crucified him. However, they should have known, because Jesus did not keep this secret.

Although Jesus' teaching was based on the common tradition of Israel, his interpretations were so unprecedented that some accused him of having rejected that tradition. Jesus insists that his interpretations really offer the fuller meaning of the tradition. The contrast that Jesus sets up is not between himself and the law, but between his interpretation of the law and that of the scribes and Pharisees. He criticizes them for insisting on the minutiae of the law at the expense of the righteousness that is at its heart. Jesus demands much more than mere external conformity. Whether it is harmony in the community, fidelity in marriage, or faithfulness to one's word, Jesus calls for radical commitment.

❖ Reflecting on the Word

We live in a country where we prize our freedom, cling to our right to choose, and even define our homeland as "the land of the free." Today's scriptures remind us that along with rights come responsibilities. We are to respond to our God who made us and calls us to be a people of the new covenant, ratified by the saving death of God's Son on the cross.

"If you choose you can keep the commandments, they will save you," says Ben Sira (Sirach 15:15). For the Jewish people the law was a blessing and those who chose to keep the law would be blessed with life. That choice is still before us today.

Jesus' teachings reveal his wisdom in understanding the law of the Mosaic covenant. His grasp of what was at the heart of the law can be clearly found in the long form of today's Gospel. While there is an option for a shorter version, spend some time with the longer reading (Matthew 5:17–37).

We are to live as kin in what has been called the "kin-dom" of God. In a world that justifies preventative strikes, Jesus forbids not only killing but even getting angry and bearing a grudge. He teaches that reconciliation takes priority over worship, that the prohibition against adultery extends even to looking with lust at another, reducing a person to an object for self-gratification. Finally, he asks us not to swear but to speak with simplicity and integrity.

Some might dismiss all this as impossible to achieve. But, as a young virgin was once told: "[N]othing will be impossible for God" (Luke 1:37).

❖ Consider/Discuss

- How does the "law of the Lord" influence my life?
- Do I consider God's law as increasing or limiting my freedom?
- Can I accept the "bottom line" that Jesus is asking of his disciples?

❖ Responding to the Word

We can pray for the Holy Spirit to open our minds to understand what is at the heart of Jesus' teachings, and that we both discern what God asks of us and respond wholeheartedly. Thus we witness to others what it means to walk in the law of the Lord.

February 20, 2011

SEVENTH SUNDAY IN ORDINARY TIME

Today's Focus: Being Holy

Jesus asks that we be perfect as our heavenly Father is perfect. The word translated as "perfect" is taken from the Latin, meaning complete, entire, full-grown. When we love our enemy, we are perfect, that is, complete, full-grown, achieving the maturity of one living "in Christ."

FIRST READING
Leviticus 19:1–2, 17–18

The LORD said to Moses, "Speak to the whole Israelite community and tell them: Be holy, for I, the LORD, your God, am holy.

"You shall not bear hatred for your brother or sister in your heart. Though you may have to reprove your fellow citizen, do not incur sin because of him. Take no revenge and cherish no grudge against any of your people. You shall love your neighbor as yourself. I am the LORD."

PSALM RESPONSE
Psalm 103:8a

The Lord is kind and merciful.

SECOND READING
1 Corinthians 3:16–23

Brothers and sisters: Do you not know that you are the temple of God, and that the Spirit of God dwells in you? If anyone destroys God's temple, God will destroy that person; for the temple of God, which you are, is holy.

Let no one deceive himself. If any one among you considers himself wise in this age, let him become a fool, so as to become wise. For the wisdom of this world is foolishness in the eyes of God, for it is written:
God catches the wise in their own ruses,
and again:
The Lord knows the thoughts of the wise,
that they are vain.
So let no one boast about human beings, for everything belongs to you, Paul or Apollos or Cephas, or the world or life or death, or the present or the future: all belong to you, and you to Christ, and Christ to God.

Jesus said to his disciples: "You have heard that it was said,
An eye for an eye and a tooth for a tooth.
But I say to you, offer no resistance to one who is evil. When someone strikes you on your right cheek, turn the other one as well. If anyone wants to go to law with you over your tunic, hand over your cloak as well. Should anyone press you into service for one mile, go for two miles. Give to the one who asks of you, and do not turn your back on one who wants to borrow.

"You have heard that it was said,
You shall love your neighbor and hate your enemy.
But I say to you, love your enemies and pray for those who persecute you, that you may be children of your heavenly Father, for he makes his sun rise on the bad and the good, and causes rain to fall on the just and the unjust. For if you love those who love you, what recompense will you have? Do not the tax collectors do the same? And if you greet your brothers only, what is unusual about that? Do not the pagans do the same? So be perfect, just as your heavenly Father is perfect."

❖ Understanding the Word

A life of holiness is patterned after the holiness of God. It requires integrity, honesty, and faithfulness. To be holy as God is holy, we must refrain from nursing hatred in our hearts; we must rebuke wrongdoers or we will share their guilt; we must not entertain vengeance; and we must love others as we love ourselves. These very demanding directives give us a glimpse into the holiness of God. Furthermore, they are all communal in nature. In other words, our likeness to God is determined by the way we relate to others.

For Paul, the temple is the collection of people who gather in God's name. Just as the presence of God made the Jerusalem temple holy, so the Spirit's presence in the people makes this new temple holy. Paul returns to an earlier discussion about the wisdom of this world (see last Sunday's second reading). As valuable as human insight might be, it is nothing compared with God's wisdom. Boasting refers to the false pride that the Corinthians took in identifying with various religious leaders. Such boasting is evidence of the wisdom of the world, a wisdom that threatened the unity of the Corinthian community.

Jesus addresses the way that disciples are to interact in any strained relationships. He instructs his disciples to offer no resistance when someone tries to take advantage of them. He employs Near Eastern exaggeration to make his point. The disciples are told to disarm others with their willingness to go beyond what is required of them. Jesus then reinterprets the law of love in a most radical manner, telling his disciples that they must love their enemies. He insists that the disciples' love must be patterned after God's love, which is given unquestioningly to the just and the unjust alike. The final exhortation succinctly sets the standard for life in the kingdom of heaven. "[B]e perfect, just as your heavenly Father is perfect" (Matthew 5:48). It is this standard that makes Jesus' interpretation of the law so radical.

A 2006 movie called *Love, Actually* has one of the best openings in recent years. It begins with two young people running toward each other and falling into each other's arms, kissing joyfully. Then you see a mother being hugged by her two little girls, then two older women, perhaps sisters, embracing. As these scenes give way to others, you become aware all this takes place in an airport at the arrivals gate. Accompanying these images is a voiceover.

Whenever he feels down about the condition of the world, the speaker goes to the arrivals gate at Heathrow airport in London. Despite the fact that there is so much hatred and greed in the world, he says, Heathrow is one place where things seem different. At Heathrow love is everywhere.

All the while you hear this voice, you are watching people rush into each other's arms. For a full minute you see the world as a welcoming, warm, loving place. You know it's something of a set-up because who goes to meet people at airports other than family, good friends, people in a loving relationship? But isn't this God's plan for the world, what God wants most from us: love God; love one another.

The voiceover concludes by noting that right before the planes hit the Twin Towers in New York City, all the calls that went out were messages of love. People chose to have their final words be professions of love. Making that choice on a daily basis is what makes us perfect—that is, full-grown, complete, holy.

✥ *Consider/Discuss*

- Do you accept Jesus' idea of what it means to be "perfect"?
- If there is someone who has given me reason not to love them, can I pray for them?

✥ *Responding to the Word*

We pray to God to continue to pour the Holy Spirit into our hearts so that we can love with God's own love, when our own ability to love fails us. We pray that we can grow into that full maturity that we see in Jesus, who prayed for his enemies from the cross.

February 27, 2011

EIGHTH SUNDAY IN ORDINARY TIME

Today's Focus: God Is Trustworthy

The Sermon on the Mount is a call for radical faith in God. Jesus' words today follow in the tradition of the prophets, especially Isaiah. Both present God to us as a loving parent. While Isaiah emphasizes that God is a loving mother, Jesus describes God as a father who provides for his children.

FIRST READING
Isaiah 49:14–15

Zion said, "The LORD has forsaken me;
　my LORD has forgotten me."
Can a mother forget her infant,
　be without tenderness for the child of her womb?
Even should she forget,
　I will never forget you.

PSALM RESPONSE
Psalm 62:6a

Rest in God alone, my soul.

SECOND READING
1 Corinthians 4:1–5

Brothers and sisters: Thus should one regard us: as servants of Christ and stewards of the mysteries of God. Now it is of course required of stewards that they be found trustworthy. It does not concern me in the least that I be judged by you or any human tribunal; I do not even pass judgment on myself; I am not conscious of anything against me, but I do not thereby stand acquitted; the one who judges me is the Lord. Therefore do not make any judgment before the appointed time, until the Lord comes, for he will bring to light what is hidden in darkness and will manifest the motives of our hearts, and then everyone will receive praise from God.

GOSPEL
Matthew 6:24–34

Jesus said to his disciples: "No one can serve two masters. He will either hate one and love the other, or be devoted to one and despise the other. You cannot serve God and mammon.

"Therefore I tell you, do not worry about your life, what you will eat or drink, or about your body, what you will wear. Is not life more than food and the body more than clothing? Look at the birds in the sky; they do not sow or reap, they gather nothing into barns, yet your heavenly Father feeds them. Are not you more important than they? Can any of you by worrying add a single moment to your life-span? Why are you anxious about clothes? Learn from the way the wild flowers grow. They do not work or spin. But I tell you that not even Solomon in all his splendor was clothed like one of them.

If God so clothes the grass of the field, which grows today and is thrown into the oven tomorrow, will he not much more provide for you, O you of little faith? So do not worry and say, 'What are we to eat?' or 'What are we to drink?'or 'What are we to wear?' All these things the pagans seek. Your heavenly Father knows that you need them all. But seek first the kingdom of God and his righteousness, and all these things will be given you besides. Do not worry about tomorrow; tomorrow will take care of itself. Sufficient for a day is its own evil."

✢ Understanding the Word

The metaphor that Isaiah uses to characterize the love that God has for the people is extraordinary. It compares this love to the relationship between a mother and the nursing child of her womb. Such a metaphor could have been considered presumptuous had it not been placed by the prophet in the mouth of God. It is improbable, though possible, that a woman would forget the child of her flesh. However, God will never forget this people. Therefore, though Zion may feel abandoned and forgotten, it is only a feeling; it is not a fact. God's attachment to the people will never be severed.

Paul speaks about ministerial accountability and judgment. Stewards were responsible for the goods of the household of another. Paul claims that as such a steward he is indeed trustworthy. He has committed himself wholeheartedly to the proclamation of the gospel, to the distribution of the mysteries of God, and he stands by this claim regardless of what others might think. Acknowledging that he is obliged to give an account of his stewardship, he insists that it is the Lord who will be his judge. Such judgment is bound to be much more demanding than mere human judgment. Human beings can be wrong, but the Lord knows the motives of the heart.

Jesus is not naive about the human need for food and clothing and shelter and material support. Nor does he advocate passivity or laziness in the face of hard work. He is talking about setting one's priorities straight, appreciating humankind's place in the natural world, trusting in the goodness and providence of God. He uses two examples from nature to demonstrate what he means: God's care for birds and God's artistry in clothing the lilies. The point of this teaching is confidence in God. People prone to anxiety need to be reminded that they are precious in God's eyes and they must learn to trust in God's providence.

I am writing this in the aftermath of the earthquake that shattered Haiti. The devastation has been beyond words. Newspapers and telecasts were filled with pictures of the dead and heart-breaking stories. As of this writing over 150,000 are presumed dead—perhaps many more—and thousands upon thousands are wounded. There is little food, water, or shelter, and few medical supplies. Yet even in the face of this tragic event, an evening news program two nights after the earthquake had footage of a large group in Port au Prince lifting their voices and hands in prayer, praising God.

This radical faith in God is what Jesus calls his disciples to have. The Father did not intervene to save his Son from death, but neither did he allow death to have the final word. He raised his Son from the dead. This saving death has remained the sign above all signs that God wills us to have eternal life. It can seem impossible at times not to worry about tomorrow. But Jesus assures us that the Father does not abandon us—ever!

We are all called to be stewards of the mysteries of the faith that is centered in the person and saving death and resurrection of Jesus Christ. We are to hand on what has been handed down to us: that Jesus is God's only Son, who suffered and died and was raised for our salvation, and by our baptism we are brought into this mystery of living, dying, and rising in Christ.

❖❖ *Consider/Discuss*

- Has your faith in God's care been tested?
- How do you respond to Jesus' words about God as a loving father and to Isaiah's words about God as a loving mother?
- Do you need to ask God to restore your trust in God?

❖❖ *Responding to the Word*

Today's psalm response is a wonderful prayer of the heart to carry through the week: "Rest in God alone, my soul" (Psalm 62:6a). We can pray with the psalmist that we find our peace in God who is our rock and our salvation, our stronghold. Let us trust in God at all times and pour out our hearts to our loving God.

March 6, 2011

NINTH SUNDAY IN ORDINARY TIME

Today's Focus: Words to Build a Life On

A disciple's life may begin with listening to Jesus' words, but it cannot end there. The importance of both hearing and living out the words of the Lord receives emphasis in this conclusion of the Sermon on the Mount. When we hear today's Gospel, we should bear in mind all that we have heard Jesus say over the last few Sundays.

FIRST READING
Deuteronomy 11:18, 26–28, 32

Moses told the people, "Take these words of mine into your heart and soul. Bind them at your wrist as a sign, and let them be a pendant on your forehead.

"I set before you here, this day, a blessing and a curse: a blessing for obeying the commandments of the LORD, your God, which I enjoin on you today; a curse if you do not obey the commandments of the LORD, your God, but turn aside from the way I ordain for you today, to follow other gods, whom you have not known. Be careful to observe all the statutes and decrees that I set before you today."

PSALM RESPONSE
Psalm 31:3b

Lord, be my rock of safety.

SECOND READING
Romans 3: 21–25, 28

Brothers and sisters: Now the righteousness of God has been manifested apart from the law, though testified to by the law and the prophets, the righteousness of God through faith in Jesus Christ for all who believe. For there is no distinction; all have sinned and are deprived of the glory of God. They are justified freely by his grace through the redemption in Christ Jesus, whom God set forth as an expiation, through faith, by his blood. For we consider that a person is justified by faith apart from works of the law.

GOSPEL
Matthew 7:21–27

Jesus said to his disciples: "Not everyone who says to me, 'Lord, Lord,' will enter the kingdom of heaven, but only the one who does the will of my Father in heaven. Many will say to me on that day, 'Lord, Lord, did we not prophesy in your name? Did we not drive out demons in your name? Did we not do mighty deeds in your name?' Then I will declare to them solemnly, 'I never knew you. Depart from me, you evildoers.'

"Everyone who listens to these words of mine and acts on them will be like a wise man who built his house on rock. The rain fell, the floods came, and the winds blew and buffeted the house. But it did not collapse; it had been set solidly on rock. And everyone who listens to these words of mine but does not act on them will be like a fool who built his house on sand. The rain fell, the floods came, and the winds blew and buffeted the house. And it collapsed and was completely ruined."

❖ Understanding the Word

Today Moses directs the people to commit themselves totally to God. The blessings promised for fidelity include numerous progeny and a good name, abundant crops and a multitude of flocks, peace and security from enemies. Curses include childlessness and premature death, family illness and diseased flocks, pestilence and drought, defeat by another nation and devastation of the land. The words Moses delivers are to be bound on their wrists and displayed as a pendant on their foreheads. This custom identified them as observant members of the covenant community and reminded them of their responsibility to commit themselves mind and heart to the covenant.

Contrary to what some have contended, Paul does not pit righteousness against the law. He insists that the Romans must conform to certain Christian principles. Nonetheless, he argues that adherence to the law does not produce righteousness. Only faith yields righteousness. According to Paul, all have sinned, and so all are in need of redemption. However, redemption and justification are received, not earned, and they are received precisely while one is a sinner. Furthermore, justification is given gratuitously, freely, without cause. God accomplishes this through the blood of Christ. Thus, by its very name, grace is an undeserved gift.

Jesus teaches that the disciples' service must be grounded in solid commitment to him. Not signs of respect, forms of religiosity, or spectacular deeds, but adherence to his words is essential for entrance into the reign of heaven. Discipleship requires a life of righteousness, not merely charismatic activities. In order to illustrate this point, Jesus contrasts the way of the wise with the way of the foolish. The wise build the house on the solid ground of Jesus' words, while the fool's house is constructed on sand. The implications of Jesus' words are quite clear. In order to be his disciples, people must follow Jesus' instructions carefully and faithfully. Those who do will be invited into the reign of God. Those who do not will be denied entry.

The poet Anne Sexton once wrote that words may be both daisies and bruises. We live in a time when words seem to wound and divide people more than heal and unite them. Whether in the realm of politics or religion, words have become weapons more often than bridges to understanding and cooperation. But we are a people who over the centuries have been formed by the word of God in both the Old and New Testament.

Both Moses and Jesus knew the power of words that have taken root in the human heart and carry over into action. In the book of Deuteronomy Moses gives his final speech to the people he has led out of bondage and brought to the border of the Promised Land. He calls them not only to wear these words on their body as emblems of faith, but to "take these words of mine into your heart and soul" (Deuteronomy 11:18).

Jesus begins by saying that words alone are not enough; what matters in the end is doing the will of the Father. And what is the Father's will? Go back and read the entire Sermon on the Mount (Matthew 5:1 — 7:29). The call to live in a way that brings the law of Moses to fulfillment is to be heard, taken to heart, and carried into action. The instruction given to the disciples remains an urgent command to bring about the kingdom of heaven now. Jesus' words will be a sturdy shelter that protects them when battering storms threaten to overwhelm.

✤✤ Consider/Discuss

Take some time to reread the Sermon on the Mount.
- Which of Jesus' words do you find most challenging?
- Which do you feel are particularly addressed to you at this time of your life?
- Is there a word that you are hearing for the first time?

✤✤ Responding to the Word

We pray that our lives will have a strong foundation on the teachings of Jesus. We pray that his words will be seeds that bear fruit in lives of justice, mercy, compassion, and forgiveness. We ask that these words find a home in our heart and soul.

Although Lent has traditionally been understood as a time of repentance and penance, the liturgical readings for the Sundays of this year focus our attention in a different way. They would have us reflect on the goodness of God and the blessings that flow from this goodness rather than on human sinfulness and any attempts to make amends for it through Lenten practices. This is not to deny human failure, but to refocus our gaze from ourselves to God.

The mystery of divine graciousness unfolds in the readings. There we see that God created the first human beings and placed them in a garden filled with trees that were delightful to look at and good for food. Despite this graciousness, the first couple sinned. However, human sinfulness could not deter God's love. Time and again, God responded to sin with graciousness: Abram was chosen by God to be both the beneficiary of God's blessing and the agent of blessing for others; God provided food and drink for the murmuring people in the wilderness; David was chosen king to lead the people to God; God promised to re-create a broken nation, opening their graves and filling the dead with God's own spirit so that they might live; a prophetic servant of the LORD allowed himself to be the object of the hatred of others. The Lenten readings suggest that not even our sinfulness can cause God to turn away from us. Instead, we are inundated with divine blessings. This is a profound, if often overlooked, Lenten message.

The ultimate example of God's unconditional love is found in the salvation won for us by Jesus. We are assured that sin cannot imperil grace. Instead, the obedience of Jesus has made even sinners righteous. Through Jesus, God saved us and called us to a life of holiness. Because of Jesus we can live as children of light. All of this is accomplished by the Spirit who dwells within us. The Sunday readings clearly point to divine graciousness as a major theme of the season.

The last three Sundays of Lent mark the period of scrutiny for the catechumens. It is also a time for the rest of us to open ourselves to transformation. With the Samaritan woman we are astonished at Jesus' revelation of himself as messiah, and we are eager to reform our lives. Like the man restored to sight, we too open ourselves to the enlightenment that comes from God. Like Lazarus, we emerge from the tomb ready to live new lives. If we reflect on God's graciousness, we will not simply do penance for our sins. Rather, we will open ourselves to be transformed by God's uncompromising love.

March 13, 2011

FIRST SUNDAY OF LENT

Today's Focus: Destination 1—The Desert

Going to the desert might not sound too appealing: hot during the day, cold at night, inhabited by rattlesnakes, tarantulas, and scorpions. In the Bible, however, the desert is one of those special places where God is at work. This Sunday we are invited to accompany Jesus out to the desert.

FIRST READING
Genesis 2:7–9; 3:1–7

The Lord God formed man out of the clay of the ground and blew into his nostrils the breath of life, and so man became a living being.

Then the Lord God planted a garden in Eden, in the east, and placed there the man whom he had formed. Out of the ground the Lord God made various trees grow that were delightful to look at and good for food, with the tree of life in the middle of the garden and the tree of the knowledge of good and evil.

Now the serpent was the most cunning of all the animals that the Lord God had made. The serpent asked the woman, "Did God really tell you not to eat from any of the trees in the garden?" The woman answered the serpent: "We may eat of the fruit of the trees in the garden; it is only about the fruit of the tree in the middle of the garden that God said, 'You shall not eat it or even touch it, lest you die.' " But the serpent said to the woman: "You certainly will not die! No, God knows well that the moment you eat of it your eyes will be opened and you will be like gods who know what is good and what is evil." The woman saw that the tree was good for food, pleasing to the eyes, and desirable for gaining wisdom. So she took some of its fruit and ate it; and she also gave some to her husband, who was with her, and he ate it. Then the eyes of both of them were opened, and they realized that they were naked; so they sewed fig leaves together and made loincloths for themselves.

PSALM RESPONSE
Psalm 51:3a

Be merciful, O Lord, for we have sinned.

SECOND READING
*Romans 5:
12–19
or 5:12, 17–19*

Brothers and sisters: Through one man sin entered the world, and through sin, death, and thus death came to all men, inasmuch as all sinned—[for up to the time of the law, sin was in the world, though sin is not accounted when there is no law. But death reigned from Adam to Moses, even over those who did not sin after the pattern of the trespass of Adam, who is the type of the one who was to come.

But the gift is not like the transgression. For if by the transgression of the one, the many died, how much more did the grace of God and the gracious gift of the one man Jesus Christ overflow for the many. And the gift is not like the result of the one who sinned. For after one sin there was the judgment that brought condemnation; but the gift, after many transgressions, brought acquittal.] For if, by the transgression of the one, death came to reign through that one, how much more will those who receive the abundance of grace and of the gift of justification come to reign in life through the one Jesus Christ. In conclusion, just as through one transgression condemnation came upon all, so, through one righteous act, acquittal and life came to all. For just as through the disobedience of the one man the many were made sinners, so, through the obedience of the one, the many will be made righteous.

GOSPEL
*Matthew 4:
1–11*

At that time Jesus was led by the Spirit into the desert to be tempted by the devil. He fasted for forty days and forty nights, and afterwards he was hungry. The tempter approached and said to him, "If you are the Son of God, command that these stones become loaves of bread." He said in reply, "It is written:
One does not live on bread alone,
  but on every word that comes forth
  from the mouth of God."

Then the devil took him to the holy city, and made him stand on the parapet of the temple, and said to him, "If you are the Son of God, throw yourself down. For it is written:
He will command his angels concerning you
  and with their hands they will support you,
  lest you dash your foot against a stone."
Jesus answered him, "Again it is written,
You shall not put the Lord, your God, to the test."

Then the devil took him up to a very high mountain, and showed him all the kingdoms of the world in their magnificence, and he said to him, "All these I shall give to you, if you will prostrate yourself and worship me." At this, Jesus said to him, "Get away, Satan! It is written:
The Lord, your God, shall you worship
  and him alone shall you serve."

Then the devil left him and, behold, angels came and ministered to him.

The reading from Genesis is the first account of sin. The sin itself was disobedience, but the inclination that gave rise to it was a form of hubris—the desire to be like gods. The cunning serpent should not be confused with the devil who appears much later in the biblical tradition. This mysterious creature has been used by the writer to point out how vulnerable to temptation humans are. The tree of knowledge plays no role except that it was very enticing, yet forbidden. The subtlety of temptation is obvious. It is admirable to want to be like God, but it is hubris to take things into one's own hands and make decisions contrary to God's will.

Paul speaks of the incomparable nature of God's salvific grace. He compares the universal effects of sin and death with the all-encompassing power of forgiveness and life. He then contrasts Adam, "the type of the one who was to come," to Christ, his unrivaled counterpart (Romans 5:14). Sin entered the world through Adam. The evidence of this is the universal reign of death. All die, therefore all must have sinned. As universal death entered the world through the sin of one—Adam—so grace was won for all through the gift of one—Christ. However, grace is much more powerful than sin.

The place of Jesus' testing is the desert, traditionally believed to be the abode of evil spirits. Reminiscent of Israel's forty years in the wilderness, Jesus fasted for forty days and forty nights. The devil challenges Jesus' identity as Son of God, urging him to turn stones into bread. The devil then proposes that Jesus test God's promise of protection by throwing himself from the pinnacle of the temple. Finally, the devil offers Jesus dominion over the world. Jesus' responses outline a very different approach. He will allow the word of God to direct his actions, he will rely on God's providence, and he will remain faithful to God. Jesus is steadfast in the face of temptation.

❖❖ *Reflecting on the Word*

Twice a year the Gospels take us to the desert. John the Baptist cries out on two Sundays every Advent, and Jesus encounters Satan every Lent. What makes the desert so ideal a setting as we prepare to celebrate the two great mysteries of our faith?

The desert is a place of testing, as God's people learned when they wandered around it for forty years. With hardened hearts, they had rejected the God who had liberated them from slavery in Egypt, losing faith even while God was talking to Moses and setting down the conditions for their adoption. Up went the golden calf and out went the memory of what God had just done for them.

Even Eden wasn't enough to keep the human heart open. Even there it was clear that we could be seduced by anything that looked good and promised more than it could deliver. But Jesus showed that one of us could measure up to the test and reveal himself as the "beloved Son" that he had been called at his baptism (Matthew 3:17).

The desert is also for wooing. The prophet Hosea quotes God saying, "So I will allure her [Israel]; I will lead her into the desert and speak to her heart" (Hosea 2:16). And when Satan left Jesus, God sent "angels [who] came and ministered to him" (Matthew 4:11).

So we come to this Lent and the possibility that God wishes to draw us out into a quiet, lonely place to have us meet the One who made us, redeemed us, and continues to shape us into temples of the Holy Spirit.

✤ Consider/Discuss

- What do you associate with the desert?
- Is there any particular place you consider "the desert" where God meets you?
- Are you being tested today in terms of living out the baptismal call to be a beloved son or daughter?

✤ Responding to the Word

We pray that this Lent will be a time of deeper understanding of what it means to be God's beloved child. We ask God to open our eyes to recognize those things that draw us away and to be open to how God might be drawing us closer.

March 20, 2011

SECOND SUNDAY OF LENT

Today's Focus: Destination 2—The Mountain

This week we are invited to go forth once again, first with Abram, who is told to leave the land of his kinsfolk. No destination is given. God simply says to "[g]o forth . . . to a land I will show you" (Genesis 12:1). Then we go with Jesus, not into the desert, but up a mountain for a glimpse of glory.

FIRST READING
Genesis 12:1–4a

The LORD said to Abram: "Go forth from the land of your kinsfolk and from your father's house to a land that I will show you.

"I will make of you a great nation,
    and I will bless you;
I will make your name great,
    so that you will be a blessing.
I will bless those who bless you
    and curse those who curse you.
All the communities of the earth
    shall find blessing in you."

Abram went as the LORD directed him.

PSALM RESPONSE
Psalm 33:22

Lord, let your mercy be on us, as we place our trust in you.

SECOND READING
2 Timothy 1: 8b–10

Beloved: Bear your share of hardship for the gospel with the strength that comes from God.

He saved us and called us to a holy life, not according to our works but according to his own design and the grace bestowed on us in Christ Jesus before time began, but now made manifest through the appearance of our savior Christ Jesus, who destroyed death and brought life and immortality to light through the gospel.

GOSPEL
Matthew 17: 1–9

Jesus took Peter, James, and John his brother, and led them up a high mountain by themselves. And he was transfigured before them; his face shone like the sun and his clothes became white as light. And behold, Moses and Elijah appeared to them, conversing with him. Then Peter said to Jesus in reply, "Lord, it is good that we are here. If you wish, I will make three tents here, one for you, one for Moses, and one for Elijah." While he was still speaking, behold, a bright cloud cast a shadow over them, then from the cloud came a voice that said, "This is my beloved Son, with whom I am well pleased; listen to him." When the disciples heard this, they fell prostrate and were very much afraid.

But Jesus came and touched them, saying, "Rise, and do not be afraid." And when the disciples raised their eyes, they saw no one else but Jesus alone.

As they were coming down from the mountain, Jesus charged them, "Do not tell the vision to anyone until the Son of Man has been raised from the dead."

❖ Understanding the Word

The reading from Genesis expressly states that Abram is directed by God to travel from the land of his kinsfolk to one that is foreign to him. God then promises a fivefold blessing: Abram will be a great nation; he will be blessed; his name will be great; those who bless him will be blessed; those who curse him will be cursed. The directives from God require profound faith on Abram's part. They determine his identity (his past), his place in society (his present), and his legacy (his future). God is asking him to start anew. No questions are asked, no long period of preparation is suggested. God directs and Abram responds.

Paul exhorts his disciple Timothy to suffer with him the misfortunes that come from fidelity to the gospel and accompany righteous living. The Christian hymn that follows outlines what God has done for us and what Christ has done on our behalf. There is no question in Paul's mind that the wondrous blessings are all God's doing. Neither salvation nor the call to holiness is the fruit of any deed that we might have performed. They are not rewards for good behavior; they come to us freely out of the goodness of God.

Jesus is transformed before Peter, James, and John, the apparent inner circle of the apostles. Most scholars maintain that this account is not a vision of the future glorification of Jesus but an insight into the identity that was his during his public life. Jesus converses with Moses and Elijah, the representatives of the law and the prophets. Jesus' teaching is authenticated by the words that are spoken from the cloud: "listen to him" (Matthew 17:5). The apostles want to prolong Jesus' transfiguration. Jesus will not hear of it. Then, identifying himself as the mysterious Son of Man, he directs the three to remain silent about this experience until after his resurrection.

❖ Reflecting on the Word

Lent is an invitation to journey more deeply into the heart of God. What God asks of Abram is a willingness to trust that God will lead him. Abram is called from the very beginning to place his trust in the Lord and in the Lord's promises. We are told that Abram is seventy years old at the time he goes forth. I remember someone remarking, "Imagine coming in the house and saying to your wife, 'Honey, we have to pack up and go I know not where.' " We are told simply: "Abram went as the LORD directed him" (Genesis 12:4a). Abram's faith translates into trust that God is leading him.

Jesus brought the three apostles up a high mountain. Mountains often served as the meeting place of God and the prophets—Moses and Elijah come to mind. When Jesus and the three reach their destination, Jesus is transformed before them, face and clothes shining. Suddenly Moses and Elijah are talking with him. You can understand Peter wanting to stay there. But this is not journey's end. That will happen on a hill outside Jerusalem. For now they hear words meant also for us this day: "This is my beloved Son . . . listen to him" (Matthew 17:5).

We are asked to journey with Jesus for forty days—sometimes it may be into the desert of testing, sometimes up a mountain for a moment of blinding clarity. In both places we know Jesus as the beloved Son who trusts in the Father's will. Lent invites us to make that same journey into trusting the Father.

❖ Consider/Discuss

- Have you had a "mountain experience" when you came to know Jesus as God's beloved Son? Was your reaction similar to that of Peter, who did not want it to end?
- How is God calling you to trust? How is God calling you to listen to Jesus?

❖ Responding to the Word

God has called us to a holy life (1 Timothy 1:9). This week, as we journey with Jesus into the presence of the Father, listen for how the Father may be speaking to you now. Ask God to open your ears and eyes to recognize the beloved Son's presence.

March 27, 2011

THIRD SUNDAY OF LENT

Today's Focus: Lent as Inner Journey

Not all journeys take place in the outer world; there are important inner journeys that we need to make. We witness one in the story of the Samaritan woman. She thought she was only going out to get water. She ended up going on a journey of faith.

FIRST READING
Exodus 17:3–7

In those days, in their thirst for water, the people grumbled against Moses, saying, "Why did you ever make us leave Egypt? Was it just to have us die here of thirst with our children and our livestock?" So Moses cried out to the LORD, "What shall I do with this people? A little more and they will stone me!" The LORD answered Moses, "Go over there in front of the people, along with some of the elders of Israel, holding in your hand, as you go, the staff with which you struck the river. I will be standing there in front of you on the rock in Horeb. Strike the rock, and the water will flow from it for the people to drink." This Moses did, in the presence of the elders of Israel. The place was called Massah and Meribah, because the Israelites quarreled there and tested the LORD, saying, "Is the LORD in our midst or not?"

PSALM RESPONSE
Psalm 95:8

If today you hear his voice, harden not your hearts.

SECOND READING
Romans 5:1–2, 5–8

Brothers and sisters: Since we have been justified by faith, we have peace with God through our Lord Jesus Christ, through whom we have gained access by faith to this grace in which we stand, and we boast in hope of the glory of God.

And hope does not disappoint, because the love of God has been poured out into our hearts through the Holy Spirit who has been given to us. For Christ, while we were still helpless, died at the appointed time for the ungodly. Indeed, only with difficulty does one die for a just person, though perhaps for a good person one might even find courage to die. But God proves his love for us in that while we were still sinners Christ died for us.

GOSPEL
John 4:5–42 or
4:5–15, 19b–26,
39a, 40–42

Jesus came to a town of Samaria called Sychar, near the plot of land that Jacob had given to his son Joseph. Jacob's well was there. Jesus, tired from his journey, sat down there at the well. It was about noon.

A woman of Samaria came to draw water. Jesus said to her, "Give me a drink." His disciples had gone into the town to buy food. The Samaritan woman said to him, "How can you, a Jew, ask me, a Samaritan woman, for a drink?"—For Jews use nothing in common with Samaritans.—Jesus answered and said to her, "If you knew the gift of God and who is saying to you, 'Give me a drink,' you would have asked him and he would have given you living water." The woman said to him, "Sir, you do not even have a bucket and the cistern is deep; where then can you get this living water? Are you greater than our father Jacob, who gave us this cistern and drank from it himself with his children and his flocks?" Jesus answered and said to her, "Everyone who drinks this water will be thirsty again; but whoever drinks the water I shall give will never thirst; the water I shall give will become in him a spring of water welling up to eternal life." The woman said to him, "Sir, give me this water, so that I may not be thirsty or have to keep coming here to draw water."

[Jesus said to her, "Go call your husband and come back." The woman answered and said to him, "I do not have a husband." Jesus answered her, "You are right in saying, 'I do not have a husband.' For you have had five husbands, and the one you have now is not your husband. What you have said is true." The woman said to him,] "Sir, I can see that you are a prophet. Our ancestors worshiped on this mountain; but you people say that the place to worship is in Jerusalem." Jesus said to her, "Believe me, woman, the hour is coming when you will worship the Father neither on this mountain nor in Jerusalem. You people worship what you do not understand; we worship what we understand, because salvation is from the Jews. But the hour is coming, and is now here, when true worshipers will worship the Father in Spirit and truth; and indeed the Father seeks such people to worship him. God is Spirit, and those who worship him must worship in Spirit and truth." The woman said to him, "I know that the Messiah is coming, the one called the Christ; when he comes, he will tell us everything." Jesus said to her, "I am he, the one speaking with you."

[At that moment his disciples returned, and were amazed that he was talking with a woman, but still no one said, "What are you looking for?" or "Why are you talking with her?" The woman left her water jar and went into the town and said to the people, "Come see a man who told me everything I have done. Could he possibly be the Christ?" They went out of the town and came to him. Meanwhile, the disciples urged him, "Rabbi, eat." But he said to them, "I have food to eat of which you do not know." So the disciples said to one another, "Could someone have brought him something to eat?" Jesus said to them, "My food is to do the will of the one who sent me and to finish his work. Do you not say, 'In four months the harvest will be here'? I tell you, look up and see the fields ripe for the harvest. The reaper is already receiving payment and gathering crops for eternal life, so that the sower and reaper can rejoice together. For here the saying is verified that 'One sows and another reaps.' I sent you to reap what you have not worked for; others have done the work, and you are sharing the fruits of their work."]

Many of the Samaritans of that town began to believe in him because of the word of the woman who testified, "He told me everything I have done." When the Samaritans came to him, they invited him to stay with them; and he stayed there two days. Many more began to believe in him because of his word, and they said to the woman, "We no longer believe because of your word; for we have heard for ourselves, and we know that this is truly the savior of the world."

✛ Understanding the Word

The murmuring of the people in the wilderness lays bare their resistance to the leadership of Moses, and the shallowness of their trust in God. Still, just as God delivered the people from the bondage of Egypt through the leadership of Moses, so now, again through the actions of Moses, God gives them the water they demand. One wonders how a people who were the beneficiaries of God's abiding concern and miraculous protection could be so faithless and lacking in trust. After all that God has done, they still put God to the test. This is but another example of God's boundless and compassionate love for sinners.

Paul's teaching on justification is quite clear. It is based on the righteousness that originates in God, a righteousness that gives and sustains life, security, and well being. Human beings are righteous when they respect and enhance that life, security, and well being. They can only do this if they are in right relationship with God and, through this relationship, share in God's righteousness. According to Paul, we have no right to this relationship with God. It has been given to us, won for us by the Lord Jesus Christ. In fact, we have never deserved it. Yet, out of love, God gives it to us.

Jesus asks the Samaritan woman for water when in fact he is the one who will give her "living water." His knowledge of her marital situation prompts her to call him a prophet and to engage him in a discussion about the proper place to worship God. Jesus moves this conversation from a discussion of the place of worship to one that characterizes the manner of worship. Jesus' discussion with the woman is curious. She is a questionable member (a sinner) of a subordinate group (a woman) of a despised people (a Samaritan). Yet she is the one whom Jesus approaches; she is the one to whom he reveals himself as Messiah; and she is the one who heralds this good news to the people in the town.

✤ Reflecting on the Word

Sometimes a journey of great significance covers a very short distance, geographically speaking. Flannery O'Connor once said that everything important happened to her between the back door of the house and the chicken coop. Moses led the people of Israel from grumbling and complaining to a renewed faith by walking a few feet to tap a rock.

The journey in today's Gospel is an inner journey into faith in Jesus. Notice how the woman's perspective changes as the story progresses. With that change of perception comes a change of heart. Her first response to Jesus' request for a drink of water is curt: "How can you, a Jew, ask me, a Samaritan woman, for a drink?" (John 4:9). But after Jesus speaks about being able to give her living water, she sees him as one who will relieve her of the burdensome daily trip to the well, or even of ever being thirsty again.

Another shift comes after he tells her of her broken marriages. She recognizes him as a prophet. There is yet one more step to take, and Jesus helps her by offering a vision of a future time when all will worship together, and then confessing to her that he is the Messiah, the Christ. Through her witness, the village comes to meet Jesus and then finally to recognize him as savior of the world.

Lent invites us to journey with this woman and recognize Jesus in his fullness: as one who thirsts for us, who also brings us the life-giving water of baptism, who is a prophet speaking for God, who is the promised Messiah, and most especially, who has come to save us.

✤ Consider/Discuss

- What do you thirst for?
- How do you relate to Jesus? Do you recognize him as truly human, as a prophet, as the promised Messiah, as the Savior and Son of God?

✤ Responding to the Word

We can pray that Jesus will bring us to see him as living water that can satisfy us. We pray for all those preparing to be washed in the waters of baptism, that they will recognize in Jesus the source of eternal life.

April 3, 2011

FOURTH SUNDAY OF LENT

Today's Focus: Lent as a Journey from Darkness to Light

The journey from darkness to light, from blindness to sight, is found in all the readings today. Samuel learns that even prophets need to have their eyesight checked. A man born blind comes to sight twice when Jesus lays hands on him. And a community is told that, though they were once darkness, now they are light in the Lord.

FIRST READING
1 Samuel 16: 1b, 6–7, 10–13a

The LORD said to Samuel: "Fill your horn with oil, and be on your way. I am sending you to Jesse of Bethlehem, for I have chosen my king from among his sons."

As Jesse and his sons came to the sacrifice, Samuel looked at Eliab and thought, "Surely the Lord's anointed is here before him." But the LORD said to Samuel: "Do not judge from his appearance or from his lofty stature, because I have rejected him. Not as man sees does God see, because man sees the appearance but the LORD looks into the heart." In the same way Jesse presented seven sons before Samuel, but Samuel said to Jesse, "The LORD has not chosen any one of these." Then Samuel asked Jesse, "Are these all the sons you have?" Jesse replied, "There is still the youngest, who is tending the sheep." Samuel said to Jesse, "Send for him; we will not begin the sacrificial banquet until he arrives here." Jesse sent and had the young man brought to them. He was ruddy, a youth handsome to behold and making a splendid appearance. The LORD said, "There—anoint him, for this is the one!" Then Samuel, with the horn of oil in hand, anointed David in the presence of his brothers; and from that day on, the spirit of the LORD rushed upon David.

PSALM RESPONSE
Psalm 23:1

The Lord is my shepherd; there is nothing I shall want.

SECOND READING
Ephesians 5: 8–14

Brothers and sisters: You were once darkness, but now you are light in the Lord. Live as children of light, for light produces every kind of goodness and righteousness and truth. Try to learn what is pleasing to the Lord. Take no part in the fruitless works of darkness; rather expose them, for it is shameful even to mention the things done by them in secret; but everything exposed by the light becomes visible, for everything that becomes visible is light. Therefore, it says:

"Awake, O sleeper,
and arise from the dead,
and Christ will give you light."

GOSPEL
John 9:1–41
or 9:1, 6–9,
13–17, 34–38

As Jesus passed by he saw a man blind from birth. [His disciples asked him, "Rabbi, who sinned, this man or his parents, that he was born blind?" Jesus answered, "Neither he nor his parents sinned; it is so that the works of God might be made visible through him. We have to do the works of the one who sent me while it is day. Night is coming when no one can work. While I am in the world, I am the light of the world." When he had said this,] he spat on the ground and made clay with the saliva, and smeared the clay on his eyes, and said to him, "Go wash in the Pool of Siloam"—which means Sent—. So he went and washed, and came back able to see.

His neighbors and those who had seen him earlier as a beggar said, "Isn't this the one who used to sit and beg?" Some said, "It is," but others said, "No, he just looks like him." He said, "I am." [So they said to him, "How were your eyes opened?" He replied, "The man called Jesus made clay and anointed my eyes and told me, 'Go to Siloam and wash.' So I went there and washed and was able to see." And they said to him, "Where is he?" He said, "I don't know."]

They brought the one who was once blind to the Pharisees. Now Jesus had made clay and opened his eyes on a sabbath. So then the Pharisees also asked him how he was able to see. He said to them, "He put clay on my eyes, and I washed, and now I can see." So some of the Pharisees said, "This man is not from God, because he does not keep the sabbath." But others said, "How can a sinful man do such signs?" And there was a division among them. So they said to the blind man again, "What do you have to say about him, since he opened your eyes?" He said, "He is a prophet."

[Now the Jews did not believe that he had been blind and gained his sight until they summoned the parents of the one who had gained his sight. They asked them, "Is this your son, who you say was born blind? How does he now see?" His parents answered and said, "We know that this is our son and that he was born blind. We do not know how he sees now, nor do we know who opened his eyes. Ask him, he is of age; he can speak for himself." His parents said this because they were afraid of the Jews, for the Jews had already agreed that if anyone acknowledged him as the Christ, he would be expelled from the synagogue. For this reason his parents said, "He is of age; question him."

So a second time they called the man who had been blind and said to him, "Give God the praise! We know that this man is a sinner." He replied, "If he is a sinner, I do not know. One thing I do know is that I was blind and now I see." So they said to him, "What did he do to you? How did he open your eyes?"

He answered them, "I told you already and you did not listen. Why do you want to hear it again? Do you want to become his disciples, too?" They ridiculed him and said, "You are that man's disciple; we are disciples of Moses! We know that God spoke to Moses, but we do not know where this one is from." The man answered and said to them, "This is what is so amazing, that you do not know where he is from, yet he opened my eyes. We know that God does not listen to sinners, but if one is devout and does his will, he listens to him. It is unheard of that anyone ever opened the eyes of a person born blind. If this man were not from God, he would not be able to do anything."] They answered and said to him, "You were born totally in sin, and are you trying to teach us?" Then they threw him out.

When Jesus heard that they had thrown him out, he found him and said, "Do you believe in the Son of Man?" He answered and said, "Who is he, sir, that I may believe in him?" Jesus said to him, "You have seen him, the one speaking with you is he." He said, "I do believe, Lord, " and he worshiped him. [Then Jesus said, "I came into this world for judgment, so that those who do not see might see, and those who do see might become blind."

Some of the Pharisees who were with him heard this and said to him, "Surely we are not also blind, are we?" Jesus said to them, "If you were blind, you would have no sin; but now you are saying, 'We see,' so your sin remains."]

❖ Understanding the Word

Samuel's choice of David as king was determined by direct command of God. The anointing was a solemn and sacred action that ceremonially sealed his election by God. Following the ritual, "the spirit of the LORD rushed upon David." This spirit was understood as a principle of dynamic divine action, a force that had unique effects in human history. Those seized by the spirit were empowered to act within the community in a unique fashion determined by the particular needs of the community. The spirit took hold of judges (Judges 3:10) and prophets (Isaiah 61:1). This story recounts how it took hold of a future king.

The move from darkness to light is the principal metaphor used by the author of Ephesians to describe the radical change that takes place in the lives of those who commit themselves to Christ. Three qualities produced by the light—goodness, righteousness, truth—are symbolic of the complete transformation that this light can effect. Three phrases describe the transition from a state of inertia to one of vibrancy: from sleep to wakefulness, from death to new life, and from darkness to illumination. Christians have entered into a new state of being, and it will require of them a new way of living.

Jesus' cure of the man born blind suggests a new creation. The struggle here is between darkness and light, between blindness and sight. Jesus underscores the urgency of his ministry. He and his disciples must do God's work while it is yet day, for the night will come when such work will have to cease. Jesus identifies himself as the light of the world. The man, who is gradually brought from physical blindness to sight, also progressively moves from spiritual blindness to religious insight. This is not true of the Pharisees. They prided themselves on being disciples of Moses, but they were blind to the truth that the newly cured man saw so clearly. The one who was blind sees, and those who can see are really blind.

❖ Reflecting on the Word

Most of us can recognize times when we are "in the dark" and occasions when we carry darkness in our hearts, just as there are moments when we feel enlightened and find that our vision is clear. It is quite another thing to become identified with darkness or with light. The first words of today's reading from the Letter to the Ephesians stand out for their boldness: "You were once darkness, but now you are light in the Lord" (Ephesians 5:8).

We get a glimpse of what it means to be light in the Lord both from Samuel, who finally sees as God sees, and in the courageous behavior of the man born blind after Jesus has healed him. Samuel anoints Israel's greatest king, David, and the man born blind comes to faith in Jesus as Lord.

The man born blind is one of those strong figures found in John's Gospel. Like the woman at the well, we never learn his name but we come to know his heart. His speech is straightforward, whether speaking to his neighbors, the Pharisees, or Jesus. You can hear the gradual dawning of faith as he responds to those around him, from the simple "He put clay on my eyes, and I washed, and now I can see" to "He is a prophet," to his answer to Jesus' question about having faith in the Son of man standing before him, "I do believe, Lord" (John 9:15, 17, 38).

In the beginning God spoke. Those first words have never stopped bringing about what they said: "Let there be light" (Genesis 1:3).

❖ Consider/Discuss

- What does it mean to be darkness? To be light?
- Are you open to the light as Samuel and the man born blind were, willing to submit to it when it speaks to or touches you?
- Are you part of a community that strives to live in the light?

❖ Responding to the Word

We pray to God as the ineffable light shining forth in the darkness, ever creating anew, calling forth from the darkness of fear and prejudice and hatred a community of men and women who choose to live in the light of Christ. We pray God to remove our attraction to the darkness, replacing it with a love for the Light.

April 10, 2011

FIFTH SUNDAY OF LENT

Today's Focus: The Journey from Death to Life

Death comes not only to individuals like Lazarus, but also to nations. Ezekiel's vision points to death not only as a physical event but, perhaps just as often, a spiritual one. Nevertheless, the Spirit of the Lord can overthrow the power of death even now. The Spirit carries us into new life.

FIRST READING
Ezekiel 37: 12–14

Thus says the LORD GOD: O my people, I will open your graves and have you rise from them, and bring you back to the land of Israel. Then you shall know that I am the LORD, when I open your graves and have you rise from them, O my people! I will put my spirit in you that you may live, and I will settle you upon your land; thus you shall know that I am the LORD. I have promised, and I will do it, says the LORD.

PSALM RESPONSE
Psalm 130:7

With the Lord there is mercy and fullness of redemption.

SECOND READING
Romans 8:8–11

Brothers and sisters: Those who are in the flesh cannot please God. But you are not in the flesh; on the contrary, you are in the spirit, if only the Spirit of God dwells in you. Whoever does not have the Spirit of Christ does not belong to him. But if Christ is in you, although the body is dead because of sin, the spirit is alive because of righteousness. If the Spirit of the one who raised Jesus from the dead dwells in you, the one who raised Christ from the dead will give life to your mortal bodies also, through his Spirit dwelling in you.

In the shorter form of the reading, the passages in brackets are omitted.

GOSPEL
John 11:1–45
or 11:3–7, 17,
20–27, 33b–45

[Now a man was ill, Lazarus from Bethany, the village of Mary and her sister Martha. Mary was the one who had anointed the Lord with perfumed oil and dried his feet with her hair; it was her brother Lazarus who was ill.] So the sisters sent word to him saying, "Master, the one you love is ill." When Jesus heard this he said, "This illness is not to end in death, but is for the glory of God, that the Son of God may be glorified through it." Now Jesus loved Martha and her sister and Lazarus. So when he heard that he was ill, he remained for two days in the place where he was. Then after this he said to his disciples, "Let us go back to Judea." [The disciples said to him, "Rabbi, the Jews were just trying to stone you, and you want to go back there?" Jesus answered, "Are there not twelve hours in a day? If one walks during the day, he does not stumble, because he sees the light of this world. But if one walks at night, he stumbles, because the light is not in him." He said this, and then told them, "Our friend Lazarus is asleep, but I am going to awaken him." So the disciples said to him, "Master, if he is asleep, he will be saved." But Jesus was talking about his death, while they thought that he meant ordinary sleep. So then Jesus said to them clearly, "Lazarus has died. And I am glad for you that I was not there, that you may believe. Let us go to him." So Thomas, called Didymus, said to his fellow disciples, "Let us also go to die with him."]

When Jesus arrived, he found that Lazarus had already been in the tomb for four days. [Now Bethany was near Jerusalem, only about two miles away. And many of the Jews had come to Martha and Mary to comfort them about their brother.] When Martha heard that Jesus was coming, she went to meet him; but Mary sat at home. Martha said to Jesus, "Lord, if you had been here, my brother would not have died. But even now I know that whatever you ask of God, God will give you." Jesus said to her, "Your brother will rise." Martha said to him, "I know he will rise, in the resurrection on the last day." Jesus told her, "I am the resurrection and the life; whoever believes in me, even if he dies, will live, and everyone who lives and believes in me will never die. Do you believe this?" She said to him, "Yes, Lord. I have come to believe that you are the Christ, the Son of God, the one who is coming into the world."

[When she had said this, she went and called her sister Mary secretly, saying, "The teacher is here and is asking for you." As soon as she heard this, she rose quickly and went to him. For Jesus had not yet come into the village, but was still where Martha had met him. So when the Jews who were with her in the house comforting her saw Mary get up quickly and go out, they followed her, presuming that she was going to the tomb to weep there. When Mary came to where Jesus was and saw him, she fell at his feet and said to him, "Lord, if you had been here, my brother would not have died." When Jesus saw her weeping and the Jews who had come with her weeping,] he became perturbed and deeply troubled, and said, "Where have you laid him?" They said to him, "Sir, come and see." And Jesus wept. So the Jews said, "See how he loved him." But some of them said, "Could not the one who opened the eyes of the blind man have done something so that this man would not have died?"

So Jesus, perturbed again, came to the tomb. It was a cave, and a stone lay across it. Jesus said, "Take away the stone." Martha, the dead man's sister, said to him, "Lord, by now there will be a stench; he has been dead for four days." Jesus said to her, "Did I not tell you that if you believe you will see the glory of God?" So they took away the stone. And Jesus raised his eyes and said, "Father, I thank you for hearing me. I know that you always hear me; but because of the crowd here I have said this, that they may believe that you sent me." And when he had said this, he cried out in a loud voice, "Lazarus, come out!" The dead man came out, tied hand and foot with burial bands, and his face was wrapped in a cloth. So Jesus said to them, "Untie him and let him go."

Now many of the Jews who had come to Mary and seen what he had done began to believe in him.

✤ Understanding the Word

Ezekiel uses bodily resurrection as a metaphor for the reestablishment of the nation after its exile. The scene is a graveyard, the ultimate place of death and decay. Three statements of reversal are made: the sealed graves will be opened, the dead will be raised, and the exiled will return home. Both original creation and this restoration, considered a new creation, are unconditional gifts from a magnanimous God. It is clear that God controls the powers of life and death, destruction and restoration. Since the people believed that exile was punishment for sin, they viewed their restoration as yet another pure gift from God.

Paul contrasts two ways of living: life in the flesh and life in the spirit. Flesh and spirit both signify the whole person, but from particular points of view. For Paul, flesh refers to human nature in all its limitations; spirit refers to that nature attuned to God. Paul insists that life in the flesh cannot please God, while life in the spirit is a form of union with God. The real point of this passage is the resurrection of those who are in union with God. Just as Christ conquered death and lives anew, so those joined to Christ share in his victory and enjoy new life.

The resurrection of Lazarus points to the future death of Jesus. The parable about day and night can be understood in at least three ways. First is the literal meaning. The second metaphorically points to an inner light that guides the person. Finally, light can refer to Jesus. All of this cryptic speech prepares for Jesus' instruction on resurrection. With a self-revelatory exclamation, Jesus proclaims that he is the resurrection and the life, and faith in him guarantees life for others. The resurrection of Lazarus cannot be denied, but it can be misunderstood. Jesus is not merely a wonder-worker; he himself has the power of resurrection and he is the source of eternal life.

❖ Reflecting on the Word

Caravaggio painted an image of Lazarus coming forth from the tomb. Eugene O'Neill wrote a play called *Lazarus Laughed*. Sylvia Plath wrote a poem called "Lady Lazarus." Poets, playwrights, and artists have been attracted to this story from John's Gospel through the centuries. For some two millennia Lazarus has been the symbol of someone brought back from the dead, revealing the power of God at work in Jesus of Nazareth.

Over the centuries Lazarus has been a figure of hope for countless generations, especially at the time of a loved one's death. Are there any more comforting words than those that Jesus says to Martha? "I am the resurrection and the life; whoever believes in me, even if he dies, will live, and everyone who lives and believes in me will never die" (John 11:25–26).

Death comes not only at the end of life, but sometimes within life. This is true both for individuals and whole nations. Israel in exile was like a field of dry bones, sealed up in tombs, cut off from life completely, lacking all hope. But God promised to bring Israel back to life and return the people to their home. God promised the spirit that would bring them back home and restore life.

Paul's words to the community at Rome serve to remind us that death will not have the last word. For all the death that we see in our world from war and earthquakes, sickness and human violence and cruelty, there is a power stronger than death: the Spirit of God.

❖ Consider/Discuss

- How do you think of death, as the end or as a transition?
- Are you being called to die to something in your life, so that you can live more fully in the power of the Spirit?

❖ Responding to the Word

We pray to the Lord of the living and the dead that we might not lose hope even now in the face of so much sadness in our world. We pray for a strengthening of trust in God that removes any fear of death threatening us or those we love.

April 17, 2011

PALM SUNDAY OF THE LORD'S PASSION

Today's Focus: Jesus' Last Journeys

Today we accompany Jesus on his last two journeys: the triumphal ride into Jerusalem and the sorrowful walk from the room of the Last Supper to the hill of Calvary. One is a journey of joy; the other, of sorrow. Both invite us to know Jesus more deeply.

FIRST
READING
Isaiah 50:4–7

The Lord GOD has given me
  a well-trained tongue,
that I might know how to speak to the weary
  a word that will rouse them.
Morning after morning
  he opens my ear that I may hear;
and I have not rebelled,
  have not turned back.
I gave my back to those who beat me,
  my cheeks to those who plucked my beard;
my face I did not shield
  from buffets and spitting.

The Lord GOD is my help,
  therefore I am not disgraced;
I have set my face like flint,
  knowing that I shall not be put to shame.

PSALM
RESPONSE
Psalm 22:2a

My God, my God, why have you abandoned me?

SECOND
READING
Philippians 2:
6–11

Christ Jesus, though he was in the form of God,
  did not regard equality with God
  something to be grasped.
Rather, he emptied himself,
  taking the form of a slave,
  coming in human likeness;
  and found human in appearance,
  he humbled himself,
  becoming obedient to the point of death,
  even death on a cross.
Because of this, God greatly exalted him
  and bestowed on him the name
  which is above every name,
  that at the name of Jesus
  every knee should bend,
  of those in heaven and on earth and under the earth,
  and every tongue confess that
  Jesus Christ is Lord,
  to the glory of God the Father.

GOSPEL
Matthew 26:
14 — 27:66
or 27:11–54

[One of the Twelve, who was called Judas Iscariot, went to the chief priests and said, "What are you willing to give me if I hand him over to you?" They paid him thirty pieces of silver, and from that time on he looked for an opportunity to hand him over.

On the first day of the Feast of Unleavened Bread, the disciples approached Jesus and said, "Where do you want us to prepare for you to eat the Passover?" He said, "Go into the city to a certain man and tell him, 'The teacher says, "My appointed time draws near; in your house I shall celebrate the Passover with my disciples." ' " The disciples then did as Jesus had ordered, and prepared the Passover.

When it was evening, he reclined at table with the Twelve. And while they were eating, he said, "Amen, I say to you, one of you will betray me." Deeply distressed at this, they began to say to him one after another, "Surely it is not I, Lord?" He said in reply, "He who has dipped his hand into the dish with me is the one who will betray me. The Son of Man indeed goes, as it is written of him, but woe to that man by whom the Son of Man is betrayed. It would be better for that man if he had never been born." Then Judas, his betrayer, said in reply, "Surely it is not I, Rabbi?" He answered, "You have said so."

While they were eating, Jesus took bread, said the blessing, broke it, and giving it to his disciples said, "Take and eat; this is my body." Then he took a cup, gave thanks, and gave it to them, saying, "Drink from it, all of you, for this is my blood of the covenant, which will be shed on behalf of many for the forgiveness of sins. I tell you, from now on I shall not drink this fruit of the vine until the day when I drink it with you new in the kingdom of my Father." Then, after singing a hymn, they went out to the Mount of Olives.

Then Jesus said to them, "This night all of you will have your faith in me shaken, for it is written:

I *will strike the shepherd,*
    and the sheep of the flock will be dispersed;

but after I have been raised up, I shall go before you to Galilee." Peter said to him in reply, "Though all may have their faith in you shaken, mine will never be." Jesus said to him, "Amen, I say to you, this very night before the cock crows, you will deny me three times." Peter said to him, "Even though I should have to die with you, I will not deny you." And all the disciples spoke likewise.

Then Jesus came with them to a place called Gethsemane, and he said to his disciples, "Sit here while I go over there and pray." He took along Peter and the two sons of Zebedee, and began to feel sorrow and distress. Then he said to them, "My soul is sorrowful even to death. Remain here and keep watch with me." He advanced a little and fell prostrate in prayer, saying, "My Father, if it is possible, let this cup pass from me; yet, not as I will, but as you will." When he returned to his disciples he found them asleep. He said to Peter, "So you could not keep watch with me for one hour?

Watch and pray that you may not undergo the test. The spirit is willing, but the flesh is weak." Withdrawing a second time, he prayed again, "My Father, if it is not possible that this cup pass without my drinking it, your will be done!" Then he returned once more and found them asleep, for they could not keep their eyes open. He left them and withdrew again and prayed a third time, saying the same thing again. Then he returned to his disciples and said to them, "Are you still sleeping and taking your rest? Behold, the hour is at hand when the Son of Man is to be handed over to sinners. Get up, let us go. Look, my betrayer is at hand."

While he was still speaking, Judas, one of the Twelve, arrived, accompanied by a large crowd, with swords and clubs, who had come from the chief priests and the elders of the people. His betrayer had arranged a sign with them, saying, "The man I shall kiss is the one; arrest him." Immediately he went over to Jesus and said, "Hail, Rabbi!" and he kissed him. Jesus answered him, "Friend, do what you have come for." Then stepping forward they laid hands on Jesus and arrested him. And behold, one of those who accompanied Jesus put his hand to his sword, drew it, and struck the high priest's servant, cutting off his ear. Then Jesus said to him, "Put your sword back into its sheath, for all who take the sword will perish by the sword. Do you think that I cannot call upon my Father and he will not provide me at this moment with more than twelve legions of angels? But then how would the Scriptures be fulfilled which say that it must come to pass in this way?" At that hour Jesus said to the crowds, "Have you come out as against a robber, with swords and clubs to seize me? Day after day I sat teaching in the temple area, yet you did not arrest me. But all this has come to pass that the writings of the prophets may be fulfilled." Then all the disciples left him and fled.

Those who had arrested Jesus led him away to Caiaphas the high priest, where the scribes and the elders were assembled. Peter was following him at a distance as far as the high priest's courtyard, and going inside he sat down with the servants to see the outcome. The chief priests and the entire Sanhedrin kept trying to obtain false testimony against Jesus in order to put him to death, but they found none, though many false witnesses came forward. Finally two came forward who stated, "This man said, 'I can destroy the temple of God and within three days rebuild it.'" The high priest rose and addressed him, "Have you no answer? What are these men testifying against you?" But Jesus was silent. Then the high priest said to him, "I order you to tell us under oath before the living God whether you are the Christ, the Son of God." Jesus said to him in reply, "You have said so. But I tell you:

From now on you will see 'the Son of Man
    seated at the right hand of the Power'
    and 'coming on the clouds of heaven.'"

Then the high priest tore his robes and said, "He has blasphemed! What further need have we of witnesses? You have now heard the blasphemy; what is your opinion?" They said in reply, "He deserves to die!" Then they spat in his face and struck him, while some slapped him, saying, "Prophesy for us, Christ: who is it that struck you?"

Now Peter was sitting outside in the courtyard. One of the maids came over to him and said, "You too were with Jesus the Galilean." But he denied it in front of everyone, saying, "I do not know what you are talking about!" As he went out to the gate, another girl saw him and said to those who were there, "This man was with Jesus the Nazarene." Again he denied it with an oath, "I do not know the man!" A little later the bystanders came over and said to Peter, "Surely you too are one of them; even your speech gives you away." At that he began to curse and to swear, "I do not know the man." And immediately a cock crowed. Then Peter remembered the word that Jesus had spoken: "Before the cock crows you will deny me three times." He went out and began to weep bitterly.

When it was morning, all the chief priests and the elders of the people took counsel against Jesus to put him to death. They bound him, led him away, and handed him over to Pilate, the governor.

Then Judas, his betrayer, seeing that Jesus had been condemned, deeply regretted what he had done. He returned the thirty pieces of silver to the chief priests and elders, saying, "I have sinned in betraying innocent blood." They said, "What is that to us? Look to it yourself." Flinging the money into the temple, he departed and went off and hanged himself. The chief priests gathered up the money, but said, "It is not lawful to deposit this in the temple treasury, for it is the price of blood." After consultation, they used it to buy the potter's field as a burial place for foreigners. That is why that field even today is called the Field of Blood. Then was fulfilled what had been said through Jeremiah the prophet,

And they took the thirty pieces of silver,
the value of a man with a price on his head,
a price set by some of the Israelites,
and they paid it out for the potter's field
just as the Lord had commanded me.

Now | Jesus stood before the governor, who questioned him, "Are you the king of the Jews?" Jesus said, "You say so." And when he was accused by the chief priests and elders, he made no answer. Then Pilate said to him, "Do you not hear how many things they are testifying against you?" But he did not answer him one word, so that the governor was greatly amazed.

Now on the occasion of the feast the governor was accustomed to release to the crowd one prisoner whom they wished. And at that time they had a notorious prisoner called Barabbas. So when they had assembled, Pilate said to them, "Which one do you want me to release to you, Barabbas, or Jesus called Christ?" For he knew that it was out of envy that they had handed him over. While he was still seated on the bench, his wife sent him a message, "Have nothing to do with that righteous man. I suffered much in a dream today because of him." The chief priests and the elders persuaded the crowds to ask for Barabbas but to destroy Jesus. The governor said to them in reply, "Which of the two do you want me to release to you?" They answered, "Barabbas!" Pilate said to them, "Then what shall I do with Jesus called Christ?" They all said, "Let him be crucified!" But he said, "Why? What evil has he done?" They only shouted the louder, "Let him be crucified!" When Pilate saw that he was not succeeding at all, but that a riot was breaking out instead, he took water and washed his hands in the sight of the crowd, saying, "I am innocent of this man's blood. Look to it yourselves." And the whole people said in reply, "His blood be upon us and upon our children." Then he released Barabbas to them, but after he had Jesus scourged, he handed him over to be crucified.

Then the soldiers of the governor took Jesus inside the praetorium and gathered the whole cohort around him. They stripped off his clothes and threw a scarlet military cloak about him. Weaving a crown out of thorns, they placed it on his head, and a reed in his right hand. And kneeling before him, they mocked him, saying, "Hail, King of the Jews!" They spat upon him and took the reed and kept striking him on the head. And when they had mocked him, they stripped him of the cloak, dressed him in his own clothes, and led him off to crucify him.

As they were going out, they met a Cyrenian named Simon; this man they pressed into service to carry his cross.

And when they came to a place called Golgotha—which means Place of the Skull—, they gave Jesus wine to drink mixed with gall. But when he had tasted it, he refused to drink. After they had crucified him, they divided his garments by casting lots; then they sat down and kept watch over him there. And they placed over his head the written charge against him: This is Jesus, the King of the Jews. Two revolutionaries were crucified with him, one on his right and the other on his left. Those passing by reviled him, shaking their heads and saying, "You who would destroy the temple and rebuild it in three days, save yourself, if you are the Son of God, and come down from the cross!" Likewise the chief priests with the scribes and elders mocked him and said, "He saved others; he cannot save himself. So he is the king of Israel! Let him come down from the cross now, and we will believe in him. He trusted in God; let him deliver him now if he wants him. For he said, 'I am the Son of God.' " The revolutionaries who were crucified with him also kept abusing him in the same way.

From noon onward, darkness came over the whole land until three in the afternoon. And about three o'clock Jesus cried out in a loud voice, "Eli, Eli, *lema sabachthani?*" which means, "My God, my God, why have you forsaken me?" Some of the bystanders who heard it said, "This one is calling for Elijah." Immediately one of them ran to get a sponge; he soaked it in wine, and putting it on a reed, gave it to him to drink. But the rest said, "Wait, let us see if Elijah comes to save him." But Jesus cried out again in a loud voice, and gave up his spirit.

And behold, the veil of the sanctuary was torn in two from top to bottom. The earth quaked, rocks were split, tombs were opened, and the bodies of many saints who had fallen asleep were raised. And coming forth from their tombs after his resurrection, they entered the holy city and appeared to many. The centurion and the men with him who were keeping watch over Jesus feared greatly when they saw the earthquake and all that was happening, and they said, "Truly, this was the Son of God!" [There were many women there, looking on from a distance, who had followed Jesus from Galilee, ministering to him. Among them were Mary Magdalene and Mary the mother of James and Joseph, and the mother of the sons of Zebedee.

When it was evening, there came a rich man from Arimathea named Joseph, who was himself a disciple of Jesus. He went to Pilate and asked for the body of Jesus; then Pilate ordered it to be handed over. Taking the body, Joseph wrapped it in clean linen and laid it in his new tomb that he had hewn in the rock. Then he rolled a huge stone across the entrance to the tomb and departed. But Mary Magdalene and the other Mary remained sitting there, facing the tomb. The next day, the one following the day of preparation, the chief priests and the Pharisees gathered before Pilate and said, "Sir, we remember that this impostor while still alive said, 'After three days I will be raised up.' Give orders, then, that the grave be secured until the third day, lest his disciples come and steal him and say to the people, 'He has been raised from the dead.' This last imposture would be worse than the first." Pilate said to them, "The guard is yours; go, secure it as best you can." So they went and secured the tomb by fixing a seal to the stone and setting the guard.]

The dynamics of hearing and speaking are featured prominently in the first reading's passage from Isaiah. God has appointed the speaker to a particular ministry and has provided him ears to hear God's word and a well-trained tongue to speak that word to others. This word is alive and fresh each day, for God opens the speaker's ears morning after morning. This means that the speaker must be always attentive to hear the word that comes from God. A heavy price is exacted of the speaker. He suffers both physical attack and personal insult. Despite this, he does not recoil from his call.

The reading from Paul is one of the New Testament's most important Christological statements. The first verse sets the tone for the actions of Christ Jesus. He did not cling to the dignity that was rightfully his, but he emptied himself of all privilege. Though in the form of God, he chose the form of a servant or slave. Without losing his Godlike being, he took on the likeness of human beings. Having taken on the form of a slave, he became obedient like a slave. The exaltation of Christ is as glorious as his humiliation was debasing. All will praise Christ, whose exaltation gives glory to God.

The Passion account from Matthew's Gospel is a collection of episodes that tell the story of Jesus' last days. Though in several episodes Jesus appears to be the passive object of the brutality of others, it is quite clear that he is really in charge of his destiny. He makes many of the major decisions. Then he hands himself over to others, allowing them to decide his fate in those cases. Jesus declares that the time of his death and resurrection is the *kairós* time, that decisive moment when the promises of God are brought to fulfillment. The reading closes at the sealed tomb. Neither Pilate nor the Jewish leaders realize that everything is now in place for the eschatological event of the Resurrection.

❖ *Reflecting on the Word*

Today's Gospel before the blessing of the palms presents an exuberant scene. Imagine the large crowd just outside Jerusalem spreading their cloaks on the road, breaking off palm fronds, strewing them about and waving them as Jesus passes by. Hear the people shouting, "Hosanna to the Son of David." As Jesus enters the city, the people there are asking, "Who is this?" The crowd accompanying him answers: "This is Jesus the prophet, from Nazareth of Galilee. This is the one who comes in the name of the Lord." A journey of joy.

But a few days later Jesus took his last journey: a winding walk from the upper room on Thursday night out to the garden to Gethsemane, then to the house of Caiaphas, on to Pilate's house and courtyard, and, finally, to the hill of Calvary. During this time, he was spat on and struck, stripped, scourged, and crowned with thorns; he was denounced, mocked, and ridiculed. Most likely some of the same crowd that cried out "Hosanna" cried out, "Crucify him!" It ended with his being nailed to a cross, and after three torturous hours, he died. At this journey's end, there was one final cry from a small group, a centurion and the men with him: "Truly, this was the Son of God!" (Matthew 27:54).

Allow some time to relive these two journeys. You might hear some things you haven't noticed before. Perhaps the words of one of the secondary characters or Jesus' response to a particular situation or his silence before another will speak to you this time.

✦ Consider/Discuss

- What does it mean to acknowledge Jesus as the Son of David, the one who comes in the name of the Lord, the prophet from Galilee, the Son of God?

- As this Lent comes to its end, where have these days taken you? What have you learned? What do you have to say to God?

✦ Responding to the Word

We pray that we will follow Jesus faithfully all the days of our life, recognizing him as the one who continues to come in the name of the Father bringing life. We ask that we may trust in God as Jesus did until we see God face to face.

Notes

The Sunday readings for the Easter season constitute a mystagogical catechesis, a formative instruction for the neophytes. Selections from the Acts of the Apostles give us insight into the character of the early Christian community. The story of this community begins on Easter Sunday itself with the proclamation of the gospel message, an overview of the life of Jesus, and the meaning of that life. This is a fitting beginning for the season because it was just such a proclamation that planted the seeds of faith out of which the community emerged.

The communitarian character of this new family of believers was extraordinary. They were together when the Spirit took possession of them, filling them with courage and determination. They prayed together and held possessions in common. When internal dissensions occurred, they did what was necessary to keep members together. Faithful to the commission they received from Jesus, they brought the message of the gospel to distant places even at great personal risk.

While the Epistle readings of this season extol various aspects of the Resurrection itself, they really describe some of the blessings that we enjoy as Christians because of it. Raised with Christ, our lives are now hidden with Christ in God. Therefore, we are told to cast out any old yeast of malice or darkness. Through the Resurrection we are granted a new birth. As our shepherd, Christ leads us to safety and guards us from harm. We are made a chosen race, a royal priesthood, ready to give an explanation for the hope that is in us.

The Gospel readings for this season are all Resurrection narratives. Beginning with the account of the empty tomb, they lead us from the locked room into which the Risen Lord came to the disciples' reception of the Holy Spirit. In each instance we see doubt and ignorance transformed into Easter faith. We accompany the disciples as they travel to Emmaus, where they recognize the Lord in the breaking of the bread. We hear him describe himself as the gate of the sheepfold and as the way, the truth, and the life. Before his ascension, we hear him assure his disciples that they will not be left without comfort. On Pentecost, this promise is fulfilled.

These Easter readings remind us of the overwhelming love of God. The Easter season proclaims aloud the fact of eschatological fulfillment. Begun at the empty tomb, it continues on the roads of our lives, at the tables where we commune with God and with each other. It dissipates our fears and strengthens our resolve. Easter is the season of unbounded joy, of realized hope, of heartfelt gratitude, and of firm determination.

April 24, 2011

EASTER SUNDAY
THE RESURRECTION OF THE LORD

Today's Focus: Resurrection Happens Now

Easter invites us to look more closely at our everyday experience. While it is true that in the resurrection of Jesus, God began something awesome, a new creation, we have intimations of resurrection even now. Like the beloved disciple, we need to take a few moments to see them.

FIRST READING
Acts 10:34a, 37–43

Peter proceeded to speak and said: "You know what has happened all over Judea, beginning in Galilee after the baptism that John preached, how God anointed Jesus of Nazareth with the Holy Spirit and power. He went about doing good and healing all those oppressed by the devil, for God was with him. We are witnesses of all that he did both in the country of the Jews and in Jerusalem. They put him to death by hanging him on a tree. This man God raised on the third day and granted that he be visible, not to all the people, but to us, the witnesses chosen by God in advance, who ate and drank with him after he rose from the dead. He commissioned us to preach to the people and testify that he is the one appointed by God as judge of the living and the dead. To him all the prophets bear witness, that everyone who believes in him will receive forgiveness of sins through his name.

PSALM RESPONSE
Psalm 118:24

This is the day the Lord has made; let us rejoice and be glad.

SECOND READING
Colossians 3: 1–4

Brothers and sisters: If then you were raised with Christ, seek what is above, where Christ is seated at the right hand of God. Think of what is above, not of what is on earth. For you have died, and your life is hidden with Christ in God. When Christ your life appears, then you too will appear with him in glory.

– or –

1 Corinthians 5: 6b–8

Brothers and sisters: Do you not know that a little yeast leavens all the dough? Clear out the old yeast, so that you may become a fresh batch of dough, inasmuch as you are unleavened. For our paschal lamb, Christ, has been sacrificed. Therefore, let us celebrate the feast, not with the old yeast, the yeast of malice and wickedness, but with the unleavened bread of sincerity and truth.

GOSPEL
John 20:1–9

On the first day of the week, Mary of Magdala came to the tomb early in the morning, while it was still dark, and saw the stone removed from the tomb. So she ran and went to Simon Peter and to the other disciple whom Jesus loved, and told them, "They have taken the Lord from the tomb, and we don't know where they put him." So Peter and the other disciple went out and came to the tomb. They both ran, but the other disciple ran faster than Peter and arrived at the tomb first; he bent down and saw the burial cloths there, but did not go in. When Simon Peter arrived after him, he went into the tomb and saw the burial cloths there, and the cloth that had covered his head, not with the burial cloths but rolled up in a separate place. Then the other disciple also went in, the one who had arrived at the tomb first, and he saw and believed. For they did not yet understand the Scripture that he had to rise from the dead.

❖ *Understanding the Word*

In today's first reading, Peter announces that the story of Jesus from his baptism, through his ministry, to his death and resurrection has been reported all over the land. He explains the mystery of Jesus in terms of prophetic expectation, at once both reinterpreting earlier prophetic tradition and developing new theological insight. With just a few words, Peter places Jesus at the heart of both the prophetic and the apocalyptic traditions of Israel. He insists that the power of the Resurrection is not circumscribed by ethnic or religious origin. It is open to all who believe in Jesus. This is truly good news to the Gentiles.

The passage from Colossians contains the fundamental teaching about the Resurrection and how it transforms the lives of Christians. It is set against the backdrop of ancient cosmology. Two different realms are delineated: the world above and the world below. Christ rose from the dead and is now in the realm of heaven, seated at God's right hand. Christians believe that they are joined to Christ. Having died with him, they have also risen with him. Here is an example of the complex eschatological view, "already, but not yet." Joined to Christ, Christians are living in the final age already, but this age of fulfillment is not yet complete.

The Resurrection stories begin with a report of Mary Magdalene's visit to the tomb. The stone had been moved, but she does not entertain the possibility of Jesus' resurrection, only the removal of his body. She runs off to tell Peter and "the other disciple" (John 20:2). The choice of this reading for Easter Sunday highlights the incomprehensibility of the event. The fact that neither Mary, probably Jesus' closest female disciple, nor Peter, the leader of the Christian community, was prepared spontaneously to embrace the truth of the Resurrection should caution us lest we too glibly presume to grasp it. There is much in the reality of the Resurrection that continues to challenge us.

Some say we are only a series of neurons that come together for a little while and eventually decompose; in the meantime, the purpose of life is to have as pleasant a time as possible. A rather limiting vision, no? Easter is my starting point for rebuttal.

Easter calls us to include resurrection in our vision of life. This is not always easy. It wasn't when it first happened. You can see why Mary Magdalene, seeing that the stone had been removed, would conclude that the body had been stolen. And you can understand how Peter never got beyond seeing a bunch of burial cloths over in the corner without concluding Jesus was raised. Only the beloved disciple "saw and believed" (John 20:8).

We are never told what the tipping point was for the beloved disciple. Was it all those times resting his head near Jesus, watching, listening . . . and knowing?

Resurrection experiences have a long history. If you have had a relationship that you thought was totally over come back to life, you know that resurrection happens. If you have had an experience of going nowhere with a project, then it suddenly kicks in, you know that resurrection happens. If you know someone held captive by an addiction and see them break free and begin the process of recovery, you know resurrection happens.

Easter invites us to consider our experiences of resurrection and move to the conclusion: resurrections have been happening for a long time. It's just a matter of seeing and believing.

❖ *Consider/Discuss*

- Have you had any resurrection experiences lately?
- What does it mean to you that you share in resurrection life even now?

❖ *Responding to the Word*

We pray through Jesus, God's Son, whose resurrection was the Father's answer to death and violence. Jesus is the Word of God, the last word of God's unconditional love for us. There is one very simple response to this: Alleluia! Praise God!

May 1, 2011

SECOND SUNDAY OF EASTER

Today's Focus: Thomas, Our Twin

Every year we hear the tale of Thomas. Next to Peter and perhaps John, he is probably the most well-known apostle, due to this story. Thomas doubted, thank God, and left room for the rest of us to have those moments when our faith falters. It reminds us that faith is a gift for which we need to keep asking.

FIRST READING
Acts 2:42–47

They devoted themselves to the teaching of the apostles and to the communal life, to the breaking of bread and to the prayers. Awe came upon everyone, and many wonders and signs were done through the apostles. All who believed were together and had all things in common; they would sell their property and possessions and divide them among all according to each one's need. Every day they devoted themselves to meeting together in the temple area and to breaking bread in their homes. They ate their meals with exultation and sincerity of heart, praising God and enjoying favor with all the people. And every day the Lord added to their number those who were being saved.

PSALM RESPONSE
Psalm 118:1

Give thanks to the Lord for he is good, his love is everlasting.

SECOND READING
1 Peter 1:3–9

Blessed be the God and Father of our Lord Jesus Christ, who in his great mercy gave us a new birth to a living hope through the resurrection of Jesus Christ from the dead, to an inheritance that is imperishable, undefiled, and unfading, kept in heaven for you who by the power of God are safeguarded through faith, to a salvation that is ready to be revealed in the final time. In this you rejoice, although now for a little while you may have to suffer through various trials, so that the genuineness of your faith, more precious than gold that is perishable even though tested by fire, may prove to be for praise, glory, and honor at the revelation of Jesus Christ. Although you have not seen him you love him; even though you do not see him now yet believe in him, you rejoice with an indescribable and glorious joy, as you attain the goal of your faith, the salvation of your souls.

GOSPEL	On the evening of that first day of the week, when the doors were

GOSPEL
John 20:19–31

On the evening of that first day of the week, when the doors were locked, where the disciples were, for fear of the Jews, Jesus came and stood in their midst and said to them, "Peace be with you." When he had said this, he showed them his hands and his side. The disciples rejoiced when they saw the Lord. Jesus said to them again, "Peace be with you. As the Father has sent me, so I send you." And when he had said this, he breathed on them and said to them, "Receive the Holy Spirit. Whose sins you forgive are forgiven them, and whose sins you retain are retained."

Thomas, called Didymus, one of the Twelve, was not with them when Jesus came. So the other disciples said to him, "We have seen the Lord." But he said to them, "Unless I see the mark of the nails in his hands and put my finger into the nailmarks and put my hand into his side, I will not believe."

Now a week later his disciples were again inside and Thomas was with them. Jesus came, although the doors were locked, and stood in their midst and said, "Peace be with you." Then he said to Thomas, "Put your finger here and see my hands, and bring your hand and put it into my side, and do not be unbelieving, but believe." Thomas answered and said to him, "My Lord and my God!" Jesus said to him, "Have you come to believe because you have seen me? Blessed are those who have not seen and have believed."

Now, Jesus did many other signs in the presence of his disciples that are not written in this book. But these are written that you may come to believe that Jesus is the Christ, the Son of God, and that through this belief you may have life in his name.

❖ Understanding the Word

Our glimpse of the Christian community in today's first reading is an idealized picture, a kind of utopian dream. It depicts the primitive church more in its eschatological fulfillment than as it probably really was. Four characteristics of that community are given: apostolic teaching, community, Eucharist, and prayer. The signs and wonders that were performed by the apostles were primarily cures, evidence that the eschatological age of fulfillment had dawned. This miraculous activity filled the bystanders with awe, the conventional response of human beings who have witnessed the extraordinary power of God. The risen Lord brought others into their midst and made their numbers increase.

The short reading from 1 Peter contains a variety of themes: praise of God, Christology, soteriology, eschatology. It opens with a doxology patterned after a Jewish hymn of praise of God. Out of this theocentric perspective, the author develops his Christology, declaring that Jesus is the mediator of the salvation that comes from God. The new life that believers receive from God is eschatological in nature, looking to the future for the fulfillment of God's promise. The hope to which the new life looks is eschatological, the inheritance that accompanies it is eschatological, and the salvation that it guarantees is eschatological. This is the living hope to which Christians are born.

Thomas is the hinge that connects the two Resurrection appearances in the Gospel. Absent for the first event, he is the central character of the second. Thomas represents the second generation of Christians who are called to believe on the testimony of others. The faith required of him is, in a way, more demanding than that required of those who actually encountered the risen Lord. Jesus states that Thomas' ultimate faith does not compare with the faith of those who do not enjoy any sensible experience of the Lord. Thomas should be remembered, not because he was absent or because he doubted, but because like us he was called to believe on the word of others.

❖ Reflecting on the Word

It is easy to feel superior to Thomas until you realize that he represents just about every person who has ever paused a moment to ask him or herself: do I really believe? Do I still believe as I used to? And some combination of your heart and mind responds: I'm not sure. Be assured, this is not the end of the world.

Thomas stood there and told the rest of the apostles, "I don't, won't, can't accept this wild tale you are telling me." When Jesus appeared again, he didn't yell or get all bent out of shape about Thomas' doubts. He invited Thomas to touch his wounds and then asked him to believe (perhaps indicating that even touching the wounds might not be enough). Then he had a word for all others who would be disciples in the future: "Blessed are those who have not seen and have believed" (John 20:29).

Everyone since that select group in the beginning has come to believe on the strength of another's word. Perhaps it was a parent or friend or teacher or some religious figure. Perhaps it was a book, a movie, or even a television show. Sometimes the invitation to believe comes out of the blue—a soul-shattering event, an unexpected experience; sometimes, from within—an inner restlessness, a seeking after answers to life's questions. But when the invitation to believe comes, it calls for a leap. It comes down to an act of trust in the word of another, ultimately in the word of God.

❖ Consider/Discuss

- Who or what called you to faith in Jesus as your Lord and God?
- How have you called others to faith? Are you being asked to do so at this time?

❖ Responding to the Word

We need to remember that faith is a gift. We do not earn it and we do not receive it as a matter of a birthright. So it is good to pray for faith: that the Lord increase it; that it not be tested beyond what we, with God's grace, can bear; and that we persevere in faith.

May 8, 2011

THIRD SUNDAY OF EASTER

Today's Focus: Resurrection Words

Certain situations can imprison us, whether in regret, sorrow, grief, or despair. But a speaker offering the right words in the right way at the right time can transform a situation and move people from apathy to engagement, from hopelessness to hope. This is what happens in two of today's readings. And it can happen in our lives.

FIRST READING
Acts 2:14, 22–33

Then Peter stood up with the Eleven, raised his voice, and proclaimed: "You who are Jews, indeed all of you staying in Jerusalem. Let this be known to you, and listen to my words. You who are Israelites, hear these words. Jesus the Nazarene was a man commended to you by God with mighty deeds, wonders, and signs, which God worked through him in your midst, as you yourselves know. This man, delivered up by the set plan and foreknowledge of God, you killed, using lawless men to crucify him. But God raised him up, releasing him from the throes of death, because it was impossible for him to be held by it. For David says of him:

I saw the Lord ever before me,
    with him at my right hand I shall not be disturbed.
Therefore my heart has been glad and my tongue has exulted;
    my flesh, too, will dwell in hope,
because you will not abandon my soul to the netherworld,
    nor will you suffer your holy one to see corruption.
You have made known to me the paths of life;
    you will fill me with joy in your presence.

"My brothers, one can confidently say to you about the patriarch David that he died and was buried, and his tomb is in our midst to this day. But since he was a prophet and knew that God had sworn an oath to him that he would set one of his descendants upon his throne, he foresaw and spoke of the resurrection of the Christ, that neither was he abandoned to the netherworld nor did his flesh see corruption. God raised this Jesus; of this we are all witnesses. Exalted at the right hand of God, he received the promise of the Holy Spirit from the Father and poured him forth, as you see and hear."

PSALM RESPONSE
Psalm 16:11a

Lord, you will show us the path of life.

SECOND READING
1 Peter 1:17–21

Beloved: If you invoke as Father him who judges impartially according to each one's works, conduct yourselves with reverence during the time of your sojourning, realizing that you were ransomed from your futile conduct, handed on by your ancestors, not with perishable things like silver or gold but with the precious blood of Christ as of a spotless unblemished lamb.

He was known before the foundation of the world but revealed in the final time for you, who through him believe in God who raised him from the dead and gave him glory, so that your faith and hope are in God.

GOSPEL
Luke 24:13–35

That very day, the first day of the week, two of Jesus' disciples were going to a village seven miles from Jerusalem called Emmaus, and they were conversing about all the things that had occurred. And it happened that while they were conversing and debating, Jesus himself drew near and walked with them, but their eyes were prevented from recognizing him. He asked them, "What are you discussing as you walk along?" They stopped, looking downcast. One of them, named Cleopas, said to him in reply, "Are you the only visitor to Jerusalem who does not know of the things that have taken place there in these days?" And he replied to them, "What sort of things?" They said to him, "The things that happened to Jesus the Nazarene, who was a prophet mighty in deed and word before God and all the people, how our chief priests and rulers both handed him over to a sentence of death and crucified him. But we were hoping that he would be the one to redeem Israel; and besides all this, it is now the third day since this took place. Some women from our group, however, have astounded us: they were at the tomb early in the morning and did not find his body; they came back and reported that they had indeed seen a vision of angels who announced that he was alive. Then some of those with us went to the tomb and found things just as the women had described, but him they did not see." And he said to them, "Oh, how foolish you are! How slow of heart to believe all that the prophets spoke! Was it not necessary that the Christ should suffer these things and enter into his glory?" Then beginning with Moses and all the prophets, he interpreted to them what referred to him in all the Scriptures. As they approached the village to which they were going, he gave the impression that he was going on farther. But they urged him, "Stay with us, for it is nearly evening and the day is almost over." So he went in to stay with them. And it happened that, while he was with them at table, he took bread, said the blessing, broke it, and gave it to them. With that their eyes were opened and they recognized him, but he vanished from their sight. Then they said to each other, "Were not our hearts burning within us while he spoke to us on the way and opened the Scriptures to us?" So they set out at once and returned to Jerusalem where they found gathered together the eleven and those with them who were saying, "The Lord has truly been raised and has appeared to Simon!" Then the two recounted what had taken place on the way and how he was made known to them in the breaking of bread.

Peter's speech today proclaiming Jesus as Lord and Messiah follows the pattern of early missionary preaching: announcement of the arrival of the age of fulfillment; summary of events in the ministry, death, and resurrection of Jesus; recourse to the Old Testament showing Jesus as fulfillment of the promises. Only the call to repentance is absent. It is clear from the text that Peter is speaking to a Jewish community. This should be remembered lest we understand his accusation as anti-Judaic. This speech also proclaims Jesus' resurrection and ascension and the descent of the Spirit. Finally, it provides us with an early statement about the inner workings of the Trinity.

The author of 1 Peter speaks of the cost of salvation and the responsibilities that accompany it. He reminds the audience that calling God "father" is comparable to asking God to act as disciplinarian. This presents a picture different from that of a tender parent. It points to our obligation to live the new life in Christ with integrity. The author insists that the death and resurrection of Christ have ransomed believers from the futile manner of living they inherited from their ancestors, patterns of living into which they had been socialized. Christians must now live differently.

The disciples on the road to Emmaus are probably returning from the celebration of Passover, and they doubtless assume that the unrecognized Jesus is on the road for the same reason. Although Cleopas' companion is not named, several clues suggest it is his wife. As Jesus shows how the scriptures point to him, the hearts of the disciples burn within them. Their religious tradition is being interpreted in an exciting new way. Finally, it is in the breaking of the bread that their eyes are opened, and they recognize him. The account underscores several important issues: glory comes by way of suffering; remembering the tradition is not enough—in new situations it must be reinterpreted; and we come to know Christ in the breaking of the bread.

✦ Reflecting on the Word

The power of words spoken by a person with great conviction can be transformative. I have heard various presidents of our country speak, and many preachers of the gospel. Most memorable were those who offered not only a well-written speech but one communicated with what has been called "fire in the belly." This does not translate necessarily into a lot of shouting or banging of the podium, but more an experience of word becoming flesh.

Jesus certainly had this ability, as we hear today in the disciples' reaction: "Were not our hearts burning within us while he spoke to us on the way and opened the Scriptures to us?" (Luke 24:32). The same sense of heat being generated is in today's first reading when Peter raises his voice and proclaims: "You who are Israelites, hear these words" (Acts 2:22). Peter then goes on to preach Jesus Christ whom "God raised . . . up, releasing him from the throes of death, because it was impossible for him to be held by it" (2:24). This is a far cry from Peter in the courtyard the night Jesus was arrested.

We spend seven weeks celebrating the Easter event so that the awareness of this mystery might occupy a bigger place in our heart. Like the disciples on the road, we may find ourselves losing hope that our belief in Jesus really matters in today's world, but seven weeks of Easter can help us recover a stronger sense of what we heard in 1 Peter today, that truly our "faith and hope are in God" (1 Peter 1:21).

❖ Consider/Discuss

- Can you think of a time when the words of another have transformed how you were thinking or feeling?
- What impact do the words "He has been raised!" have on you?

❖ Responding to the Word

We can pray that we will be welcoming to anyone through whom Jesus continues to meet us on the road and bring us to deeper understanding of what his death and resurrection mean for our lives and the life of the world. We pray for liberation from whatever prevents us from recognizing him.

FOURTH SUNDAY OF EASTER

Today's Focus: Following the Shepherd

The comforting image of Jesus the Good Shepherd was found in the catacombs. It is one of the oldest images Christians turned to for understanding why God became human: to seek out and search for the lost. Today's Gospel emphasizes how the sheep hear the shepherd's voice and follow where he leads, to fullness of life.

FIRST READING
Acts 2:14a, 36–41

Then Peter stood up with the Eleven, raised his voice, and proclaimed: "Let the whole house of Israel know for certain that God has made both Lord and Christ, this Jesus whom you crucified."

Now when they heard this, they were cut to the heart, and they asked Peter and the other apostles, "What are we to do, my brothers?" Peter said to them, "Repent and be baptized, every one of you, in the name of Jesus Christ for the forgiveness of your sins; and you will receive the gift of the Holy Spirit. For the promise is made to you and to your children and to all those far off, whomever the Lord our God will call." He testified with many other arguments, and was exhorting them, "Save yourselves from this corrupt generation." Those who accepted his message were baptized, and about three thousand persons were added that day.

PSALM RESPONSE
Psalm 23:1

The Lord is my shepherd; there is nothing I shall want.

SECOND READING
1 Peter 2:20b–25

Beloved: If you are patient when you suffer for doing what is good, this is a grace before God. For to this you have been called, because Christ also suffered for you, leaving you an example that you should follow in his footsteps.
He committed no sin, and no deceit was found in his mouth.

When he was insulted, he returned no insult; when he suffered, he did not threaten; instead, he handed himself over to the one who judges justly. He himself bore our sins in his body upon the cross, so that, free from sin, we might live for righteousness. By his wounds you have been healed. For you had gone astray like sheep, but you have now returned to the shepherd and guardian of your souls.

Jesus said: "Amen, amen, I say to you, whoever does not enter a sheepfold through the gate but climbs over elsewhere is a thief and a robber. But whoever enters through the gate is the shepherd of the sheep. The gatekeeper opens it for him, and the sheep hear his voice, as the shepherd calls his own sheep by name and leads them out. When he has driven out all his own, he walks ahead of them, and the sheep follow him, because they recognize his voice. But they will not follow a stranger; they will run away from him, because they do not recognize the voice of strangers." Although Jesus used this figure of speech, the Pharisees did not realize what he was trying to tell them.

So Jesus said again, "Amen, amen, I say to you, I am the gate for the sheep. All who came before me are thieves and robbers, but the sheep did not listen to them. I am the gate. Whoever enters through me will be saved, and will come in and go out and find pasture. A thief comes only to steal and slaughter and destroy; I came so that they might have life and have it more abundantly."

❖ Understanding the Word

When Peter declares that God made Jesus both Lord and Christ, the people are cut to the heart with remorse. They realize that they put to death the Holy One, God's anointed. The openness with which they receive Peter's words of testimony and accusation shows that all of the Jewish people were not hard–hearted, as some have suggested. Peter then exhorts them to repent and be baptized. The promise of which Peter speaks is probably a reference to the promise of the Spirit that was initially made to the ancestors of the people in Peter's audience. The promise of the Spirit is now made to them.

The author of First Peter claims that when we suffer precisely for having done what is good, we have the example of Christ to follow. Afflicted though innocent, he did not resort to vengeance. The description of the innocent suffering of Christ recalls a passage from one of the Suffering Servant Songs of the prophet Isaiah (53:4–7). This passage also contains the image of the shepherd. It is employed here to indicate that Jesus is the shepherd and his disciples are the sheep. Although at times they wander away from him, they will be safe and will prosper only if they follow his lead.

In the Gospel, Jesus uses figures of speech to make his points. Characterizing himself as a shepherd, he contrasts himself with those who try to steal into the sheepfold. He seeks to guide, guard, and nurture the sheep; strangers want to snatch the sheep. The true shepherd will be recognized by both the gatekeeper and the sheep. Then, using the technical phrase "I am", he characterizes himself as the gate. Those who go through Jesus will be safe within the pen. As both shepherd and gate, Jesus shows concern for the welfare of the sheep. He insists that he has come so that they may have life and have it more abundantly.

At the end of the day, shepherds would bring their sheep to a common sheep-fold, leading them through a gate that was guarded during the night. Shepherds would give names to their sheep and call to them when daylight came, leading them back out to pasture. Because the sheep recognized the shepherd's voice there was no mix-up with sheep that belonged to others.

The idea that shepherds had a name for each of their sheep brings home the difference between a good shepherd and a stranger. The good shepherd was concerned not only for the flock but for each sheep in it. He knew them and they knew him. "They will not follow a stranger; they will run away from him, because they do not recognize the voice of strangers" (John 10:5).

There are two words in Greek for "good"—*agathos* and *kalos*. *Agathos* refers to moral goodness, as in being a "good person." *Kalos* refers to being "good at" something. Certainly Jesus is the Good Shepherd in both senses, but the word used here is *kalos*, emphasizing his being "good at" shepherding.

Jesus knows his sheep by name, leads them to safety when darkness falls, and returns them to pasture. He was willing to lay down his life for them. Most comforting of all, he came then and comes now so we might have life and have it more abundantly. This image challenges all who have been called to be shepherds in today's church, to be good shepherds and to be good at shepherding.

✦ Consider/Discuss

- What does the image of Jesus as the good shepherd say to you in your life?
- What does the promise of "abundant life" mean for you?
- Have you come to know the difference between the voice of the good shepherd and the voice of "a stranger"?

✦ Responding to the Word

Jesus, our shepherd, not only cares and searches us out, but he "bore our sins in his body upon the cross so that, free from sin, we might live for righteousness" (1 Peter 2:24). We praise the Father for giving us Jesus as "the shepherd and guardian of our souls" and we pray for all who have taken up ministering to God's people.

May 22, 2011

FIFTH SUNDAY OF EASTER

Today's Focus: A House of Living Stones

The night before his death Jesus promised to prepare a home for his disciples and that he would return and take them there. The community of believers can also be thought of as a "spiritual house," its members "living stones," built with Christ as its cornerstone, offering shelter to those burdened.

FIRST READING
Acts 6:1–7

As the number of disciples continued to grow, the Hellenists complained against the Hebrews because their widows were being neglected in the daily distribution. So the Twelve called together the community of the disciples and said, "It is not right for us to neglect the word of God to serve at table. Brothers, select from among you seven reputable men, filled with the Spirit and wisdom, whom we shall appoint to this task, whereas we shall devote ourselves to prayer and to the ministry of the word." The proposal was acceptable to the whole community, so they chose Stephen, a man filled with faith and the Holy Spirit, also Philip, Prochorus, Nicanor, Timon, Parmenas, and Nicholas of Antioch, a convert to Judaism. They presented these men to the apostles who prayed and laid hands on them. The word of God continued to spread, and the number of the disciples in Jerusalem increased greatly; even a large group of priests were becoming obedient to the faith.

PSALM RESPONSE
Psalm 33:22

Lord, let your mercy be on us, as we place our trust in you.

SECOND READING
1 Peter 2:4–9

Beloved: Come to him, a living stone, rejected by human beings but chosen and precious in the sight of God, and, like living stones, let yourselves be built into a spiritual house to be a holy priesthood to offer spiritual sacrifices acceptable to God through Jesus Christ. For it says in Scripture:
Behold, I am laying a stone in Zion,
a cornerstone, chosen and precious,
and whoever believes in it shall not be put to shame.
Therefore, its value is for you who have faith, but for those without faith:
The stone that the builders rejected
has become the cornerstone,
and
A stone that will make people stumble,
and a rock that will make them fall.
They stumble by disobeying the word, as is their destiny.

You are "a chosen race, a royal priesthood, a holy nation, a people of his own, so that you may announce the praises" of him who called you out of darkness into his wonderful light.

GOSPEL
John 14:1–12 Jesus said to his disciples: "Do not let your hearts be troubled. You have faith in God; have faith also in me. In my Father's house there are many dwelling places. If there were not, would I have told you that I am going to prepare a place for you? And if I go and prepare a place for you, I will come back again and take you to myself, so that where I am you also may be. Where I am going you know the way." Thomas said to him, "Master, we do not know where you are going; how can we know the way?" Jesus said to him, "I am the way and the truth and the life. No one comes to the Father except through me. If you know me, then you will also know my Father. From now on you do know him and have seen him." Philip said to him, "Master, show us the Father, and that will be enough for us." Jesus said to him, "Have I been with you for so long a time and you still do not know me, Philip? Whoever has seen me has seen the Father. How can you say, 'Show us the Father'? Do you not believe that I am in the Father and the Father is in me? The words that I speak to you I do not speak on my own. The Father who dwells in me is doing his works. Believe me that I am in the Father and the Father is in me, or else, believe because of the works themselves. Amen, amen, I say to you, whoever believes in me will do the works that I do, and will do greater ones than these, because I am going to the Father."

❖ Understanding the Word

Today's scriptures observe tension within the early Christian community. Both the Greek-speakers and Hebrew-speakers were probably Jewish-Christians, separated by language rather than by religious background. At issue is some practical matter, not a point of doctrine. Peter does not stand as sole leader. Rather, the entire group of apostles, known as the Twelve, addresses the problem. Besides this collegiality, the community practiced subsidiarity, for the community selected men to exercise the ministry. The diversity that accompanied the growth of the community both enriched it and was the cause of the tension described here.

The second reading characterizes Christ as a living stone and describes Christians as living stones as well. The stone is living because of who Christ is and not because of what he does. When "living" describes Christians, it refers to the life that is theirs because of their relationship with Christ. As cornerstone, Christ is the underpinning of the building, the church. This stone is sometimes considered the capstone, the stone that holds the two pillars of an arch together. This passage clearly related the way they understand Christ and how they understand the church.

Jesus seeks to strengthen his followers who are troubled at the thought of his departure. He urges them to trust. He does not focus on the end of his life, only on the joyful events that will follow it. He leaves to prepare a place for the others with God. The passage is open to both an apocalyptic and a mystical interpretation. In the first, he is referring to his return at the end of time; in the second, he is alluding to the indwelling of his spirit enjoyed in this life by those united with him. Neither Thomas nor Philip fully understands what he means. Jesus ends his discourse with a promise that those who believe in him will be able to perform deeds that are even more wondrous than those he has performed.

❖ Reflecting on the Word

Over the years several television shows have focused on rebuilding and reshaping houses. For over thirty years PBS's *This Old House* has offered tips on repairing homes. More recently, *Extreme Makeover* takes a team into someone's home and transforms it to meet the serious needs of its occupants, often dealing with health or disability issues or trying to serve the larger community in some way.

From the beginning the church has been imagined as a house of living stones, built on Jesus Christ, a dwelling place where people come for shelter and sustenance, where they can set down their burdens and find comfort and consolation before being sent back out in the world to make it a better place to live.

The risen Christ is truly one who offers an "extreme makeover." He can be trusted to shape us into a dwelling place where the Spirit of the Lord takes up permanent residence, bringing gifts to benefit the world. From the beginning there have been challenges for those who form the church, and an ongoing need for renovation to meet the needs of the time.

Our efforts to make the church a home where love, mercy, justice, and peace will be found should lead us to build more firmly on Jesus our cornerstone. When the time comes, the home he promised to prepare for us and take us to should be easily recognizable. It should not be that much different from the church we have been living in all our lives.

❖ Consider/Discuss

- What does it mean to be a community of "living stones"?
- What are the "works" that Jesus empowers us to do, perhaps even greater than what he did?

❖ Responding to the Word

We pray the Lord to give us confidence to trust in his word that he has gone to prepare a permanent dwelling place for us, where we will be with him and all those who have gone ahead of us. We pray that this assurance may strengthen us to live as if we were already there.

May 29, 2011

SIXTH SUNDAY OF EASTER

Today's Focus: Living into the Mystery

Christian life is not simply a matter of following commands from the Bible. At the heart of responding to Jesus Christ is the decision to open our hearts to receive the Spirit of truth, allowing the Spirit to take up permanent residence within us. By doing this, we live in communion with the Father and the Son.

FIRST READING
Acts 8:5–8, 14–17

Philip went down to the city of Samaria and proclaimed the Christ to them. With one accord, the crowds paid attention to what was said by Philip when they heard it and saw the signs he was doing. For unclean spirits, crying out in a loud voice, came out of many possessed people, and many paralyzed or crippled people were cured. There was great joy in that city.

Now when the apostles in Jerusalem heard that Samaria had accepted the word of God, they sent them Peter and John, who went down and prayed for them, that they might receive the Holy Spirit, for it had not yet fallen upon any of them; they had only been baptized in the name of the Lord Jesus. Then they laid hands on them and they received the Holy Spirit.

PSALM RESPONSE
Psalm 66:1

Let all the earth cry out to God with joy.

SECOND READING
1 Peter 3:15–18

Beloved: Sanctify Christ as Lord in your hearts. Always be ready to give an explanation to anyone who asks you for a reason for your hope, but do it with gentleness and reverence, keeping your conscience clear, so that, when you are maligned, those who defame your good conduct in Christ may themselves be put to shame. For it is better to suffer for doing good, if that be the will of God, than for doing evil. For Christ also suffered for sins once, the righteous for the sake of the unrighteous, that he might lead you to God. Put to death in the flesh, he was brought to life in the Spirit.

GOSPEL
John 14:15–21   Jesus said to his disciples: "If you love me, you will keep my commandments. And I will ask the Father, and he will give you another Advocate to be with you always, the Spirit of truth, whom the world cannot accept, because it neither sees nor knows him. But you know him, because he remains with you, and will be in you. I will not leave you orphans; I will come to you. In a little while the world will no longer see me, but you will see me, because I live and you will live. On that day you will realize that I am in my Father and you are in me and I in you. Whoever has my commandments and observes them is the one who loves me. And whoever loves me will be loved by my Father, and I will love him and reveal myself to him."

❖ Understanding the Word

Philip, one of the seven men appointed by the Jerusalem community to attend to the needs of the Hellenistic widows, travels north to Samaria. Though Jews and Samaritans pursued different paths, they both lived in expectation of a messiah. This shared hope explains their openness to Philip's preaching, which is supported by exorcisms and healings. By their baptism, the Samaritans were incorporated into the community. Whether the Spirit was conferred on them when they were baptized or when the apostles laid hands on them is a lesser matter. What is important is the reconciliation in Christ between the Jews and the Samaritans.

The First Letter of Peter tells the Christians that they must respond to the suffering they will endure for their faith in a way that will enhance the spread of the gospel. Peter offers the sufferings of Christ as an example to follow. He places their sufferings within the context of the holiness of Christ, which gives them both strength and courage. He explains how the suffering of Christ was a vicarious sacrifice that effected redemption for all. The reading ends with a traditional formula of Christian faith in the Resurrection, built on the classical contrast between flesh and spirit. Though he died in the flesh, Christ is alive in the Spirit. Following his example, even though they die in the flesh, they can hope to live in the Spirit.

Jesus calls for self-sacrifice, as was his own love. He insists that if the disciples truly love him, they will keep his commandments. Though his departure might leave them feeling abandoned, he reassures them that he will return. The real marvel of this passage is found in the description of mutual indwelling. Jesus is in the Father; Jesus is in the disciples and they are in him; both the Spirit and Jesus will remain in the disciples. This is the manifestation of the love that begins and ends this reading.

The Easter season keeps offering us pictures of what happens when the power of resurrected life, given by Jesus to his disciples, enters the world. Sometimes it led to a recognition that one group should not be favored over another, whether they were widows or Samaritans. All were to be served; all were to receive the gospel.

When the deacon Philip began to preach Jesus as the Messiah, the people of Samaria listened. They not only heard Philip's message but also saw the power of God's salvation at work as he cast out demons and cured people who were crippled and paralyzed. With the new birth of faith came baptism and a reception of the Holy Spirit, when Peter and John laid hands on them.

The Holy Spirit continues to bring the truth of who God is and the strength to help us live in that truth, fully revealed in Jesus. Because of the Spirit, we dwell with the Father and the Son. Jesus' promises come to fulfillment in us; we are not orphans but beloved sons and daughters, the divine life of the Trinity flowing in us. In the Eucharist Jesus comes to be with us, and brings the Father, for he is in the Father and we are in him and he in us.

Resurrection life commits us to living out the command "Always be ready to give an explanation to anyone who asks you for a reason for your hope" (1 Peter 3:15). The Spirit brings hope and, as Pope Benedict XVI wrote in his encyclical "Saved in Hope" *(Spe Salvi)*, "The one who has hope lives differently."

❖ Consider/Discuss

- What does it mean to have the Holy Spirit with you as an "Advocate," that is, a "counselor" or "protector"?
- Jesus says the world cannot accept the Spirit of truth "because it neither sees nor knows him." Does this mean the world is beyond hope?

❖ Responding to the Word

We ask the Holy Spirit to be with us always, so we may live more fully in an awareness of the truth that is Jesus Christ, beloved Son, who came to teach us what it means to be children of God. Pray to be more aware of your intimate communion with the Father and the Son.

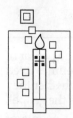

June 2 or 5, 2011

THE ASCENSION OF THE LORD

Many dioceses in the United States celebrate the Ascension on June 5, replacing the Seventh Sunday of Easter

Today's Focus: The Work Goes On

Two scenes feature Jesus' last words to his disciples from Matthew's Gospel and from Luke's Acts of the Apostles. The feast of the Ascension reminds us that the work of spreading the gospel goes on, with Jesus now interceding for us as we continue to bring good news to others.

FIRST READING
Acts 1:1–11

In the first book, Theophilus, I dealt with all that Jesus did and taught until the day he was taken up, after giving instructions through the Holy Spirit to the apostles whom he had chosen. He presented himself alive to them by many proofs after he had suffered, appearing to them during forty days and speaking about the kingdom of God. While meeting with them, he enjoined them not to depart from Jerusalem, but to wait for "the promise of the Father about which you have heard me speak; for John baptized with water, but in a few days you will be baptized with the Holy Spirit."

When they had gathered together they asked him, "Lord, are you at this time going to restore the kingdom to Israel?" He answered them, "It is not for you to know the times or seasons that the Father has established by his own authority. But you will receive power when the Holy Spirit comes upon you, and you will be my witnesses in Jerusalem, throughout Judea and Samaria, and to the ends of the earth." When he had said this, as they were looking on, he was lifted up, and a cloud took him from their sight. While they were looking intently at the sky as he was going, suddenly two men dressed in white garments stood beside them. They said, "Men of Galilee, why are you standing there looking at the sky? This Jesus who has been taken up from you into heaven will return in the same way as you have seen him going into heaven."

PSALM RESPONSE
Psalm 47:6

God mounts his throne to shouts of joy: a blare of trumpets for the Lord.

Brothers and sisters: May the God of our Lord Jesus Christ, the Father of glory, give you a Spirit of wisdom and revelation resulting in knowledge of him. May the eyes of your hearts be enlightened, that you may know what is the hope that belongs to his call, what are the riches of glory in his inheritance among the holy ones, and what is the surpassing greatness of his power for us who believe, in accord with the exercise of his great might, which he worked in Christ, raising him from the dead and seating him at his right hand in the heavens, far above every principality, authority, power, and dominion, and every name that is named not only in this age but also in the one to come. And he put all things beneath his feet and gave him as head over all things to the church, which is his body, the fullness of the one who fills all things in every way.

GOSPEL
Matthew
28:16–20
The eleven disciples went to Galilee, to the mountain to which Jesus had ordered them. When they saw him, they worshiped, but they doubted. Then Jesus approached and said to them, "All power in heaven and on earth has been given to me. Go, therefore, and make disciples of all nations, baptizing them in the name of the Father, and of the Son, and of the Holy Spirit, teaching them to observe all that I have commanded you. And behold, I am with you always, until the end of the age."

❖ *Understanding the Word*

According to Acts of the Apostles, Jesus remained on earth for forty days after his resurrection, appearing to his apostles and speaking about the reign of God. The activity of the Spirit is a characteristic of the new age, the time between the Resurrection and the time of complete fulfillment. The apostles' misunderstanding of this presented an opportunity for Jesus to instruct them. He tells them to concern themselves with being his witnesses, and not to worry about the limited restoration of one nation. Furthermore, it is not for them to know when the end will occur. He assures them that they will have the power of the Spirit to guide them for whatever length of time God desires.

The second reading consists of a series of prayers. The first is a prayer for a spirit of wisdom and revelation so believers might possess insight and understanding. Another is for a threefold spiritual enlightenment that includes hope in the calling they have received from God, the riches of God's inheritance, and the surpassing greatness of God's power. The depiction of Christ is quite exalted. Having been raised from the dead, Christ now sits at God's right hand, high above all other heavenly creatures. His rule is universal in scope and duration. Exalted by God, Christ is made the head of the church, which is his body.

The disciples see Jesus on the mountain and they worship him, reminiscent of his earlier transfiguration. Jesus declares that all power in heaven and on earth has been given to him, a reference to the Son of Man who was exalted by God and granted eschatological authority. Employing that power, he commissions them. The great missionary commission is straightforward and all-encompassing.

The disciples are told to go out and make disciples of all nations. Jesus inaugurates the reign of God, at the heart of which is a radically different way of life. This reign is to be the essence of the teaching of the disciples.

✤ Reflecting on the Word

We can get caught up in the details and miss the heart of the message today. Where did Jesus go? Is heaven "up there"? Why doesn't Matthew's Gospel have Jesus being taken up? Doesn't this feast remove Jesus from us, to some place where he "sits at the right hand of the Father"? Sound a little disengaged?

In his introduction to the writings of St. Bernard of Clairvaux, Jean Leclercq writes that the mystery of the Ascension fulfilled the mystery of love in which Jesus returns to the glory of the Father. The Son then sends this Spirit to unite us with the Father in love. Thus, in Bernard's thought, the Ascension is a symbol for the passage of Christ from his life in mortal flesh to glorious life in the Spirit. This same transition from flesh to Spirit can also be accomplished in us, since it has already taken place in Christ.

But we are not simply passive recipients. There is work to be done. Luke's angels bluntly tell the apostles to get moving. Matthew's final scene spells out the work: "Go forth and make disciples, baptizing them in the name of the Father, Son, and Holy Spirit, and teaching others to observe all that I have commanded you." Witness to Jesus, in word and deed.

The task of spreading the good news that is Jesus Christ, teaching others about him, can seem daunting. But we are not alone. We have the promise that the Holy Spirit will work with us; in Matthew, Jesus' final words are reassuring: "I am with you always." That is reason enough to work with confidence.

✤ Consider/Discuss

- Does the image of Jesus ascending to sit at the right hand of the Father comfort you? Challenge you?
- When is the last time you witnessed to Christ, sharing what he means to you?

✤ Responding to the Word

We pray: Loving Father, give us your Spirit of wisdom and revelation to enlighten the eyes of our hearts, so we may have the hope that accompanies your call and come to the glory that is our inheritance. May your great power be at work in us, raising us to new life as it did your Son Jesus. Amen.

June 5, 2011

SEVENTH SUNDAY OF EASTER

Today's Focus: Giving God Glory

In John's Gospel, Jesus' final words at the Last Supper are a prayer to the Father. In the beginning of it, Jesus recognizes that the long-awaited "hour" has come, when he will reveal God's love for the world. Jesus lifted up on the cross is the hour of glory.

FIRST READING
Acts 1:12–14

After Jesus had been taken up to heaven the apostles returned to Jerusalem from the mount called Olivet, which is near Jerusalem, a sabbath day's journey away.

When they entered the city they went to the upper room where they were staying, Peter and John and James and Andrew, Philip and Thomas, Bartholomew and Matthew, James son of Alphaeus, Simon the Zealot, and Judas son of James. All these devoted themselves with one accord to prayer, together with some women, and Mary the mother of Jesus, and his brothers.

PSALM RESPONSE
Psalm 27:13

I believe that I shall see the good things of the Lord in the land of the living.

SECOND READING
1 Peter 4:13–16

Beloved: Rejoice to the extent that you share in the sufferings of Christ, so that when his glory is revealed you may also rejoice exultantly. If you are insulted for the name of Christ, blessed are you, for the Spirit of glory and of God rests upon you. But let no one among you be made to suffer as a murderer, a thief, an evildoer, or as an intriguer. But whoever is made to suffer as a Christian should not be ashamed but glorify God because of the name.

GOSPEL
John 17:1–11a

Jesus raised his eyes to heaven and said, "Father, the hour has come. Give glory to your son, so that your son may glorify you, just as you gave him authority over all people, so that your son may give eternal life to all you gave him. Now this is eternal life, that they should know you, the only true God, and the one whom you sent, Jesus Christ. I glorified you on earth by accomplishing the work that you gave me to do. Now glorify me, Father, with you, with the glory that I had with you before the world began.

"I revealed your name to those whom you gave me out of the world. They belonged to you, and you gave them to me, and they have kept your word. Now they know that everything you gave me is from you, because the words you gave to me I have given to them, and they accepted them and truly understood that I came from you, and they have believed that you sent me. I pray for them. I do not pray for the world but for the ones you have given me, because they are yours, and everything of mine is yours and everything of yours is mine, and I have been glorified in them. And now I will no longer be in the world, but they are in the world, while I am coming to you."

✦ Understanding the Word

Those who were with Jesus as he ascended return to the city and devote themselves to prayer. The list of apostles in the first reading corresponds with other lists found in the Gospel accounts, with the exception of Judas Iscariot. Simon is identified as a member of the Zealots, a militant wing of the Jewish independence movement. The women who accompany these men might be their wives or women followers of Jesus who came with him from Galilee and who attended to his burial. His mother was there along with his brothers. These latter no longer questioned the authenticity of Jesus' ministry. They now join his disciples in prayer, open to the unfolding of God's plan.

The author of the Letter of Peter is very clear about the reason for the suffering of the Christians. They are either defamed for the name of Christ or persecuted for being Christians. Since their religious teaching and values frequently prevent them from engaging in behavior that is part of pagan culture, they often have to endure misunderstanding, mistrust, and resentment. Their way of living is considered antisocial at best, treasonable at worst. The author of the letter tells them to bear the name "Christian" proudly, and to endure any misfortune that might befall them because of it.

This passage from John's Gospel is commonly known as the High Priestly prayer. Jesus speaks of having accomplished his work and of returning to his Father. It is clearly a farewell message in which Jesus prays for himself and for his disciples. The theme upon which most other themes depend is the unparalleled relationship between Jesus and God. The glorification for which Jesus prays can now be seen within the context of this unique relationship. While on earth, Jesus revealed the name of his Father through the life that he lived and the ministry that he performed. Finally, in leaving the world, Jesus prays for his disciples who remain within it.

There are moments of life that we call "glorious," special times beyond ordinary experience, that give us a hint of transcendence, a glimpse of glory, whether it is a "glorious day" in spring or a "glorious occasion" like a wedding. Such times lift our spirits and hearts, and we feel transported to a different level of awareness and know a joy beyond words. Such are moments of glory.

We hear the words "glory" and "glorify" five times in the opening verses of today's Gospel as Jesus prays to his Father. In John's Gospel this is the last recorded prayer of Jesus, since John does not have Jesus praying in the garden.

Jesus begins his prayer by telling the Father the "hour" has come, that is, the hour of revelation, the time when the Father will give glory to the Son and the Son will glorify the Father. It is the moment when the Son is "lifted up," which refers to both the lifting up on the cross and the Resurrection. Jesus has said: "And when I am lifted up, I will draw all things to myself" (John 12:32).

This mutual glorifying that characterizes the relationship between the Father and the Son also embraces the disciples. Jesus says at the end of today's reading that he prays "for the ones you have given me, because they are yours, and everything of mine is yours and everything of yours is mine and I have been glorified in them" (John 17:10).

❖ Consider/Discuss

- Do you see your life as one that gives glory to God by what you say and do?
- Do you follow the example of Jesus by encouraging others to glorify God?

❖ Responding to the Word

We pray this final Sunday in the Easter season that the prayer of Jesus can also be ours: Father, give glory to your children, so that your children may glorify you. Help us to know you, the only true God, and the one whom you sent, Jesus Christ. Alleluia. Amen.

June 12, 2011

PENTECOST

Today's Focus: Three Gifts of Pentecost

When the risen Jesus suddenly stood before the disciples that first Easter evening, he came bearing gifts. Like the magi's gifts, there were three of them: peace, a mission, and the Holy Spirit. These same gifts are given to us, so we might live as faithful disciples in our world.

FIRST READING
Acts 2:1–11

When the time for Pentecost was fulfilled, they were all in one place together. And suddenly there came from the sky a noise like a strong driving wind, and it filled the entire house in which they were. Then there appeared to them tongues as of fire, which parted and came to rest on each one of them. And they were all filled with the Holy Spirit and began to speak in different tongues, as the Spirit enabled them to proclaim.

Now there were devout Jews from every nation under heaven staying in Jerusalem. At this sound, they gathered in a large crowd, but they were confused because each one heard them speaking in his own language. They were astounded, and in amazement they asked, "Are not all these people who are speaking Galileans? Then how does each of us hear them in his native language? We are Parthians, Medes, and Elamites, inhabitants of Mesopotamia, Judea and Cappadocia, Pontus and Asia, Phrygia and Pamphylia, Egypt and the districts of Libya near Cyrene, as well as travelers from Rome, both Jews and converts to Judaism, Cretans and Arabs, yet we hear them speaking in our own tongues of the mighty acts of God."

PSALM RESPONSE
Psalm 104:30

Lord, send out your Spirit, and renew the face of the earth.

SECOND READING
1 Corinthians 12:3b–7, 12–13

Brothers and sisters: No one can say, "Jesus is Lord," except by the Holy Spirit. There are different kinds of spiritual gifts but the same Spirit; there are different forms of service but the same Lord; there are different workings but the same God who produces all of them in everyone. To each individual the manifestation of the Spirit is given for some benefit.

As a body is one though it has many parts, and all the parts of the body, though many, are one body, so also Christ. For in one Spirit we were all baptized into one body, whether Jews or Greeks, slaves or free persons, and we were all given to drink of one Spirit.

GOSPEL
John 20:19–23
On the evening of that first day of the week, when the doors were locked, where the disciples were, for fear of the Jews, Jesus came and stood in their midst and said to them, "Peace be with you." When he had said this, he showed them his hands and his side. The disciples rejoiced when they saw the Lord. Jesus said to them again, "Peace be with you. As the Father has sent me, so I send you." And when he had said this, he breathed on them and said to them, "Receive the Holy Spirit. Whose sins you forgive are forgiven them, and whose sins you retain are retained."

❖ Understanding the Word

The Jewish feast of Pentecost was one of the three major pilgrimage festivals of Israel. This feast explains why there was a crowd gathered in Jerusalem. This is the crowd that heard a loud noise and was confused, astonished, and amazed. They knew that those speaking were Galileans, yet the hearers could understand the message in their own dialect. The exact nature of this marvel is less significant than its meaning. It was clearly a manifestation of the universal presence and power of the Spirit. The outpouring of the Spirit and the preaching of the gospel to all nations are seen by some as initiating the reunion of the human race and the gathering of all into the reign of God.

The acclamation "Jesus is Lord!" is rich in both Jewish and early Christian meaning. "Lord" was the official title of the Roman emperor. To proclaim Jesus as Lord was to set up a rivalry between the followers of Jesus and the ruling political authority. The title "Lord" is also used in the Greek-language version of the Old Testament as a substitute for God's personal name. To use this title for Jesus is also to ascribe to him the attributes of God. Paul next launches into a discourse on the varieties of functions within the Christian community. The diversity of gifts is compared to the complexity of the human body. This metaphor exemplifies unity in diversity and interdependence.

John's account of the risen Lord treats the Resurrection and the bestowal of the Spirit as occurring on the same day. The locked doors, meant to secure the disciples from those who put Jesus to death, also underscore the mysterious character of his risen body. The image of breathing life into another is reminiscent of the creation of Adam (Genesis 2:7) and restoration of Israel after the Exile (Ezekiel 37:9). The disciples are commissioned to go forth, to declare salvation and judgment. With the bestowal of the Spirit, the disciples are authorized to continue the mission of Jesus.

The disciples were cowering behind locked doors. Fear has a way of imprisoning, away from the outer world, but also from our inner world, taking away our freedom to hope, imagine, and dream. We can become comfortable working in cramped spaces, isolated and unattached, removed from life and contact with others.

But then along comes the risen Lord, arms outstretched, heart wide open, bearing gifts to transform our lives. The first gift of the risen Lord is peace (*shalom*), which translates as all good things, physically, mentally, and spiritually—all that is needed to be alive inside. This peace is a gift that the world cannot give.

The second gift is a mission: we are sent, as Jesus was sent, by the Father. Where? To the world. "For God so loved the world that he gave his only Son, so that everyone who believes in him may not perish but may have eternal life. Indeed, God did not send the Son into the world to condemn the world but in order that the world might be saved through him" (John 3:16–17). Now the Son sends the disciples—us!—to bring life.

The third gift is the Holy Spirit, given for the forgiveness of sins. The Holy Spirit is the gift of the Father and the Son, given to us at baptism, again at confirmation, and whose gifts are given to the church and its members for the good of all, within and outside the church. Primary among these gifts is the gift of forgiveness.

❖ Consider/Discuss

- Have I received the gift of the Holy Spirit who brings the forgiveness of my own sins?
- Have I made use of this gift of the Holy Spirit who calls me to bring forgiveness to others?

❖ Responding to the Word

During this week, pray the Sequence used at Mass for Pentecost before the Gospel, "Come, Holy Spirit, come!" Notice especially these words: "Heal our wounds, our strength renew/On our dryness pour your dew/Wash the stains of guilt away/Bend the stubborn heart and will/Melt the frozen, warm the chill."

There are ways that the readings for this section of Ordinary Time reinforce the idea of the ordinary. We are not in the midst of a specific liturgical season, nor are we anticipating one. The Lectionary readings seem particularly focused on issues and concerns of the ordinary life of ordinary people. It is a time for us to listen to the teachings of Jesus and to look into our own lives to see what kind of disciples we are, or what kind we are called to be. As we move toward the end of the liturgical year, the exhortations seem to have greater urgency, and our reflections become more serious.

The portions of Matthew's Gospel that are read in this segment of Ordinary Time show the care that Jesus took in instructing his disciples. Their formation continues in his instruction through parables. With the crowds they hear his teaching, but away from the crowds they learn the fuller meaning of that teaching. It is only to the disciples that the mysteries of the kingdom are revealed. Their eyes are opened, because it will be their responsibility in the future to proclaim that same message to others. On the last three Sundays of Ordinary Time, Jesus teaches his disciples how they are to live their lives as they await the dawning of the eschatological age. This message challenges us as well. Since we do not know exactly when the Lord will return, we must be vigilant; we must be prepared.

The first readings for this section of Ordinary Time provide us with a kind of collage, an artistic creation composed of diverse snippets from various biblical books. At times a theme seems to correspond to a similar theme in the second reading or the Gospel. At other times this is not the case. What we have is an unspecified collection of discrete passages, each of which contributes a unique insight into our rich and broad religious tradition.

With few exceptions, this section of Ordinary Time moves us through Paul's Letter to the Romans. Though he is convinced of the universal effectiveness of the death of Jesus, he also speaks very positively about the destiny of the Jews. He insists that Christians must reject the standards of the world and conform themselves to the standards of the gospel, the entire ethical program of which can be summarized in the admonition to love.

The readings that carry us to the end of the liturgical year are both comforting and challenging. While there is frequent mention of the judgment that will take place at the endtime, God is depicted as provident and caring, and God will be partial toward those who humbly acknowledge that they are the beneficiaries of divine mercy.

June 19, 2011

THE MOST HOLY TRINITY

Today's Focus: Who Are You? What Do You Do?

Meeting people for the first time usually involves offering our name and what we do. This happens on today's feast. We return to Ordinary Time by listening to three texts that attempt to tell us who our Triune God is and what God has done and continues to do for us.

FIRST READING
Exodus 34:4b–6, 8–9

Early in the morning Moses went up Mount Sinai as the LORD had commanded him, taking along the two stone tablets.

Having come down in a cloud, the LORD stood with Moses there and proclaimed his name, "LORD." Thus the LORD passed before him and cried out, "The LORD, the LORD, a merciful and gracious God, slow to anger and rich in kindness and fidelity." Moses at once bowed down to the ground in worship. Then he said, "If I find favor with you, O LORD, do come along in our company. This is indeed a stiff-necked people; yet pardon our wickedness and sins, and receive us as your own."

PSALM RESPONSE
Dn 3:52b

Glory and praise for ever!

SECOND READING
2 Corinthians 13:11–13

Brothers and sisters, rejoice. Mend your ways, encourage one another, agree with one another, live in peace, and the God of love and peace will be with you. Greet one another with a holy kiss. All the holy ones greet you.

The grace of the Lord Jesus Christ and the love of God and the fellowship of the Holy Spirit be with all of you.

GOSPEL
John 3:16–18

God so loved the world that he gave his only Son, so that everyone who believes in him might not perish but might have eternal life. For God did not send his Son into the world to condemn the world, but that the world might be saved through him. Whoever believes in him will not be condemned, but whoever does not believe has already been condemned, because he has not believed in the name of the only Son of God.

The readings for Trinity Sunday do not really explain the mystery of the Trinity. Rather, they underscore several divine characteristics that are relational and that throw light on ways that the Triune God interacts with us. Some of them traditionally have been associated with one of the three persons more than with the others.

In the first reading, though the cloud upon which God descends onto the mountain conceals God, God's declaration to Moses is self-revelatory: "The LORD, a merciful and gracious God, slow to anger and rich in kindness and fidelity" (Exodus 42:6). Moses' response to this spectacular revelation is worship. He prostrates himself on the ground in profound adoration. In this appearance, God reveals those divine traits that are associated with the covenant, namely, mercy, steadfast love, and fidelity.

Paul promises that if the Corinthian Christians follow his admonitions and live in the way he instructs them, they will experience the presence of God. The blessing with which he ends this letter embodies an early Trinitarian emphasis. It notes the gift of grace that is received through Jesus Christ, the love that God has for all of creation, a love that is the source of all good things, and the community of the Holy Spirit within which believers are rooted. There is no more meaningful benediction that Paul might have chosen.

In the Gospel reading, the extent of God's love is drawn in bold lines in two significant ways. The first is the scope of divine love, and the second is the price that God is willing to pay because of that love. The passage is remarkable in its explicit declaration of God's love for the entire world. This love for the world is so deep and so magnanimous that, for the world to be saved, nothing is spared, not even God's only Son. Those who believe in that Son are saved; those who do not believe in him call down judgment upon themselves.

❖❖ Responding to the Word

Once a young priest was giving a blessing in our seminary chapel and he left out the *ands* separating the Father and the Son and the Holy Spirit. An older priest loudly whispered: "Modalism!" This was a heresy in the early church that taught that there was one God but not three distinct persons, only three modes or ways of experiencing God. Thus, those *ands* were important, giving emphasis to three distinct persons. We believe in one God who is three: the Father and the Son and the Holy Spirit.

Your head can hurt trying to wrap your mind around this mystery. Today's readings don't try to "figure it out." They simply allow God to be introduced. First God gives Moses a name: "LORD." God then spells out what that means for Moses and a people liberated from slavery. God is "merciful and gracious, slow to anger and rich in kindness and fidelity."

The Gospel of John reveals Jesus as beloved Son sent into the world. For "God so loved the world he gave his only Son, so that everyone who believes in him might not perish but have eternal life" (3:16). God really loves creation and all that continues to be created in love.

Finally, Paul's farewell to the Corinthians refers to the Lord Jesus who graces, the Father who loves, and the Holy Spirit who draws everyone into community. In brief, at the heart of God is found love, grace, mercy, community, kindness, and fidelity. Not a bad introduction. More ways to know the Trinity will be discovered as we move through "ordinary" time.

✤ Consider/Discuss

- Do you have a favorite name for God? How do you think of the Father, and the Son, and the Holy Spirit?
- How would you "introduce" the Father and the Son and the Holy Spirit to someone who does not know them?

✤ Responding to the Word

We place ourselves before the most Holy Trinity, praying for a faith that can humbly bow before this mystery, accepting that we have been given to know God as three in one, that God is drawing us ever more deeply into sharing the life and love that flow between and among these three Persons. We pray our lives may witness to this love.

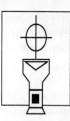

June 26, 2011

THE MOST HOLY BODY AND BLOOD OF CHRIST

Today's Focus: Eternal Life-giving Food

Our celebration of the Trinity last week reminded us that at our baptism we entered into the life shared by the Trinity. Today's feast calls us to celebrate the intimate communion we have with Jesus when we receive his Body and Blood under the signs of bread and wine in the Eucharist.

FIRST READING
Deuteronomy 8:2–3, 14b–16a

Moses said to the people: "Remember how for forty years now the LORD, your God, has directed all your journeying in the desert, so as to test you by affliction and find out whether or not it was your intention to keep his commandments. He therefore let you be afflicted with hunger, and then fed you with manna, a food unknown to you and your fathers, in order to show you that not by bread alone does one live, but by every word that comes forth from the mouth of the LORD.

"Do not forget the LORD, your God, who brought you out of the land of Egypt, that place of slavery; who guided you through the vast and terrible desert with its saraph serpents and scorpions, its parched and waterless ground; who brought forth water for you from the flinty rock and fed you in the desert with manna, a food unknown to your fathers."

PSALM RESPONSE
Psalm 147:12

Praise the Lord, Jerusalem.

SECOND READING
1 Corinthians 10:16–17

Brothers and sisters: The cup of blessing that we bless, is it not a participation in the blood of Christ? The bread that we break, is it not a participation in the body of Christ? Because the loaf of bread is one, we, though many, are one body, for we all partake of the one loaf.

GOSPEL	Jesus said to the Jewish crowds: "I am the living bread that came
John 6:51–58	down from heaven; whoever eats this bread will live forever; and
	the bread that I will give is my flesh for the life of the world."

The Jews quarreled among themselves, saying, "How can this man give us his flesh to eat?" Jesus said to them, "Amen, amen, I say to you, unless you eat the flesh of the Son of Man and drink his blood, you do not have life within you. Whoever eats my flesh and drinks my blood has eternal life, and I will raise him on the last day. For my flesh is true food, and my blood is true drink. Whoever eats my flesh and drinks my blood remains in me and I in him. Just as the living Father sent me and I have life because of the Father, so also the one who feeds on me will have life because of me. This is the bread that came down from heaven. Unlike your ancestors who ate and still died, whoever eats this bread will live forever."

✥ Understanding the Word

The reading from Deuteronomy shows that God's graciousness is not to be squandered. The people are told to remember the past in order to act in a certain way in the present. Though the time of their sojourn in the wilderness is over, there are still lessons that they must learn from it. Moses directs the people to remember how God delivered them from bondage, guided them through the wilderness, miraculously gave them water, and provided them with mysterious food. The trials in the wilderness did not so much test their obedience to the commandments as their total dependence on God.

Paul's discourse on the Eucharist not only identifies the symbolic potential of the substances of bread and wine, but it also describes actions that are rich in symbolism. It is by sharing the cup that is blessed that one participates in the blood of Christ. Eating food with another establishes a bond of companionship, a bond that includes mutual obligations. Paul further insists that breaking bread together may form us into a community, but sharing eucharistic bread forms us into the body of Christ. The acts of blessing the cup and breaking the bread have profound significance for salvation and the life of the church.

Jesus identifies his flesh as the bread of heaven, thus giving manna a new meaning. His flesh and blood are the source of life for those who partake of them. In other words, eternal life comes from feeding on Jesus, not simply from believing in him. He insists that it is not something that believers merely hope to enjoy in the future. Rather, those who share in this meal already possess eternal life. Furthermore, just as we and whatever we eat and drink become one, so Jesus and those who feed on him form an intimate union. In a mutually intimate way, they abide in him and he abides in them. Jesus does not merely visit them, but he dwells with them permanently.

God feeding a hungry people is a cherished memory in the Jewish tradition. In his farewell speech to the Israelites, Moses calls upon the people to remember how God gave them food and drink during their many years in the desert. The manna was "something unknown to your fathers," and the water flowed forth from a "flinty rock." The water and manna were wondrous signs of God's presence and care as the Israelites journeyed to a new land.

Jesus proclaimed himself as the living bread come down from heaven, bringing eternal life to all who eat it. We approach the table of the Eucharist to receive the bread and drink the wine, the Body and Blood of Christ made present through the power of the Holy Spirit. Again, something wondrous is happening.

We remember that Jesus did this on the night before he died, and told his disciples to "do this in memory of me." When we do this, the saving event of Christ's death and resurrection is made present in the broken bread and wine poured out for us. We enter into communion with the risen Lord and one another.

Through our sharing in the memorial meal, Christ re-members us as his body and sends us out to witness to God's fidelity in the past and God's promise for the future: a world renewed, restored, reborn in the Spirit. God continues to feed us on the road from slavery to freedom, from death to life.

✢ Consider/Discuss

- Are you able to see beyond the morsel of bread and sip from the cup to recognize God feeding you and drawing you into communion with the Son and all who are fed?
- Do you connect the Eucharist with the mission of the Church in the world, when you hear: "Go in peace to love and serve the Lord"?

✢ Responding to the Word

Today's feast has a special hymn called a "Sequence" before the Gospel. Some of the images and ideas are: Jesus good shepherd and true bread, have mercy on us; feed us and guard us. Grant that we find happiness in the land of the living. Make us your guests in heaven, co-heirs with you and companions of heaven's citizens.

July 3, 2011

FOURTEENTH SUNDAY IN ORDINARY TIME

Today's Focus: Home Schooling

Truly knowing another person can take a lifetime; knowing God will take an eternity. Even so, Jesus reminds us that even now we can know the Father by looking and listening to Jesus himself. As Jesus turned to the Hebrew scriptures to understand the Father's plan for him, so we turn to Jesus and listen to his words.

FIRST READING
Zechariah 9:9–10

Thus says the LORD:
  Rejoice heartily, O daughter Zion,
    shout for joy, O daughter Jerusalem!
See, your king shall come to you;
  a just savior is he,
meek, and riding on an ass,
  on a colt, the foal of an ass.
He shall banish the chariot from Ephraim,
  and the horse from Jerusalem;
the warrior's bow shall be banished,
  and he shall proclaim peace to the nations.
His dominion shall be from sea to sea,
  and from the River to the ends of the earth.

PSALM RESPONSE
Psalm 145:1

I will praise your name for ever, my king and my God.

SECOND READING
Romans 8:9, 11–13

Brothers and sisters: You are not in the flesh; on the contrary, you are in the spirit, if only the Spirit of God dwells in you. Whoever does not have the Spirit of Christ does not belong to him. If the Spirit of the one who raised Jesus from the dead dwells in you, the one who raised Christ from the dead will give life to your mortal bodies also, through his Spirit that dwells in you. Consequently, brothers and sisters, we are not debtors to the flesh, to live according to the flesh. For if you live according to the flesh, you will die, but if by the Spirit you put to death the deeds of the body, you will live.

GOSPEL
Matthew
11:25–30

At that time Jesus exclaimed: "I give praise to you, Father, Lord of heaven and earth, for although you have hidden these things from the wise and the learned you have revealed them to little ones. Yes, Father, such has been your gracious will. All things have been handed over to me by my Father. No one knows the Son except the Father, and no one knows the Father except the Son and anyone to whom the Son wishes to reveal him.

"Come to me, all you who labor and are burdened, and I will give you rest. Take my yoke upon you and learn from me, for I am meek and humble of heart; and you will find rest for yourselves. For my yoke is easy, and my burden light."

❖ Understanding the Word

The passage from Zechariah is an oracle of salvation, containing an idealized picture of an Israelite king and the peaceful kingdom over which he will rule. Though this is a vision of the future, the verbs are prophetic perfect, indicating that in God's time the future is already present. The king is seated on the foal of an ass, a purebred animal born of a female ass rather than of a mule. While this may be a depiction of a victory march, it is devoid of military ostentation. Instead, the king proclaims peace to all nations. This king is the agent of God's blessings to all people.

Paul contrasts two ways of living: life in the flesh and life in the spirit. For Paul, flesh is human nature in all of the limitations that sometimes incline one away from God; by spirit he means a life that is attuned to God. Paul argues that life in the flesh cannot please God, while life in the spirit is a form of union with God. Sin may still exact physical death, but it cannot quench the spirit that lives because of righteousness. Just as Christ conquered death and lives anew, so those joined to Christ will share in his victory and through the Spirit will enjoy new life.

Jesus describes the intimate relationship that he shares with God in terms that can only be considered a high Christology, an emphasizing of his divine rather than his human nature. He claims that only the Father can really know him, because only God has this kind of experiential knowledge of him. Correspondingly, only he can really know God, for only he has experiential knowledge of the Father. If anyone else knows the Father it is only because Jesus has revealed God to that person. In this sense, Jesus is the mediator of knowledge of God. If his hearers learn from him, they too will be blessed with the revelation of the Father.

✢ *Reflecting on the Word*

When you think of a king coming before his people, the image of someone riding on a donkey does not come to mind. If the Lone Ranger had Silver and Roy Rogers had Trigger, a similar white stallion would seem most fitting for a king. Not an ass, even a purebred one. But this image from the prophet Zechariah is one that must have planted itself in the imagination of Jesus, for that is how he made his great entrance into Jerusalem and was greeted as the Messiah. It was not the entrance of a powerful warrior, but of a gentle king whose rule would bring peace to the nations.

I have sometimes regretted the loss of St. Christopher from the calendar of saints. That legendary saint, whose name means "Christ-bearer," signaled that the risen Lord had now chosen to be carried by his disciples. We bear him in our bodies, minds, and hearts. We bring him to the world when we work to bring peace and healing and knowledge of the Father.

This necessitates being willing to take on the yoke of Jesus. I remember once hearing that the yokes Jesus made in the carpenter shop under Joseph's guidance rode easily on the shoulders of the animals, distributing evenly the weight they pulled. The yoke Jesus offers us is his teaching about the kingdom of heaven and how to live in it while in the world. This means putting on his attitude and spirit of attentive listening for the will of the Father—home schooling in the best sense.

✢ *Consider/Discuss*

• How do you believe Jesus will return at the end of time?
• Have you accepted the yoke of the Lord? How does it guide you?

✢ *Responding to the Word*

Lord, give us the rest only you can give when we feel burdened by life's labors and sorrows. Open our hearts so that we learn from you to seek and accept the yoke that is easy. Give us the strength to help others with the burdens that weigh them down.

July 10, 2011

FIFTEENTH SUNDAY IN ORDINARY TIME

Today's Focus: Rejuvenating Sluggish Hearts

Jesus came preaching the word of God, proclaiming the kingdom of heaven. Not everyone listened—then or now. Receiving God's word is challenging in a world that has so many voices competing for our attention. But if we give it a place to settle in our hearts, the yield will be great.

FIRST READING
Isaiah 55:10–11

Thus says the LORD:
Just as from the heavens
   the rain and snow come down
and do not return there
   till they have watered the earth,
   making it fertile and fruitful,
giving seed to the one who sows
   and bread to the one who eats,
so shall my word be
   that goes forth from my mouth;
my word shall not return to me void,
   but shall do my will,
   achieving the end for which I sent it.

PSALM RESPONSE
Luke 8:8

The seed that falls on good ground will yield a fruitful harvest.

SECOND READING
Romans 8:18–23

Brothers and sisters: I consider that the sufferings of this present time are as nothing compared with the glory to be revealed for us. For creation awaits with eager expectation the revelation of the children of God; for creation was made subject to futility, not of its own accord but because of the one who subjected it, in hope that creation itself would be set free from slavery to corruption and share in the glorious freedom of the children of God. We know that all creation is groaning in labor pains even until now; and not only that, but we ourselves, who have the firstfruits of the Spirit, we also groan within ourselves as we wait for adoption, the redemption of our bodies.

GOSPEL
Matthew
13:1–23
or 13:1–9

On that day, Jesus went out of the house and sat down by the sea. Such large crowds gathered around him that he got into a boat and sat down, and the whole crowd stood along the shore. And he spoke to them at length in parables, saying: "A sower went out to sow. And as he sowed, some seed fell on the path, and birds came and ate it up. Some fell on rocky ground, where it had little soil. It sprang up at once because the soil was not deep, and when the sun rose it was scorched, and it withered for lack of roots. Some seed fell among thorns, and the thorns grew up and choked it. But some seed fell on rich soil, and produced fruit, a hundred or sixty or thirtyfold. Whoever has ears ought to hear."

[The disciples approached him and said, "Why do you speak to them in parables?" He said to them in reply, "Because knowledge of the mysteries of the kingdom of heaven has been granted to you, but to them it has not been granted. To anyone who has, more will be given and he will grow rich; from anyone who has not, even what he has will be taken away. This is why I speak to them in parables, because

they look but do not see and hear but do not listen or understand.
Isaiah's prophecy is fulfilled in them, which says:
You shall indeed hear but not understand,
  you shall indeed look but never see.
Gross is the heart of this people,
  they will hardly hear with their ears,
  they have closed their eyes,
  lest they see with their eyes
  and hear with their ears
and understand with their hearts and be converted,
  and I heal them.

"But blessed are your eyes, because they see, and your ears, because they hear. Amen, I say to you, many prophets and righteous people longed to see what you see but did not see it, and to hear what you hear but did not hear it.

"Hear then the parable of the sower. The seed sown on the path is the one who hears the word of the kingdom without understanding it, and the evil one comes and steals away what was sown in his heart. The seed sown on rocky ground is the one who hears the word and receives it at once with joy. But he has no root and lasts only for a time. When some tribulation or persecution comes because of the word, he immediately falls away. The seed sown among thorns is the one who hears the word, but then worldly anxiety and the lure of riches choke the word and it bears no fruit. But the seed sown on rich soil is the one who hears the word and understands it, who indeed bears fruit and yields a hundred or sixty or thirtyfold."]

Isaiah provides us with a glimpse of what ecologists today would refer to as the integrity of creation. Focusing on precipitation in the forms of rain and snow, he traces the cycle that it takes. His understanding comes from observation of nature, the primary source of wisdom. This metaphor assures us that we can be as confident of the power of the word of God as we can be of the working of the natural world. Just as nature produces miracles upon which we can rely and because of which we can survive, so the word of God can effect miracles upon which we can rely and because of which we can live.

Paul's teaching on the end of time takes a very interesting turn. He maintains that the new life of which he speaks is not limited to the human sphere. Rather, the entire created world participates in this transformation. The entire created world is somehow swept up with humankind into this eschatological drama, awaiting the revelation that will be granted the children of God, not as spectators, but as participants. Paul assures the Christians that they already possess the first fruits of the Spirit, a pledge that guarantees they will be brought into full transformation. By implication, all of creation will be brought along with them.

The Gospel parable focuses neither on the sower nor on the seed, but on the receptivity of the soil. The parable is not a difficult story to understand. But what does it really mean? Jesus provides his disciples an allegorical interpretation of the parable. In each case described, the sown word is actually heard; to some extent it is accepted. Jesus is not referring to outright rejection from outsiders, but to the way followers receive the word of God. When one understands the meaning of the parable, one is apt to wonder: What kind of soil am I? How receptive am I to the word of God?

❖   *Reflecting on the Word*

Some words we welcome into our hearts; some we don't. Consider how the heart responds differently to "I love you" or "I have no time for you." But our reaction to words depends not only on what is said but also on who is saying it and for what purpose. When God speaks, the goal is to bring life.

The power of God's word is like the rain and snow watering and making the earth fertile and fruitful, bringing life and nourishment. God says, "My word shall do my will." Yet when Jesus came preaching God's word, many rejected it. "They look but do not see," says Jesus, "listen but do not hear . . . Sluggish indeed is this people's heart."

In Jesus' Israel, the land was first plowed and turned over. Then the sower went forth scattering seed generously, tossing it with abandon. That is why it lands all over the place—on the footpath, on rocky ground, among weeds, and on fertile land.

A sluggish heart can be lazy, weary, or sick. Every heart can bear different crops or no crops at all. I used to ask, "What kind of field is my heart?" as if the answer were restricted to only one possibility. Now I think my heart is all four places mentioned. Some parts of God's word I have missed completely, some I have heard but they have not taken root, some I responded to at one time, but then other things got my attention, and then there are those too few words of Jesus that I have embraced wholeheartedly.

❖ Consider/Discuss

- Do I believe and trust in the power of God's word to change my life?
- What parts of God's word have I ignored, barely listened to, acted on but only for a while, allowed to take root in my heart?
- How does this parable speak to my community?

❖ Responding to the Word

Loving God, we thank you for sending your Son Jesus to sow the seed of your life-giving word in our hearts, so that it might do your will and achieve your purpose in our world. Open our hearts to receive this word. Increase our desire to live it out wholeheartedly. Amen.

July 17, 2011

SIXTEENTH SUNDAY IN ORDINARY TIME

Today's Focus: The Patience and Power of God

"God reigns" is the message of the scriptures. God's word assures us that the rule of God is a reality, though it might not often seem that way. The Gospel speaks of the patience and power of God. We are called to reflect God's patient kindness in life.

FIRST READING
Wisdom 12:13, 16–19

There is no god besides you who have the care of all,
    that you need show you have not unjustly condemned.
For your might is the source of justice;
    your mastery over all things makes you lenient to all.
For you show your might when the perfection
        of your power is disbelieved;
    and in those who know you, you rebuke temerity.
But though you are master of might,
        you judge with clemency,
    and with much lenience you govern us;
    for power, whenever you will, attends you.
And you taught your people, by these deeds,
        that those who are just must be kind;
and you gave your children good ground for hope
    that you would permit repentance for their sins.

PSALM RESPONSE
Psalm 86:5a

Lord, you are good and forgiving.

SECOND READING
Romans 8:26–27

Brothers and sisters: The Spirit comes to the aid of our weakness; for we do not know how to pray as we ought, but the Spirit himself intercedes with inexpressible groanings. And the one who searches hearts knows what is the intention of the Spirit, because he intercedes for the holy ones according to God's will.

GOSPEL
Matthew
13:24–43

Jesus proposed another parable to the crowds, saying: "The kingdom of heaven may be likened to a man who sowed good seed in his field. While everyone was asleep his enemy came and sowed weeds all through the wheat, and then went off. When the crop grew and bore fruit, the weeds appeared as well. The slaves of the householder came to him and said, 'Master, did you not sow good seed in your field? Where have the weeds come from?' He answered, 'An enemy has done this.' His slaves said to him, 'Do you want us to go and pull them up?' He replied, 'No, if you pull up the weeds you might uproot the wheat along with them. Let them grow together until harvest; then at harvest time I will say to the harvesters, "First collect the weeds and tie them in bundles for burning; but gather the wheat into my barn." ' "

[He proposed another parable to them. "The kingdom of heaven is like a mustard seed that a person took and sowed in a field. It is the smallest of all the seeds, yet when full-grown it is the largest of plants. It becomes a large bush, and the 'birds of the sky come and dwell in its branches.' "

He spoke to them another parable. "The kingdom of heaven is like yeast that a woman took and mixed with three measures of wheat flour until the whole batch was leavened."

All these things Jesus spoke to the crowds in parables. He spoke to them only in parables, to fulfill what had been said through the prophet:

> I *will open my mouth in parables,*
>> I *will announce what has lain hidden from the*
>> *foundation of the world.*

Then, dismissing the crowds, he went into the house. His disciples approached him and said, "Explain to us the parable of the weeds in the field." He said in reply, "He who sows good seed is the Son of Man, the field is the world, the good seed the children of the kingdom. The weeds are the children of the evil one, and the enemy who sows them is the devil. The harvest is the end of the age, and the harvesters are angels. Just as weeds are collected and burned up with fire, so will it be at the end of the age. The Son of Man will send his angels, and they will collect out of his kingdom all who cause others to sin and all evildoers. They will throw them into the fiery furnace, where there will be wailing and grinding of teeth. Then the righteous will shine like the sun in the kingdom of their Father. Whoever has ears ought to hear."]

The author of Wisdom lists forceful divine characteristics. Beginning with the total and exclusive providence of God, he states that only the God of Israel exercises care over all. Because God has neither peer nor rival, God is accountable to no one for the way justice is practiced. God's might is tempered by leniency. The righteous trust in God's power at work in the world. However, those who do not trust this power are fearful. The people of Israel are exhorted to pattern their treatment of others after God's treatment of them, to temper their own might with leniency, to regulate their own justice with kindness.

Paul provides us with a bold and moving explanation of prayer. He describes human limitation and how the Spirit comes to the assistance of human beings precisely in this limitation. He maintains that we do not know how to pray as we ought. Still, such weakness need not prevent us from accomplishing great things through the Spirit who works in and through us. This Spirit acts as intermediary between God and us. Since God searches hearts, God knows that it is the Spirit who makes intercession for us. God has a purpose, and though we do not know what that purpose is, the enabling Spirit of God moves us toward it.

Three parables illustrate aspects of the growth of the reign of God: the field sown with weeds, the mustard seed, and the yeast in the dough. In the first parable, good seed is sown, but weeds grow up along with the crops. This represents a community that includes both good and bad. Purging should be delayed. The time of harvest will come when separation will take place. The second and third parables address the reign's unimpressive beginnings, its gradual and imperceptible growth, and the extraordinary yield that it will ultimately produce. Jesus' teaching ends with a solemn admonishment: Whoever has ears ought to hear and understand this.

✤ Reflecting on the Word

Our experience of the world is often an experience of opposites: truth and lies, goodness and evil, beauty and ugliness. They are found in intimate proximity, often on the same page of the newspaper or in the same half-hour news report, and intertwined in the same human heart. Their existence is connected to human freedom as well as to the power of sin and evil in our world.

Jesus tells a parable that makes the same point as the author of Wisdom: God's exercise of power is tempered by leniency and mercy; God's justice is balanced by loving-kindness. Our desire to pull up and destroy the weeds prematurely could destroy the good wheat. While the interpretation in the Gospel applies this image to different groups in a community, we can also hear this parable as referring to the weeds and wheat, the evil and goodness residing in the heart.

Jesus says God's active presence in the world is something as small as a mustard seed and as fragile as a pinch of yeast, yet each contains a power that, when released, will bring about growth and expansion.

In the meantime, the challenge is being as patient with others as God is, while working with God to purify our own hearts. Last week Jesus warned about the sluggish heart; today he pictures a contaminated heart, good interpenetrated by evil. But the power of God is stronger than the power of evil and death. Be patient, and remain open to the workings of God's grace.

✤ Consider/Discuss

- What do you see as "weeds" in your life, in the community, in the world?
- Where have you seen the power of God at work in small and hidden ways?
- How can the patience and kindness of God work through you?

✤ Responding to the Word

We respond by praying: "O God, you have given us the gift of life; continue to keep us alive in Christ Jesus. Bring us from death to grow in faith, hope, and love. We remain patient in prayer and faithful to your word, until your glory is revealed."

July 24, 2011

SEVENTEENTH SUNDAY IN ORDINARY TIME

Today's Focus: In Search Of: A Wise Heart

Once again, God's word calls us to attend to the condition of our hearts. Today we are invited to consider what our hearts most desire, and what we are willing to give in exchange for it. The Gospel points to the treasure God wishes us to have, if we are wise enough "to seek and sell all" to attain it.

FIRST READING
1 Kings 3:5, 7–12

The LORD appeared to Solomon in a dream at night. God said, "Ask something of me and I will give it to you." Solomon answered: "O LORD, my God, you have made me, your servant, king to succeed my father David; but I am a mere youth, not knowing at all how to act. I serve you in the midst of the people whom you have chosen, a people so vast that it cannot be numbered or counted. Give your servant, therefore, an understanding heart to judge your people and to distinguish right from wrong. For who is able to govern this vast people of yours?"

The LORD was pleased that Solomon made this request. So God said to him: "Because you have asked for this—not for a long life for yourself, nor for riches, nor for the life of your enemies, but for understanding so that you may know what is right—I do as you requested. I give you a heart so wise and understanding that there has never been anyone like you up to now, and after you there will come no one to equal you."

PSALM RESPONSE
Psalm 119:97a

Lord, I love your commands.

SECOND READING
Romans 8:28–30

Brothers and sisters: We know that all things work for good for those who love God, who are called according to his purpose. For those he foreknew he also predestined to be conformed to the image of his Son, so that he might be the firstborn among many brothers and sisters. And those he predestined he also called; and those he called he also justified; and those he justified he also glorified.

146

GOSPEL
Matthew
13:44–52
or 13:44–46

Jesus said to his disciples: "The kingdom of heaven is like a treasure buried in a field, which a person finds and hides again, and out of joy goes and sells all that he has and buys that field. Again, the kingdom of heaven is like a merchant searching for fine pearls. When he finds a pearl of great price, he goes and sells all that he has and buys it. [Again, the kingdom of heaven is like a net thrown into the sea, which collects fish of every kind. When it is full they haul it ashore and sit down to put what is good into buckets. What is bad they throw away. Thus it will be at the end of the age. The angels will go out and separate the wicked from the righteous and throw them into the fiery furnace, where there will be wailing and grinding of teeth.

"Do you understand all these things?" They answered, "Yes." And he replied, "Then every scribe who has been instructed in the kingdom of heaven is like the head of a household who brings from his storeroom both the new and the old."]

❖ Understanding the Word

Solomon asks for an understanding heart so that he can rule his people wisely. This request shows his concern for God's people, not merely for himself. It is no wonder that God is pleased with him. The very last verse of the passage reinforces the tradition of Solomon's wisdom, claiming that no one before him or anyone after him could compare with him. The wisdom referred to here is not experiential wisdom, the kind that stems from reflection on experience; it is really a gift from God. God chose Solomon to be king, and gave him the wisdom he needed to rule wisely.

Paul's insistence that all things work for good should not be misunderstood as meaning that everything will work out in the end. Rather, it implies a profound trust that God can bring good even out of misfortune. Paul's teaching on predestination has often been misunderstood. He states that God foreknew from the beginning of time and with divine power predetermined who would be called, justified, and glorified. And who are the ones called? Nowhere does Paul suggest that some are predestined to salvation and others to perdition. Rather, the entire Christian tradition provides the answer to the question. All are called to be justified and glorified.

The parables of the treasure in the field and the pearl of great price both suggest that the kingdom of God is present though unperceived. However, only the very shrewd discover it and sacrifice everything in order to possess it. The parable of the net is quite different. Like the parable of the wheat and the weeds (see Matthew 13:40b–42, Sixteenth Sunday), it describes a community consisting of both good and bad. Only at the end of the catch will the fish be separated. Jesus asks if the disciples understand his teaching, because they must see that, like the old and new treasures of the householder, the teaching of Jesus, though radically different, is grounded in the original tradition.

If God were to offer you your heart's desire, what would you ask for? Solomon did not request health or wealth. Nor did he ask God to remove his enemies—either those inherited from his father or those acquired when he was given the crown at a very young age. Solomon asked for wisdom, for a heart that understands or listens. Such wisdom included the ability to judge justly and to distinguish right from wrong. God was pleased.

The gift of wisdom allows the heart to see; the letter to the Ephesians refers to "seeing with the eyes of the heart." And wisdom brings the ability to hear the word of the Lord even when spoken in the sound of silence, as Elijah did. Such seeing and hearing lie at the heart of the first two parables. Seeing God's reign is likened to finding a treasure in a field or seeking a most valuable pearl—when one sees where it is hidden or hears where it can be found, one gives all one has to make it one's own.

The heart can spend many years and look in many places for happiness. We can bypass the kingdom again and again, going off into various dead ends, cul de sacs, and blind alleys. Paul reminds the Romans that all things work for good for those who look to God. God, who has predestined us to share the image of the Son, wishes to give us the wisdom needed to discover where the kingdom is hidden.

✥ Consider/Discuss

- What is your heart's desire?
- Have you asked for that wisdom that is a gift of the Holy Spirit?
- Of the different parables you have heard these last three weeks, which one speaks most to your heart?

✥ Responding to the Word

Remembering that "the revelation of [God's] words sheds light" (Psalm 119), ask God to give you the wisdom needed in your life to seek out the divine presence and to respond wholeheartedly to that presence, so that God rules in your heart, mind, and spirit as you grow into the image of Jesus Christ.

July 31, 2011

EIGHTEENTH SUNDAY IN ORDINARY TIME

Today's Focus: "Come and Get It!"

What a perfect set of readings for summertime: God throws a picnic—water, wine, milk, grain bread, rich fare. And Jesus does the same. But the stakes (pardon the pun!) are more serious. We are fed to have fullness of life and to join in the work of salvation.

FIRST READING
Isaiah 55:1–3

Thus says the LORD:
All you who are thirsty,
    come to the water!
You who have no money,
    come, receive grain and eat;
Come, without paying and without cost,
    drink wine and milk!
Why spend your money for what is not bread;
    your wages for what fails to satisfy?
Heed me, and you shall eat well,
    you shall delight in rich fare.
Come to me heedfully,
    listen, that you may have life.
I will renew with you the everlasting covenant,
    the benefits assured to David.

PSALM RESPONSE
Psalm 145:16

The hand of the Lord feeds us; he answers all our needs.

SECOND READING
Romans 8:35, 37–39

Brothers and sisters: What will separate us from the love of Christ? Will anguish, or distress, or persecution, or famine, or nakedness, or peril, or the sword? No, in all these things we conquer overwhelmingly through him who loved us. For I am convinced that neither death, nor life, nor angels, nor principalities, nor present things, nor future things, nor powers, nor height, nor depth, nor any other creature will be able to separate us from the love of God in Christ Jesus our Lord.

149

GOSPEL
Matthew 14:13–21

When Jesus heard of the death of John the Baptist, he withdrew in a boat to a deserted place by himself. The crowds heard of this and followed him on foot from their towns. When he disembarked and saw the vast crowd, his heart was moved with pity for them, and he cured their sick. When it was evening, the disciples approached him and said, "This is a deserted place and it is already late; dismiss the crowds so that they can go to the villages and buy food for themselves." Jesus said to them, "There is no need for them to go away; give them some food yourselves." But they said to him, "Five loaves and two fish are all we have here." Then he said, "Bring them here to me," and he ordered the crowds to sit down on the grass. Taking the five loaves and the two fish, and looking up to heaven, he said the blessing, broke the loaves, and gave them to the disciples, who in turn gave them to the crowds. They all ate and were satisfied, and they picked up the fragments left over—twelve wicker baskets full. Those who ate were about five thousand men, not counting women and children.

❖❖ *Understanding the Word*

God is cast in the role of a street vendor, who offers food and drink at no cost both to those who are able to pay and to those who are not. All are invited to come to the Lord in order to be nourished. What God has to offer is satisfying and will be long-lasting, compared with all else for which people seem to spend their money. The real object of the invitation is God's announcement of the reestablishment of a covenant bond. This prophecy suggests that the covenant had been violated, and now God is eager to restore the severed bond.

Paul insists that nothing that can separate believers from the love of Christ. He is probably challenging the long-standing notion that a person's misfortune is the consequence of some misdeed. Paul turns this understanding upside down by insisting that the opposite can be true—that the righteous, precisely because they are righteous, enter into the sufferings of Christ. In other words, misfortune does not separate them from Christ; it can actually unite them with him. Paul makes four significant points: 1) God's love for us is basic to everything, 2) this love comes to us through Jesus, 3) Jesus is God's "anointed one," and 4) Jesus is the Lord to whom we give our allegiance.

The death of John the Baptist prompted Jesus to seek a place where he might be by himself. However, his departure did not deter the crowds, who seemed to know where he was going and arrived there before he did. Jesus' actions over the food were brief but significant. He took the bread, blessed it, broke it, and gave it as food. The eucharistic overtones are obvious. The role played here by the apostles cannot be overlooked. They were the ones through whom the crowds experienced the munificence of Jesus. The author of the Gospel shows by this that Jesus provides for his people through the agency of the church.

A TV series featured an English chef going into an elementary school in Huntington, West Virginia, trying to change the children's eating habits. The resistance he first encounters is fierce. The children choose pizza over fresh chicken, throwing the beans and salad into the trash. Even sadder was the resistance of the adults: the women who prepare lunch, the school principal, and even the food supervisor of the school system.

We see Jesus feeding people in many ways throughout the Gospels: by his words and deeds, by his preaching, teaching, and healing. In today's account, he literally feeds a crowd of over five thousand with five loaves and two fish. This event is a sign of God's ongoing desire to meet our hungers with generosity and life-giving nourishment.

This feeding reveals Jesus as his Father's Son, the God who calls people to come, eat and drink without paying, without cost. God wants to feed us so we have and share life with others. We can refuse both the food of God's word and the food of the Eucharist, even when we receive it with our ears and mouths, by not taking it into our lives.

The word "heed" comes twice in the first reading: "Heed me and you shall eat well . . . Come to me heedfully, listen, that you may have life." God cries for us to hear, to listen "that you may have life," to receive the love of God revealed in Jesus, and let it nourish us into eternal life.

❖ Consider/Discuss

- Do you take and digest the food that God feeds you at the table of the word and the table of the Eucharist?
- Are you willing to distribute the food of God's word and God's love to others, as the disciples were asked to do?

❖ *Responding to the Word*

We pray that we fully take in the food Jesus gives to us. We ask that the bread of the word and the bread of the Eucharist be nourishment that strengthens us in this life and enables us to walk in the way of the Lord. We pray that we may give this food to others.

August 7, 2011

NINETEENTH SUNDAY IN ORDINARY TIME

Today's Focus: When Sinking, Call on the Lord

Three men are sinking in today's readings: the discouraged Elijah is sinking into a cave on Mount Horeb, Paul is sinking into "great sorrow and constant anguish" as he grieves over his own people's rejection of Jesus, and Peter is sinking into the sea as fear overtakes faith. In all three cases, God raises them up.

FIRST READING
1 Kings 19:9a, 11–13a

At the mountain of God, Horeb, Elijah came to a cave where he took shelter. Then the LORD said to him, "Go outside and stand on the mountain before the LORD; the LORD will be passing by." A strong and heavy wind was rending the mountains and crushing rocks before the LORD—but the LORD was not in the wind. After the wind there was an earthquake—but the LORD was not in the earthquake. After the earthquake there was fire—but the LORD was not in the fire. After the fire there was a tiny whispering sound. When he heard this, Elijah hid his face in his cloak and went and stood at the entrance of the cave.

PSALM RESPONSE
Psalm 85:8

Lord, let us see your kindness, and grant us your salvation.

SECOND READING
Romans 9:1–5

Brothers and sisters: I speak the truth in Christ, I do not lie; my conscience joins with the Holy Spirit in bearing me witness that I have great sorrow and constant anguish in my heart. For I could wish that I myself were accursed and cut off from Christ for the sake of my own people, my kindred according to the flesh. They are Israelites; theirs the adoption, the glory, the covenants, the giving of the law, the worship, and the promises; theirs the patriarchs, and from them, according to the flesh, is the Christ, who is over all, God blessed forever. Amen.

GOSPEL	After he had fed the people, Jesus made the disciples get into a
Matthew	boat and precede him to the other side, while he dismissed the
14:22–33	crowds. After doing so, he went up on the mountain by himself

After he had fed the people, Jesus made the disciples get into a boat and precede him to the other side, while he dismissed the crowds. After doing so, he went up on the mountain by himself to pray. When it was evening he was there alone. Meanwhile the boat, already a few miles offshore, was being tossed about by the waves, for the wind was against it. During the fourth watch of the night, he came toward them walking on the sea. When the disciples saw him walking on the sea they were terrified. "It is a ghost," they said, and they cried out in fear. At once Jesus spoke to them, "Take courage, it is I; do not be afraid." Peter said to him in reply, "Lord, if it is you, command me to come to you on the water." He said, "Come." Peter got out of the boat and began to walk on the water toward Jesus. But when he saw how strong the wind was he became frightened; and, beginning to sink, he cried out, "Lord, save me!" Immediately Jesus stretched out his hand and caught Peter, and said to him, "O you of little faith, why did you doubt?" After they got into the boat, the wind died down. Those who were in the boat did him homage, saying, "Truly, you are the Son of God."

❖ Understanding the Word

Elijah has retreated into a cave, but God calls him from this place of shelter and darkness to stand before the LORD out in the open. There he witnesses the wind, the earthquake, and the fire associated with God's appearance, but he does not experience God within these natural marvels. It is only when he hears a "tiny whispering sound" that he is gripped with the realization that God is present. He covers his face in an act of reverence. Most commentators maintain that this tiny whisper points to the importance of the small and seemingly insignificant in life as the stage upon which the revelation of God is enacted.

Paul speaks about his ardent attachment to his Jewish compatriots, his kindred according to the flesh. Although he has turned from proclaiming the gospel to the Jewish people and devoted himself to the conversion of the Gentiles, he never ceases loving the people from whom he came. It is this very love that causes him such anguish, because his own people have not accepted Jesus as the Messiah whom God first promised and then sent to them. Paul lists several prerogatives that they enjoy as the chosen people of God. However, their greatest boast is that the anointed one of God came from them.

In the pre-dawn dimness the apostles saw Jesus walking toward them on the water. To portray Jesus walking on the chaotic water was to cast him in the guise of this creator-god who alone governs chaotic waters. Peter accepted Jesus' invitation to walk on the water to him. Peter is a model of both faith and lack of faith. He believed that he would be able to walk on the water, and he did; he doubted that he would be able to long endure the chaotic waters, and he did not. Ultimately, it was faith that won out, for Peter cried out to Jesus, knowing that Jesus had the power to save him, and he did.

We all have moments of feeling "down," times of discouragement, depression, loss, fear, anxiety, (fill in the blank). Such "moods" can descend unexpectedly or result from a particular event. They can pass quickly or stay longer. The three main characters in today's scriptures are having such a moment.

After Elijah had his showdown with the prophets of Baal in Israel and led the Israelites in slaughtering them, word came that Jezebel wanted him killed, so he set out into the desert. There, he sat down and said to God, "Enough! Life is unbearable. Let me die." But God wasn't finished with Elijah, and sent an angel with some food and drink and told him to walk "forty days" to Mount Horeb (Sinai). There, God appeared.

Paul would go first into the synagogues to preach about Jesus as Israel's long-awaited Messiah. But the response was not overwhelming. Often he was run out of town, beaten, or tossed into jail. We hear his grief today. Still, he trusts God will work it out, and later proclaims, "God has not rejected his people . . . For the gifts and call of God are irrevocable" (Romans 11:2, 29).

Perhaps Peter is the most instructive for our "sinking" occasions. He was doing fine until he lost focus. As long as he looked to Jesus, he walked on water. When he focused on the wind and the waves, he sank. When he re-focused on Jesus and cried out for help, Jesus' hand caught him. There seems to be a lesson here.

✤ Consider/Discuss

- What gets you "down"?
- Do you cry out to the Lord and ask for help?

✤ Responding to the Word

Today's responsorial psalm assures us that "Near indeed is his salvation to those who fear him" and "The LORD himself will give his benefits." In those times when the waves of chaos threaten to overwhelm us, we can pray: "Lord, let us see your kindness, and grant us your salvation."

August 14, 2011

TWENTIETH SUNDAY IN ORDINARY TIME

Today's Focus: God's Ever-Expanding Table

A Gentile woman comes to Jesus, boldly asking for her daughter's release from a demon. Jesus turns away from her request, then changes his mind and grants it. Does her wit win his favor or is something else going on here? Jesus' response focuses our attention on her faith.

FIRST READING
Isaiah 56:1, 6–7

Thus says the LORD:
Observe what is right, do what is just;
    for my salvation is about to come,
    my justice, about to be revealed.

The foreigners who join themselves to the LORD,
    ministering to him,
loving the name of the LORD,
    and becoming his servants—
all who keep the sabbath free from profanation
    and hold to my covenant,
them I will bring to my holy mountain
    and make joyful in my house of prayer;
their burnt offerings and sacrifices
    will be acceptable on my altar,
for my house shall be called
    a house of prayer for all peoples.

PSALM RESPONSE
Psalm 67:4

O God, let all the nations praise you!

SECOND READING
Romans 11: 13–15, 29–32

Brothers and sisters: I am speaking to you Gentiles. Inasmuch as I am the apostle to the Gentiles, I glory in my ministry in order to make my race jealous and thus save some of them. For if their rejection is the reconciliation of the world, what will their acceptance be but life from the dead?

For the gifts and the call of God are irrevocable. Just as you once disobeyed God but have now received mercy because of their disobedience, so they have now disobeyed in order that, by virtue of the mercy shown to you, they too may now receive mercy. For God delivered all to disobedience, that he might have mercy upon all.

GOSPEL
Matthew
15:21–28

At that time, Jesus withdrew to the region of Tyre and Sidon. And behold, a Canaanite woman of that district came and called out, "Have pity on me, Lord, Son of David! My daughter is tormented by a demon." But Jesus did not say a word in answer to her. Jesus' disciples came and asked him, "Send her away, for she keeps calling out after us." He said in reply, "I was sent only to the lost sheep of the house of Israel." But the woman came and did Jesus homage, saying, "Lord, help me." He said in reply, "It is not right to take the food of the children and throw it to the dogs." She said, "Please, Lord, for even the dogs eat the scraps that fall from the table of their masters." Then Jesus said to her in reply, "O woman, great is your faith! Let it be done for you as you wish." And the woman's daughter was healed from that hour.

❖ Understanding the Word

Israel's primary ethical obligation was social responsibility. Righteousness, which describes the quality of the relationship with God, is really a divine characteristic. Human beings only appropriate it when they are in right relationship with God. In response to the people's fidelity, they are encouraged to proceed to God's holy mountain. Even faithful foreigners will be allowed to rejoice here as members of the praying community. The temple is now designated as a house of prayer for all people, not merely a national shrine reserved for the elect. Now God is accessible to all, not merely to those of the bloodline of Israel.

Lest Gentile Christians think that their acceptance of Christ has made them superior to Jews, Paul emphasizes Israelite privilege. They were God's special people, and it was to them that God granted extraordinary gifts. Paul argues that if he turned to the Gentiles because some Jews would not listen to him, now Jews will be jealous because Gentiles have accepted his message and will be converted. If the Jews' rejection of the gospel brought reconciliation with God to the rest of the world, how much more will their acceptance of the gospel affect them? Gentiles have no reason to feel superior, for they too were sinners, and God granted them divine mercy.

The story of the Canaanite woman addresses several important and interrelated issues: crossing territorial and cultural boundaries, public social exchange of women and men, the Christian mission to the Gentiles, and the issue of faith. First, despite the belief that to cross into pagan territory was to leave God's holy land, Jesus deliberately crosses into Gentile territory. In addition, the woman was unattended, a fact that threatened Jesus' respectability. However, Jesus disregards the factors of gender, ethnic/religious background, and questionable lifestyle in order to reconcile to God a person who was marginalized by society.

A woman has a daughter tormented by a demon. She hears about Jesus, seeks him out, and pleads with him to pity her child. Who could turn away? Yet Jesus dismisses her, saying dogs do not get the children's food. Is Jesus really comparing her to a dog begging at table? Is he turning away because his mission to the house of Israel limits who benefits from his healing power? What was Jesus thinking?

Three things can be said here.

First of all, it is probable he was not literally calling her a dog any more than we are when we say about someone, "Every dog has its day."

Second, it is possible that *at this time* Jesus understood his mission as taking care of his own people first. We are told he grew in wisdom. Would this not include a growth in fully understanding his Father's will and how far it went?

Third, is it not even possible that this was a moment of growth, that the woman's faith pushed him further along in widening his mission, and in recognizing that everyone was welcome at the table of the kingdom, and that his work was to respond wherever he found faith?

Isaiah reminds his Jewish listeners that God will bring the foreigners who join themselves to the Lord to his holy mountain, where they will worship. Paul reminds his Gentile listeners that God's gifts and call to the Jews are irreversible. In a word, everyone has a place at the table.

❖ Consider/Discuss

- Do I believe that Jesus grew in wisdom and strength and favor?
- Are there any groups that I tend to see as not belonging at the table of the Lord?
- Do I take seriously the power of faith, my faith?

❖ Responding to the Word

We pray to look beyond categories of nationality, ethnicity, class, gender, or any other arbitrary dividing line we put up to exclude others from the mercy of God and from being treated with justice, compassion, and forgiveness. We ask for the grace to respond to others as we would have God respond to us.

August 21, 2011

TWENTY-FIRST SUNDAY IN ORDINARY TIME

Today's Focus: A Life-changing Question

Jesus' question is not only for the disciples who walked the roads of Galilee with him, but one posed to disciples of every age: "Who do you say that I am?" His question asks for a response of mind, heart, and spirit. It may well be the most important question in our lives.

FIRST READING
Isaiah 22:19–23

Thus says the LORD to Shebna, master of the palace:
"I will thrust you from your office
    and pull you down from your station.
On that day I will summon my servant
    Eliakim, son of Hilkiah;
I will clothe him with your robe,
    and gird him with your sash,
    and give over to him your authority.
He shall be a father to the inhabitants of Jerusalem,
    and to the house of Judah.
I will place the key of the House of David on Eliakim's shoulder;
    when he opens, no one shall shut
    when he shuts, no one shall open.
I will fix him like a peg in a sure spot,
    to be a place of honor for his family."

PSALM RESPONSE
Psalm 138:8bc

Lord, your love is eternal; do not forsake the work of your hands.

SECOND READING
Romans 11:33–36

Oh, the depth of the riches and wisdom and knowledge of God! How inscrutable are his judgments and how unsearchable his ways!
    For who has known the mind of the Lord
        or who has been his counselor?
    Or who has given the Lord anything
        that he may be repaid?
For from him and through him and for him are all things. To him be glory forever. Amen.

GOSPEL
Matthew
16:13–20

Jesus went into the region of Caesarea Philippi and he asked his disciples, "Who do people say that the Son of Man is?" They replied, "Some say John the Baptist, others Elijah, still others Jeremiah or one of the prophets." He said to them, "But who do you say that I am?" Simon Peter said in reply, "You are the Christ, the Son of the living God." Jesus said to him in reply, "Blessed are you, Simon son of Jonah. For flesh and blood has not revealed this to you, but my heavenly Father. And so I say to you, you are Peter, and upon this rock I will build my church, and the gates of the netherworld shall not prevail against it. I will give you the keys to the kingdom of heaven. Whatever you bind on earth shall be bound in heaven; and whatever you loose on earth shall be loosed in heaven." Then he strictly ordered his disciples to tell no one that he was the Christ.

❖ Understanding the Word

The role of leadership among the people of God is very important. In ancient Israel, those in office had religious as well as political responsibilities. Today's first reading narrates the transfer of authority from one man to another. This investiture symbolizes the man's being clothed with authority. Even if this passage does not reflect an actual historical occasion, the picture it sketches is significant. The oracle promises a person who will provide the order and stability that the kingdom of Judah must have needed. If the man being clothed with authority is not himself a messianic figure, he ensures that the kingdom—one that will produce such a figure—will survive.

Paul speaks of the mysterious ways of God in the plan of salvation. Even though human beings cannot grasp God's plan, it has meaning and purpose, and God's plan for all creation will unfold in God's way. Paul extols God the creator, the source of all that is; he acclaims God the sustainer, through whom all creation continues to be; he celebrates God the goal for whom all things were made and to whom all things proceed. Paul is certainly grounded in a very Jewish understanding of God. What is unique, however, is the way he has interpreted this theology. It is here that Christ holds a constitutive place.

Jesus asks the disciples what people are saying about him. Some believe that he is John the Baptist; others, that he is Elijah; still others, that he is one of the other prophets. Simon Peter speaks in the name of the others when he proclaims that Jesus is the Christ, the Messiah, the anointed one of God, the Son of the living God. With a play on Greek words, Jesus declares that Peter (*Petros*) is the rock (*petra*) upon which Jesus will establish his church. Although the image of a rock suggests stability and endurance, we will soon see that these characteristics are not natural to Peter.

Certain questions change lives, depending on our answer: "Do you take this person to be your husband/wife?" "Do you want this job?" "Can you forgive me?" The question Jesus asks today is one that certainly changes lives. Our response is not simply an academic exercise, a matter of knowing the right answer we learned from a book. Our answer must lead to a commitment that is to be lived out each day of our lives.

Peter's answer certainly changed the course of his life. Jesus recognized that it was not Peter's innate knowledge, or that of any other person, that had given Peter his response: "You are the Christ, the Son of the living God." It was the Father. And so Jesus declares that Peter will be the one to lead the other disciples and all who would come after. Simon, son of John, fisherman, husband, brother—and one who would deny he ever knew Christ!—he was to be the rock on which Jesus would build the church. His response was life-changing.

Peter's answer was not a perfect one, as we shall see next week. Even so, Jesus accepts it as an indication that his Father is at work in those called to be with him who would continue his work. The Father chose to work in fallible human beings. We may not think of ourselves as rocks, but the future of the church depends on how well each one of us lives out the answer to this question, "Who do you say that I am?"

✠ *Consider/Discuss*

- Who do you say Jesus is?
- Do you recognize Jesus as one who embodies the wisdom and knowledge of God?
- How does your answer to Jesus' question show up in the way you live?

✠ *Responding to the Word*

We pray that our loving Father will bring us to a deeper knowledge and understanding of his Son Jesus. We ask that this understanding will lead to a deeper commitment on our part to the work of Jesus to bring about in our own day the reign of God in our world.

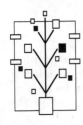

August 28, 2011

TWENTY-SECOND SUNDAY IN ORDINARY TIME

Today's Focus: The Cost of Closeness

We might think being close to God is always a warm, cozy experience. Today's readings remind us it can also be wearying, consuming, costly, feeling like a fire burning within your heart (Jeremiah), or like a thirst that makes you parched and lifeless (Psalm 63).

FIRST READING
Jeremiah 20:7–9

You duped me, O LORD, and I let myself be duped;
   you were too strong for me, and you triumphed.
All the day I am an object of laughter;
   everyone mocks me.

Whenever I speak, I must cry out,
   violence and outrage is my message;
the word of the LORD has brought me
   derision and reproach all the day.

I say to myself, I will not mention him,
   I will speak in his name no more.
But then it becomes like fire burning in my heart,
   imprisoned in my bones;
I grow weary holding it in, I cannot endure it.

PSALM RESPONSE
Psalm 63:2b

My soul is thirsting for you, O Lord my God.

SECOND READING
Romans 12:1–2

I urge you, brothers and sisters, by the mercies of God, to offer your bodies as a living sacrifice, holy and pleasing to God, your spiritual worship. Do not conform yourselves to this age but be transformed by the renewal of your mind, that you may discern what is the will of God, what is good and pleasing and perfect.

GOSPEL
Matthew 16:21–27

Jesus began to show his disciples that he must go to Jerusalem and suffer greatly from the elders, the chief priests, and the scribes, and be killed and on the third day be raised. Then Peter took Jesus aside and began to rebuke him, "God forbid, Lord! No such thing shall ever happen to you." He turned and said to Peter, "Get behind me, Satan! You are an obstacle to me. You are thinking not as God does, but as human beings do."

Then Jesus said to his disciples, "Whoever wishes to come after me must deny himself, take up his cross, and follow me. For whoever wishes to save his life will lose it, but whoever loses his life for my sake will find it. What profit would there be for one to gain the whole world and forfeit his life? Or what can one give in exchange for his life? For the Son of Man will come with his angels in his Father's glory, and then he will repay all according to his conduct."

161

Jeremiah is caught between fidelity to the vocation that is his as God's prophet and his own natural inclinations. He was called to deliver a message of violence and destruction to his own people. It is his nation that will be racked with violence and that will face destruction, and he recoils from this responsibility. He can no longer endure the burden so he decides never again to speak in God's name. However, like a roaring fire, the words seem to burn within him. He cannot restrain their fury. He must speak. Jeremiah is indeed a man of sorrows.

Paul appeals to the mercies of God as the basis of his admonition when he asks the Christians of Rome to offer themselves as a living sacrifice. He is calling them to a disciplined life, not a sacrificial death. He insists that they have entered into the final age of fulfillment. Saved through the blood of Christ and filled with the Spirit of God, they are being transformed into Christ. They have put aside the standards of this world in order to take on the standards of Christ and of the reign of God. This is the transformation and renewal of which Paul speaks.

Jesus predicts his own suffering, death, and resurrection and then discusses the need for the disciples to bear their own suffering. The idea of a suffering messiah did not conform to the expectations of the people, at least not to Peter's. He rebukes Jesus. Jesus then addresses Peter as Satan, the one who acts as an obstacle to the unfolding of God's will. Then, turning to the other disciples, Jesus says that those who follow him must, like him, deny themselves any self-interest and self-fulfillment. Those who selfishly save themselves from sufferings lose in the arena of eschatological judgment, while those who unselfishly offer themselves are saved from this judgment. This is what following Jesus means.

❖ *Reflecting on the Word*

The prophets often spoke bluntly, whether addressing the people or even God. Take Jeremiah today. He accuses God of seducing and overpowering him, making him speak a word that has led to his ridicule and persecution. He was even thrown down a cistern and left to die because of his preaching! Jeremiah confesses he has no choice in the matter. When he refuses to speak God's word, he experiences a fire burning in his heart, consuming his very bones.

The cost of drawing near to the living God can take us down a path we would rather not go. Peter saw this coming when Jesus began to speak of the suffering that lay ahead, instead of being the powerful Messiah people had been waiting for, who would cast down their enemies and restore Israel to the glory days of King David. Instead, Jesus spoke about taking up the cross, losing one's life, or, in Paul's words to the Romans, becoming "a living sacrifice, holy and acceptable to God."

God's plan for us is the transformation and renewal of our minds according to the pattern of God's Son Jesus. This transformation comes about when we "offer [our] bodies as a living sacrifice," seeking to discern and do God's will as Jesus did. Such self-offering may lead to our following Jesus on the way: finding life by losing it for the sake of others, and coming to know the living God as purifying fire, life-giving water, and nourishing food for our spirit.

- Would your reaction to Jesus' speaking of having to go to Jerusalem be like Peter's? Why or why not?
- Can you apply Paul's words to your life: "Do not conform yourselves to this age but be transformed by the renewal of your mind, that you may discern what is the will of God"?

✤ Responding to the Word

We can pray that we have the strength to respond courageously to Jesus' call to be willing to lose our life for his sake. We ask to be able to discern in our daily lives the way we can "offer [our] bodies as a living sacrifice, holy and acceptable to God, your spiritual worship."

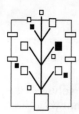

September 4, 2011

TWENTY-THIRD SUNDAY
IN ORDINARY TIME

Today's Focus: A Job Nobody Wants

God appointed Ezekiel to be a watchman, to warn anyone turning away from God or harming another. Jesus gives this task of correction to all the community, calling each person to be willing to correct someone who is committing a wrong. Fraternal correction is one face of loving another.

FIRST READING
Ezekiel 33:7–9

Thus says the LORD: You, son of man, I have appointed watchman for the house of Israel; when you hear me say anything, you shall warn them for me. If I tell the wicked, "O wicked one, you shall surely die," and you do not speak out to dissuade the wicked from his way, the wicked shall die for his guilt, but I will hold you responsible for his death. But if you warn the wicked, trying to turn him from his way, and he refuses to turn from his way, he shall die for his guilt, but you shall save yourself.

PSALM RESPONSE
Psalm 95:8

If today you hear his voice, harden not your hearts.

SECOND READING
Romans 13:8–10

Brothers and sisters: Owe nothing to anyone, except to love one another; for the one who loves another has fulfilled the law. The commandments, "You shall not commit adultery; you shall not kill; you shall not steal; you shall not covet," and whatever other commandment there may be, are summed up in this saying, namely, "You shall love your neighbor as yourself." Love does no evil to the neighbor; hence, love is the fulfillment of the law.

GOSPEL
Matthew 18:15–20

Jesus said to his disciples: "If your brother sins against you, go and tell him his fault between you and him alone. If he listens to you, you have won over your brother. If he does not listen, take one or two others along with you, so that 'every fact may be established on the testimony of two or three witnesses.' If he refuses to listen to them, tell the church. If he refuses to listen even to the church, then treat him as you would a Gentile or a tax collector. Amen, I say to you, whatever you bind on earth shall be bound in heaven, and whatever you loose on earth shall be loosed in heaven. Again, amen, I say to you, if two of you agree on earth about anything for which they are to pray, it shall be granted to them by my heavenly Father. For where two or three are gathered together in my name, there am I in the midst of them."

❖ Understanding the Word

Today's first reading is an oracle of appointment, a personal message to the prophet himself. Ezekiel is called to be a watchman. He is entrusted with keeping watch over the entire house of Israel. He fulfills this role when he proclaims God's words of warning, and God will hold him responsible if he does not protect the people by means of his proclamation. The wording of the oracle implies that there is still time for the people. The sinner can still be called back from sin. However, in a very real sense this all depends upon the prophet's fidelity to his call to be watchman.

Paul tells the Christians of Rome that on the one hand they should owe nothing, while on the other hand they should owe everything, for love requires total self-giving. The debt of love is not an obligation that can be paid once for all. It is more like interest for which we are always liable. Love will take different forms, depending upon circumstances. When we truly love others, we desire only what is good for those we love. Following the teaching of Jesus, the love that Paul exhorts is to be extended to all people without exception. According to Paul, love is the fulfillment of the law.

Reconciliation within the community is such a pressing concern that its maintenance is a matter of church discipline. The Gospel reading describes the procedure to be followed in achieving it. The importance of the community in this process is apparent. First, it is the entire group of disciples, not merely its leader, that exercises disciplinary power. Second, Jesus declares that any agreement arrived at by two members of this group will be heard. He is not here talking about prayer in general, but prayer for guidance in coming to a decision that will affect the community's well-being. Jesus promises to be present in his church if the members turn to him for guidance.

❖ Reflecting on the Word

We can respond in different ways when someone wrongs us: we can ignore the offense, cut off the offender, announce our anger or hurt, or be equally offensive. Perhaps you have tried each of these. Jesus sets out another way for his disciples. First, go to the person and point out the failure; if that doesn't work, take another with you; if that doesn't work, "refer it to the church." And if that doesn't work, "treat the person as you would a Gentile or a tax collector."

This last remark could sound like even Jesus put limits on what you had to do to bring a person around, especially since tax collectors were generally held in contempt and Gentiles kept at a distance. But this wasn't so for Jesus; these were the very ones he reached out to. So, his last remark indicates that you never stop trying to win over another.

These words are part of Jesus' fourth speech in Matthew's Gospel, focused on life within the community of his followers. They are to be a community of reconciliation. This call to engage in fraternal correction has got to be one of the more difficult aspects of living out the way of Jesus, by loving others enough to tell them when they are committing a wrong. It's frequently much easier to let it slide or move away from the person altogether.

Paul's exhortation to "owe nothing to anyone, except to love one another" finds fulfillment in this difficult area of fraternal correction. Such love fulfills the law.

✤ Consider/Discuss

- How do you react when someone wrongs you?
- Do you see any value in the process Jesus sets out here?
- Do you accept that being a church community means correcting those who do wrong?

✤ Responding to the Word

We may need to ask God for the courage to face those who have wronged us and tell them of their failure. We pray to the Spirit whose work is to bring about unity, strengthening the bonds of love between all disciples so that this love may extend to all creation.

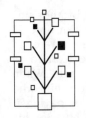

September 11, 2011

TWENTY-FOURTH SUNDAY IN ORDINARY TIME

Today's Focus: Forever Forgiving?

Last week's Gospel called us to be willing to correct each other, willing to point out to another when he or she has wronged us. This week disciples get an equally difficult mission—to forgive. Not just once but again and again. Is this really possible? With God's grace it is.

FIRST READING
Sirach 27:30 — 28:9

Wrath and anger are hateful things,
    yet the sinner hugs them tight.
The vengeful will suffer the LORD's vengeance,
    for he remembers their sins in detail.
Forgive your neighbor's injustice;
    then when you pray, your own sins will be forgiven.
Could anyone nourish anger against another
    and expect healing from the LORD?
Could anyone refuse mercy to another like himself,
    can he seek pardon for his own sins?
If one who is but flesh cherishes wrath,
    who will forgive his sins?
Remember your last days, set enmity aside;
    remember death and decay, and cease from sin!
Think of the commandments, hate not your neighbor;
    remember the Most High's covenant, and overlook faults.

PSALM RESPONSE
Psalm 103:8

The Lord is kind and merciful, slow to anger, and rich in compassion.

SECOND READING
Romans 14:7–9

Brothers and sisters: None of us lives for oneself, and no one dies for oneself. For if we live, we live for the Lord, and if we die, we die for the Lord; so then, whether we live or die, we are the Lord's. For this is why Christ died and came to life, that he might be Lord of both the dead and the living.

Peter approached Jesus and asked him, "Lord, if my brother sins against me, how often must I forgive? As many as seven times?" Jesus answered, "I say to you, not seven times but seventy-seven times. That is why the kingdom of heaven may be likened to a king who decided to settle accounts with his servants. When he began the accounting, a debtor was brought before him who owed him a huge amount. Since he had no way of paying it back, his master ordered him to be sold, along with his wife, his children, and all his property, in payment of the debt. At that, the servant fell down, did him homage, and said, 'Be patient with me, and I will pay you back in full.' Moved with compassion the master of that servant let him go and forgave him the loan. When that servant had left, he found one of his fellow servants who owed him a much smaller amount. He seized one of his fellow servants and started to choke him, demanding, 'Pay back what you owe.' Falling to his knees, his fellow servant begged him, 'Be patient with me, and I will pay you back.' But he refused. Instead, he had the fellow servant put in prison until he paid back the debt. Now when his fellow servants saw what had happened, they were deeply disturbed, and went to their master and reported the whole affair. His master summoned him and said to him, 'You wicked servant! I forgave you your entire debt because you begged me to. Should you not have had pity on your fellow servant, as I had pity on you?' Then in anger his master handed him over to the torturers until he should pay back the whole debt. So will my heavenly Father do to you, unless each of you forgives your brother from your heart."

❖ Understanding the Word

The tone of the passage from Sirach is set in the first verse. Wrath and anger may be instinctive responses to situations in life, but they are abhorrent if they are permanent dispositions of mind and heart. The certainty of death should prompt us to set aside anger or wrath. Life is too short to bear attitudes that can undermine our spirits. Sirach insists on the need to forgive others, for we too need to be forgiven. The basis of this teaching is not forgiveness by others, but forgiveness by God. We must be willing to extend to others the same gracious compassion that God has extended to us.

Paul maintains that Christ, by virtue of his death and resurrection, exercises power over life and death. In like manner, those who are joined to Christ are joined permanently. Nothing, neither life nor death, can separate them from the love of Christ (see Romans 8:38). He further insists that in every aspect of life and even in death, Christians are under the lordship of Christ. Having conquered death by means of his resurrection, Christ has gained lordship over all. Whether they live or they die, they belong to Christ and are accountable to Christ. This understanding is the bedrock of Christian ethics.

The rabbis taught that the duty to forgive was fulfilled if one forgave an offender three times. Peter must have thought that he was being extraordinarily generous if he forgave seven times. However, Jesus indicates that not even this is enough. He insists that we must be willing to forgive seventy-seven times. In other words, there must be no limit to our forgiveness. The radical nature of Jesus' parable illustrates this. With one simple statement Jesus draws a connection between the generosity of the king and that of God. If God is willing to forgive the exorbitant debt we owe God, surely we can forgive the paltry debts owed us.

❖ Reflecting on the Word

Erich Segal died at the beginning of 2010. I remember reading his best seller *Love Story* and being moved by its then famous line "Love means never having to say you're sorry." Over the years I have really come to disagree with this. I believe love means having to say you're sorry and asking for forgiveness many times in life.

Today's Gospel reminds us that love also means being willing to forgive many times in a life. We fail each other. We sin against each other. Sometimes we do this deliberately, sometimes thoughtlessly, but nonetheless it is painful for the one sinned against.

Is forgiveness ever easy—especially with a repeat offender? "Seven times?" Peter asks. "Seventy-seven times," Jesus replies. Today's readings give us the major reason to forgive others: God has forgiven us. There's more. Not to forgive is to let anger and wrath poison our hearts. Being unforgiving can imprison a person, resulting in bitterness, revenge, and a slow death of the spirit. Not to forgive can be more costly for the one offended.

Paul tells us we belong to the Lord, are called to serve him, to do his will, which is the will of the Father. And God's will is that we forgive one another. When the risen Lord first appeared to the disciples in the upper room, he wished them peace, and then gave them the power of the Spirit to forgive. This work is not limited to our going to the sacrament of reconciliation.

❖ Consider/Discuss

- Have you known the grace of being forgiven?
- Have you known the freedom of forgiving another person?

❖ Responding to the Word

We pray that we might have the gift of forgiveness, both of receiving and giving it to others in turn. We ask the Holy Spirit to empower us to be able to forgive what the world judges to be "unforgiveable." While for us it can seem impossible, with God all things are possible.

September 18, 2011

TWENTY-FIFTH SUNDAY IN ORDINARY TIME

Today's Focus: God as Giver: Generous or Unjust?

Understanding the mind of God is not within our power, especially when it comes to God's generosity. God has spoken about this tendency to confound us in the books of Isaiah and in the parables of Jesus. The challenge for us is to absorb this message in trust.

FIRST READING
Isaiah 55:6–9

Seek the LORD while he may be found,
    call him while he is near.
Let the scoundrel forsake his way,
    and the wicked his thoughts;
let him turn to the LORD for mercy;
    to our God, who is generous in forgiving.
For my thoughts are not your thoughts,
    nor are your ways my ways, says the LORD.
As high as the heavens are above the earth,
    so high are my ways above your ways
    and my thoughts above your thoughts.

PSALM RESPONSE
Psalm 145:18a

The Lord is near to all who call upon him.

SECOND READING
Philippians 1:20c–24, 27a

Brothers and sisters: Christ will be magnified in my body, whether by life or by death. For to me life is Christ, and death is gain. If I go on living in the flesh, that means fruitful labor for me. And I do not know which I shall choose. I am caught between the two. I long to depart this life and be with Christ, for that is far better. Yet that I remain in the flesh is more necessary for your benefit.

Only, conduct yourselves in a way worthy of the gospel of Christ.

Jesus told his disciples this parable: "The kingdom of heaven is like a landowner who went out at dawn to hire laborers for his vineyard. After agreeing with them for the usual daily wage, he sent them into his vineyard. Going out about nine o'clock, the landowner saw others standing idle in the marketplace, and he said to them, 'You too go into my vineyard, and I will give you what is just.' So they went off. And he went out again around noon, and around three o'clock, and did likewise. Going out about five o'clock, the landowner found others standing around, and said to them, 'Why do you stand here idle all day?' They answered, 'Because no one has hired us.' He said to them, 'You too go into my vineyard.' When it was evening the owner of the vineyard said to his foreman, 'Summon the laborers and give them their pay, beginning with the last and ending with the first.' When those who had started about five o'clock came, each received the usual daily wage. So when the first came, they thought that they would receive more, but each of them also got the usual wage. And on receiving it they grumbled against the landowner, saying, 'These last ones worked only one hour, and you have made them equal to us, who bore the day's burden and the heat.' He said to one of them in reply, 'My friend, I am not cheating you. Did you not agree with me for the usual daily wage? Take what is yours and go. What if I wish to give this last one the same as you? Or am I not free to do as I wish with my own money? Are you envious because I am generous?' Thus, the last will be first, and the first will be last."

❖ Understanding the Word

The prophecy of salvation that is read today includes a call to worship and a call to conversion. The prophet describes the sinfulness of the people. There is a pattern of sin here, not merely isolated offenses. Still, the prophet assures them that God will be compassionate toward them. On the one hand are wicked thoughts and the way of the scoundrel; on the other hand are compassion and forgiveness. This oracle both exhorts sinners to turn away from their evil lives and assures them that having turned away they will enjoy the salvation of God.

Paul shares his own inner struggle regarding life and death. Although the decision to live or die was probably not in his hands, it is his attitude toward these options that is of importance here. Paul does not consider death a way of escaping the misfortune that he may be suffering. Rather, he weighs the religious and ministerial advantages of both living and dying. At issue is the extent to which Christ will be glorified through Paul's continued life or his death. Though he prefers dying and being with Christ, he can see advantages for himself either way. Still he is willing to postpone the joyful union with Christ for the sake of his ministry.

The parable read today is particularly startling. It does not seem fair to pay all of the laborers the same wage regardless of the amount of time they put into the work. Still, all received exactly the amount for which they had contracted. The paradox of the narrative is seen in the payment policy of the owner of the vineyard. The justice with which he pays the laborers is superseded by his generosity. What is almost scandalous here is the fact that he is most generous toward the workers who were unwanted by others. The parable shows that the reign of God is based on generosity, not merely on human standards of fairness.

❖ Reflecting on the Word

If you ever felt you have not gotten what you deserve for all that you have done, or that others have been given more than they deserve for the little that they have done, this Gospel is not going to please you. It is hard not to line up with the grumblers, complaining that those who worked all day should not be given the same as the eleventh-hour crowd. Where's the justice in this?

Isaiah sets the stage for hearing the Gospel when he calls us to seek and call on God for what we need, especially mercy and forgiveness. But the prophet recognizes that God's response to this request may baffle us, especially when such overabundant mercy is shown to others.

Jesus is not telling a tale about being fair, or offering a lesson on just wages. He is teaching that God's rule is marked by generosity, especially to the last and least, the overlooked, the undervalued, the unwanted, those judged as not very capable. This master calls all to do what they can do. For some the work will last longer than for others. But all will be rewarded.

So, be generous as God is generous. We see an example of this in Paul's willingness to stay working with the early communities. While the Philippians were easy to love, he also ministered to the cantankerous Corinthians and the "stupid" Galatians (Paul's own words) who were turning away from the gospel he preached to them. Paul heard the call to act differently with these different groups of people.

❖ Consider/Discuss

- When are you being asked to be generous rather than "just"?
- Is there another way of thinking about justice than how we usually think of it, that is, as getting what we deserve?
- Have you known God's splendid generosity, going beyond anything you have "deserved"?

❖ Responding to the Word

We pray that we might be able to enter into God's compassion toward those who come later and do less. We pray that we might be able to mirror the generosity of God during the coming week if an opportunity arises.

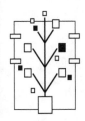

September 25, 2011

TWENTY-SIXTH SUNDAY IN ORDINARY TIME

Today's Focus: Doing "Yes"

It's all in the doing. Doing the right thing leads to life, says the LORD to Ezekiel. A child's doing what a father asks wins out over saying one will do it. Paul quotes an early hymn that sings of Christ doing the Father's will, thereby emptying himself so that the Father could fill him and exalt him.

FIRST READING
Ezekiel 18:25–28

Thus says the LORD: You say, "The LORD's way is not fair!" Hear now, house of Israel: Is it my way that is unfair, or rather, are not your ways unfair? When someone virtuous turns away from virtue to commit iniquity, and dies, it is because of the iniquity he committed that he must die. But if he turns from the wickedness he has committed, and does what is right and just, he shall preserve his life; since he has turned away from all the sins that he has committed, he shall surely live, he shall not die.

PSALM RESPONSE
Psalm 25:6a

Remember your mercies, O Lord.

In the shorter form of the reading, the passage in brackets is omitted.

SECOND READING
Philippians 2:1–11 or 2:1–5

Brothers and sisters: If there is any encouragement in Christ, any solace in love, any participation in the Spirit, any compassion and mercy, complete my joy by being of the same mind, with the same love, united in heart, thinking one thing. Do nothing out of selfishness or out of vainglory; rather, humbly regard others as more important than yourselves, each looking out not for his own interests, but also for those of others.

Have in you the same attitude
  that is also in Christ Jesus,
    [Who, though he was in the form of God,
    did not regard equality with God
    something to be grasped.
  Rather, he emptied himself,
    taking the form of a slave,
    coming in human likeness;
    and found human in appearance,
    he humbled himself,
    becoming obedient to the point of death,
    even death on a cross.

Because of this, God greatly exalted him
and bestowed on him the name
which is above every name,
that at the name of Jesus
every knee should bend,
of those in heaven and on earth and under the earth,
and every tongue confess that
Jesus Christ is Lord,
to the glory of God the Father.]

GOSPEL
Matthew
21:28–32

Jesus said to the chief priests and elders of the people: "What is your opinion? A man had two sons. He came to the first and said, 'Son, go out and work in the vineyard today.' He said in reply, 'I will not,' but afterwards changed his mind and went. The man came to the other son and gave the same order. He said in reply, 'Yes, sir,' but did not go. Which of the two did his father's will?" They answered, "The first." Jesus said to them, "Amen, I say to you, tax collectors and prostitutes are entering the kingdom of God before you. When John came to you in the way of righteousness, you did not believe him; but tax collectors and prostitutes did. Yet even when you saw that, you did not later change your minds and believe him."

❖ *Understanding the Word*

The issue in the first reading is the matter of retribution, the manner in which God rewards righteous living and punishes wicked behavior. Two situations are described. In the first one, a righteous person sins; in the second, a sinner repents. God metes out punishment in the first situation and grants a reward in the second. Actually, having chosen another path, the once righteous person now suffers the consequences of that choice. In like manner, the sinner who turns away from wickedness and chooses the path of righteousness and justice will live united with God, the source of life. Is this injustice on God's part?

The reading from Philippians is one of Christianity's most exalted hymns of praise of Christ. Paul offered this magnificent vision of Christ's self-emptying to challenge the Philippians' own attitudes of mind and heart. Not only did Christ relinquish his Godlike state, he emptied himself of it. Without losing his Godlike being, he took on the likeness of human beings, not merely resembling a human being, but actually becoming one. As a result, his exaltation is as glorious as his humiliation was debasing. Every knee shall do him homage and every tongue shall proclaim his sovereignty. The entire created universe is brought under his lordship.

The sons in the Gospel story represent two ways of responding to a father's command. The first son refuses to obey, a serious breach of protocol in a patriarchal kinship structure. However, the headstrong son repents and eventually does what his father charged him to do. The second son does not show such disrespect to his father by refusing to go as he was directed, but neither does he obey him. Jesus turns to his adversaries and asks them for an interpretation of the law: Which one did the father's will? Without knowing it, they condemned themselves with their answer, for they prided themselves on their righteousness and piety, yet they refused to accept him.

In *The Secret Life of Bees*, August, an older black woman, is talking about "the problem with people" to Lily, a younger white woman who has run away from an abusive father. Lily has said that people don't really know what matters. But August says the deeper problem is that people do know what matters, but don't *choose* it.

God tells Ezekiel that virtue's proof is in choosing to do the right thing. What you choose to do matters. So be careful not to go off the right path at the end of your days. On the other hand, you might be off the right path for years, but end up hopping back on at the very end, and you will have life. It doesn't sound very fair; nevertheless, it's where you are when the end comes that counts. And you don't know when the end will come.

Jesus confronts the religious leaders with a parable. A father asks his two sons to do some work in the vineyard. One talks a good game but never makes it into the field; the other refuses outright, but then goes and does what his father asked. In telling this parable, Jesus compares these leaders unfavorably to the tax collectors and prostitutes. The elders must have been shocked.

"Have in you that same attitude that is also in Christ Jesus," writes Paul to his beloved Philippians. The attitude he urged on them was giving oneself for the sake of others—even unto death. In this way, we not only speak but also *do* "Yes." Choose to live Christ.

❖ Consider/Discuss

- Can you think of a time when you said yes to someone's request but did not carry it out?
- Do you think of Jesus as one who emptied himself, even of life, trusting his Father to fill him?
- How is God calling you to empty yourself at this time, doing "nothing out of selfishness, but regarding others as more important than yourselves"?

❖ Responding to the Word

In the Our Father we pray that God will not lead us into temptation but deliver us from evil. We pray that we will be obedient to the Father's will to the point of death so that we will be raised into eternal life and join in the song of exaltation, confessing Jesus Christ as Lord.

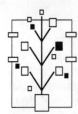

October 2, 2011

TWENTY-SEVENTH SUNDAY IN ORDINARY TIME

Today's Focus: Bearing Fruit: Not Just for Vineyards

Imagine a vineyard. Isaiah sings of one bearing only wild, unusable grapes, despite the efforts of its owner. Jesus tells the story of a vineyard entrusted to tenants who not only refuse to honor the owner's claim, but try to seize it for themselves. God's desire is for a fruitful vineyard, that is, a people lovingly tended by trustworthy leaders.

FIRST READING
Isaiah 5:1–7

Let me now sing of my friend,
    my friend's song concerning his vineyard.
My friend had a vineyard
    on a fertile hillside;
he spaded it, cleared it of stones,
    and planted the choicest vines;
within it he built a watchtower,
    and hewed out a wine press.
Then he looked for the crop of grapes,
    but what it yielded was wild grapes.

Now, inhabitants of Jerusalem and people of Judah,
    judge between me and my vineyard:
What more was there to do for my vineyard
    that I had not done?
Why, when I looked for the crop of grapes,
    did it bring forth wild grapes?
Now, I will let you know
    what I mean to do with my vineyard:
take away its hedge, give it to grazing,
    break through its wall, let it be trampled!
Yes, I will make it a ruin:
    it shall not be pruned or hoed,
    but overgrown with thorns and briers;
I will command the clouds
    not to send rain upon it.
The vineyard of the LORD of hosts is the house of Israel,
    and the people of Judah are his cherished plant;
he looked for judgment, but see, bloodshed!
    for justice, but hark, the outcry!

PSALM RESPONSE
Isaiah 5:7a

The vineyard of the Lord is the house of Israel.

SECOND
READING
*Philippians
4:6–9*
Brothers and sisters: Have no anxiety at all, but in everything, by prayer and petition, with thanksgiving, make your requests known to God. Then the peace of God that surpasses all understanding will guard your hearts and minds in Christ Jesus.

Finally, brothers and sisters, whatever is true, whatever is honorable, whatever is just, whatever is pure, whatever is lovely, whatever is gracious, if there is any excellence and if there is anything worthy of praise, think about these things. Keep on doing what you have learned and received and heard and seen in me. Then the God of peace will be with you.

GOSPEL
*Matthew
21:33–43*
Jesus said to the chief priests and the elders of the people: "Hear another parable. There was a landowner who planted a vineyard, put a hedge around it, dug a wine press in it, and built a tower. Then he leased it to tenants and went on a journey. When vintage time drew near, he sent his servants to the tenants to obtain his produce. But the tenants seized the servants and one they beat, another they killed, and a third they stoned. Again he sent other servants, more numerous than the first ones, but they treated them in the same way. Finally, he sent his son to them, thinking, 'They will respect my son.' But when the tenants saw the son, they said to one another, 'This is the heir. Come, let us kill him and acquire his inheritance.' They seized him, threw him out of the vineyard, and killed him. What will the owner of the vineyard do to those tenants when he comes?" They answered him, "He will put those wretched men to a wretched death and lease his vineyard to other tenants who will give him the produce at the proper times." Jesus said to them, "Did you never read in the Scriptures:
*The stone that the builders rejected
    has become the cornerstone;
by the Lord has this been done,
    and it is wonderful in our eyes?*
Therefore, I say to you, the kingdom of God will be taken away from you and given to a people that will produce its fruit."

❖ Understanding the Word

The first reading tells a story about a vineyard. The vine dresser diligently performed each step of the process to produce grapes. However, not only was there no abundant harvest, but wild, useless grapes sprang forth. This unnatural yield was not due to poor cultivation. Rather, the vineyard itself had failed. It becomes clear that the prophet is really talking about the Israelites. Judgment is now passed on the vineyard (the people). God invested so much in the future of this people, and they scorned the attention of the vineyard owner. What began as a poem about friendship and devotion ends as a message of doom.

The tenderness with which Paul regards the Philippians is evident here. They are anxious and Paul offers them encouragement and direction. Rather than be anxious, they are admonished to turn to God in prayer. Paul is not advising some kind of magical exercise that will right every wrong, but an openness to God that itself can help people bear trying circumstances. They will then know the peace that only God can give, the peace that surpasses all understanding. He then exhorts them to live lives patterned after Christ. Christian thinking and behavior will open the believer to the kind of peace that only God can give.

Jesus too tells a story about a vineyard. When he is finished, he turns to the leaders and asks them to provide a legal ruling on the situation. They must have known that the parable was highlighting their own resistance to God's directives, and they also would have known that whatever judgment they might suggest would fall on their heads as well. The sentence they passed was quite harsh, but it was actually no harsher than the conduct of the tenants. Just as the vineyard is taken from the wicked tenants and given to others, so the kingdom of God will be taken from the leaders and given to people who will produce fruits.

❖ Reflecting on the Word

God's relationship with people is at the heart of both the first reading and the Gospel, but there is a difference. In Isaiah, destruction comes to the vineyard; in the Gospel, it comes to those entrusted with the care of the vineyard.

Isaiah's song highlights the people's failure—the house of Israel and the people of Judah—to bear fruit, to provide the Lord who has lovingly tended this vineyard with anything more than wild grapes, that is, bloodshed and violence against each other. Because of this, the owner will turn his back on them, no longer giving care but letting it be trampled underfoot, no longer pruning or hoeing, but allowing thorns and briers to take over. This song is demanding conversion.

In Jesus' parable, the focus is on those entrusted with the care of the vineyard. Jesus addresses the chief priests and the elders in Jerusalem, not only criticizing their failure to care for the people adequately, but also their rejection of those God sent to call them to conversion. The parable calls all religious leaders to remember that authority is for service.

Bearing fruit in our lives, being true and honorable, just and pure, lovely and gracious is the fruit God desires from all, as Paul reminds the Philippians. God's people, but especially their leaders, have a responsibility to bear fruit. No one is let off the hook. God expects a return for love so lavishly given.

✤ *Consider/Discuss*

- Have you ever tended a plant or grown a garden? What did this experience teach you?
- What fruitfulness God is asking of you?
- Is there anything that prevents you from making a return to God for all that has been given to you?

✤ *Responding to the Word*

St. Paul calls us to set aside anxiety and to make known to God any requests we have for more fruitful lives. In prayer we will find that "the peace of God that surpasses all understanding will guard our hearts and minds in Christ Jesus."

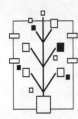

October 9, 2011

TWENTY-EIGHTH SUNDAY IN ORDINARY TIME

Today's Focus: Come to the Table Worthily

A banquet as a symbol of God's gracious invitation to draw near is found in both the Old and New Testaments. While Isaiah's banquet points to the end time, the banquet in Jesus' parable points to the past and present, reminding us of our freedom to accept the invitation, reject it, or respond in an unworthy way.

FIRST READING
Isaiah 25:6–10a

On this mountain the LORD of hosts
    will provide for all peoples
a feast of rich food and choice wines,
    juicy, rich food and pure, choice wines.
On this mountain he will destroy
    the veil that veils all peoples,
the web that is woven over all nations;
    he will destroy death forever.
The Lord GOD will wipe away
    the tears from every face;
the reproach of his people he will remove
    from the whole earth; for the LORD has spoken.
    On that day it will be said:
"Behold our God, to whom we looked to save us!
    This is the LORD for whom we looked;
    let us rejoice and be glad that he has saved us!"
For the hand of the LORD will rest on this mountain.

PSALM RESPONSE
Psalm 23:6cd

I shall live in the house of the Lord all the days of my life.

SECOND READING
Philippians 4:12–14, 19–20

Brothers and sisters: I know how to live in humble circumstances; I know also how to live with abundance. In every circumstance and in all things I have learned the secret of being well fed and of going hungry, of living in abundance and of being in need. I can do all things in him who strengthens me. Still, it was kind of you to share in my distress.

My God will fully supply whatever you need, in accord with his glorious riches in Christ Jesus. To our God and Father, glory forever and ever. Amen.

180

GOSPEL
Matthew
22:1–14 or
22:1–10
Jesus again in reply spoke to the chief priests and elders of the people in parables, saying, "The kingdom of heaven may be likened to a king who gave a wedding feast for his son. He dispatched his servants to summon the invited guests to the feast, but they refused to come. A second time he sent other servants, saying, 'Tell those invited: "Behold, I have prepared my banquet, my calves and fattened cattle are killed, and everything is ready; come to the feast." ' Some ignored the invitation and went away, one to his farm, another to his business. The rest laid hold of his servants, mistreated them, and killed them. The king was enraged and sent his troops, destroyed those murderers, and burned their city. Then he said to his servants, 'The feast is ready, but those who were invited were not worthy to come. Go out, therefore, into the main roads and invite to the feast whomever you find.' The servants went out into the streets and gathered all they found, bad and good alike, and the hall was filled with guests. [But when the king came in to meet the guests, he saw a man there not dressed in a wedding garment. The king said to him, 'My friend, how is it that you came in here without a wedding garment?' But he was reduced to silence. Then the king said to his attendants, 'Bind his hands and feet, and cast him into the darkness outside, where there will be wailing and grinding of teeth.' Many are invited, but few are chosen."]

❖ Understanding the Word

Isaiah depicts a scene of permanent victory, abundant feasting, and life without end. He sees a high mountain on which a sumptuous feast, probably the banquet of the end of time, is prepared for all people. It is also on this mountain that God destroys death. Once death is destroyed there will be no cause for tears. Instead, there will be rejoicing. On that day of fulfillment, the people will acclaim the God to whom they looked for salvation. The hand of God, the symbol of God's power, will rest on this holy mountain, bringing to fulfillment all of God's promises and blessings.

Paul is not speaking here of the ordinary trials and sufferings that invade every life. He is talking about the tribulations that will engulf all people at the onslaught of the end time, the suffering known as the "birth pangs of the Messiah." For Paul, the burdens of his ministry form the avenue by which he enters this time of tribulation. He does not make light of the help that the Philippians must have offered him. Acting this way, they actually participated in his ministerial endeavors, and he is grateful. For this reason, they too are promised a share in the glory of the new age.

Once again Jesus is in confrontation with the leaders of the people. The apocalyptic character of the parable he tells is unmistakable. The metaphor of a banquet to describe the delights of the age of fulfillment can be traced as far back as the ancient prophets (see Isaiah 25:6). An interim exists between the initial invitation to the wedding banquet and the announcement that the banquet is ready. This interim resembles the period of time between the invitation to participate in the age of fulfillment and one's entrance into that age. The point of the parable is clear: enjoyment of the time of fulfillment is open to all, but guaranteed to none.

A newspaper columnist expressed his chagrin at friends not responding to his "e-vites" (e-mail invitations), even after repeated requests. He speculated that some might have held off responding in case "something better" came along.

Jesus tells a tale of invited guests refusing to come to a wedding feast for a king's son. This parable is aimed once again at the religious leaders, confronting them with their refusal to accept him as one sent by God. Matthew's violent version of the parable differs from Luke's peaceful one (14:16–24), since it reflects the destruction of Jerusalem that happened decades later. But it reminded both communities that the invitation to the kingdom of God could be refused.

Matthew also includes the expulsion of a man who comes in without a wedding garment. This seems seem a little strange since people had been called in off the streets. It serves as a reminder that showing up is not enough. The grace of being invited to the Lord's table, then as now, does not excuse us from wearing the appropriate garment—that is, "putting on" Christ.

Every Eucharist tells us that we have a place at the table, and this table prepares us for another table at the end of time, when all peoples will gather and the Lord will move among us, wiping every tear away, and death shall be no more. We are a people of many tables—of the word, the Eucharist, the world, and the kingdom of God.

✦ *Consider/Discuss*

- Do you see yourself as one who has been invited to have a place at many tables?
- What does "putting on" Christ mean to you?
- How do you think about the end time when all will gather?

✦ *Responding to the Word*

We pray to respond wholeheartedly to God's invitation to that final gathering place where rich food and choice wines will be served and our shepherd God, who even now spreads a table before us, will move among us. We can ask the Spirit to help us wear Christ well.

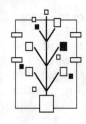

October 16, 2011

TWENTY-NINTH SUNDAY
IN ORDINARY TIME

Today's Focus: God's Currency

While many kings of antiquity insisted on being called divine, Israel's God was not fussy about who would be anointed for divine works. They were all God's currency, to be spent at God's will. Jesus' words remind us that we too are God's currency, set apart to carry God's image and presence into the world.

FIRST READING
Isaiah 45:1, 4–6

Thus says the LORD to his anointed, Cyrus,
    whose right hand I grasp,
subduing nations before him,
    and making kings run in his service,
opening doors before him
    and leaving the gates unbarred:
For the sake of Jacob, my servant,
    of Israel, my chosen one,
I have called you by your name,
    giving you a title, though you knew me not.
I am the LORD and there is no other,
    there is no God besides me.
It is I who arm you, though you know me not,
    so that toward the rising and the setting of the sun
    people may know that there is none besides me.
I am the LORD, there is no other.

PSALM RESPONSE
Psalm 96:7b

Give the Lord glory and honor.

SECOND READING
1 Thessalonians 1:1–5b

Paul, Silvanus, and Timothy to the church of the Thessalonians in God the Father and the Lord Jesus Christ: grace to you and peace. We give thanks to God always for all of you, remembering you in our prayers, unceasingly calling to mind your work of faith and labor of love and endurance in hope of our Lord Jesus Christ, before our God and Father, knowing, brothers and sisters loved by God, how you were chosen. For our gospel did not come to you in word alone, but also in power and in the Holy Spirit and with much conviction.

The Pharisees went off and plotted how they might entrap Jesus in speech. They sent their disciples to him, with the Herodians, saying, "Teacher, we know that you are a truthful man and that you teach the way of God in accordance with the truth. And you are not concerned with anyone's opinion, for you do not regard a person's status. Tell us, then, what is your opinion: Is it lawful to pay the census tax to Caesar or not?" Knowing their malice, Jesus said, "Why are you testing me, you hypocrites? Show me the coin that pays the census tax." Then they handed him the Roman coin. He said to them, "Whose image is this and whose inscription?" They replied, "Caesar's." At that he said to them, "Then repay to Caesar what belongs to Caesar and to God what belongs to God."

❖ Understanding the Word

Cyrus was the Persian ruler who permitted the Israelites to return from captivity in Babylon. He is called God's anointed, a title ascribed to Israelite kings, and particularly Davidic kings. Cyrus the foreigner is the agent of the release of the Israelites, but their release is for the sake of the enlightenment of the foreign nations. It is not by accident that Cyrus plays this role. God has specially chosen him. This call occurred even though Cyrus did not know the God of Israel. God works through people without their even knowing that it is really God who is directing the events of history.

Paul writes in his own name and in the names of two missionary companions, Silvanus and Timothy. Apparently they were the three men who founded the church in Thessalonica and now they are writing back to their own converts. Paul speaks for all three men when he tells the Thessalonians how grateful the missionaries are for their fidelity to the gospel that was preached to them. The converts are remarkable for their show of faith, love, and hope. Theirs is an active faith, one that produces fruits. Probably the most significant expression of faith is the love that they show to others.

The Pharisees hoped to set a trap to ensnare Jesus. They ask him to interpret a point of law: Should the Jews pay taxes to Rome? If Jesus answers no, he can be accused of political insubordination of the type that might incite others to respond in kind. If he says yes, he will appear to have relinquished Israel's boast of being a people bound only to God. He says neither yes nor no, but directs them to "give back" or "repay" what is owed to both Caesar and God. Jesus' response suggests that one can indeed be loyal to both a religious tradition and a secular power. It may be very difficult at times, especially when their claims seem to conflict, but it is possible.

❖ Reflecting on the Word

In a country that has a strong commitment to separation of church and state, it is noteworthy that our money, both bills and coins, is inscribed with the words "In God We Trust." The history of this motto and its relation to our currency goes back to the Civil War. Changing it has never gotten much support. It serves as a helpful reminder about where our true security lies.

In the Gospel, the Pharisees, along with some supporters of the Roman regime called Herodians, get into the act of trying to trap Jesus into taking a stand that would get him in trouble with either the Roman authorities or his own people. But Jesus, as much the fox as Herod was reputed to be, slips out of their net by noting that there can be different loyalties without a loss of priorities.

Jesus calls on them to produce the idolatrous coin that no devout Jew should carry, since it declared Caesar to be a god. Then he advises them to return to the emperor the coin that bears his image but to return to God what bears God's image, that is, themselves, made in the image of God.

A new order is revealed when we give God's image back to God by our words and deeds, showing God's image to others. When this happens, the motto "In God We Trust" becomes not merely stamped on paper or branded on copper, but encountered in living flesh and blood.

❖ Consider/Discuss

- Do you ever reflect on the words stamped on the money in your pocket?
- When have you experienced the tension between "repay[ing] to Caesar what belongs to Caesar and to God what belongs to God"?

❖ Responding to the Word

We pray to recognize what it means to be a good citizen, giving to our country what is needed for the support of the common good. And we pray to discern wisely when loyalty to Christ and the building up of the kingdom of God may call for a response that challenges what civil authorities propose.

October 23, 2011

THIRTIETH SUNDAY IN ORDINARY TIME

Today's Focus: Living in God

God's word calls us to love God with all our heart, mind, and soul—that is, with our total person—and to love one another. God is the source of all love, the love we receive and the love we give. When we love, we live in and are the image of the invisible God.

FIRST READING
Exodus 22:20–26

Thus says the LORD: "You shall not molest or oppress an alien, for you were once aliens yourselves in the land of Egypt. You shall not wrong any widow or orphan. If ever you wrong them and they cry out to me, I will surely hear their cry. My wrath will flare up, and I will kill you with the sword; then your own wives will be widows, and your children orphans.

"If you lend money to one of your poor neighbors among my people, you shall not act like an extortioner toward him by demanding interest from him. If you take your neighbor's cloak as a pledge, you shall return it to him before sunset; for this cloak of his is the only covering he has for his body. What else has he to sleep in? If he cries out to me, I will hear him; for I am compassionate."

PSALM RESPONSE
Psalm 18:2

I love you, Lord, my strength.

SECOND READING
1 Thessalonians 1:5c–10

Brothers and sisters: You know what sort of people we were among you for your sake. And you became imitators of us and of the Lord, receiving the word in great affliction, with joy from the Holy Spirit, so that you became a model for all the believers in Macedonia and in Achaia. For from you the word of the Lord has sounded forth not only in Macedonia and in Achaia, but in every place your faith in God has gone forth, so that we have no need to say anything. For they themselves openly declare about us what sort of reception we had among you, and how you turned to God from idols to serve the living and true God and to await his Son from heaven, whom he raised from the dead, Jesus, who delivers us from the coming wrath.

When the Pharisees heard that Jesus had silenced the Sadducees, they gathered together, and one of them, a scholar of the law, tested him by asking, "Teacher, which commandment in the law is the greatest?" He said to him, "You shall love the Lord, your God, with all your heart, with all your soul, and with all your mind. This is the greatest and the first commandment. The second is like it: You shall love your neighbor as yourself. The whole law and the prophets depend on these two commandments."

❖ Understanding the Word

Israel's law was quite humane. It exhorted the Israelites to be especially attentive to those within their community who were the most vulnerable, defenseless, and disadvantaged. It singled out the alien, the widow, and the orphan, because in a patriarchal society these groups had very little legal recourse. If they were further oppressed and they cried out to God, God would hear their cry just as God had heard the cry of the Israelites when they were in bondage in Egypt. The law is also concerned with those burdened with financial hardship. Every attempt must be made to ensure that they undergo no added humiliation or distress.

Paul insists that, as important as the transmission of the gospel might be, it is really handed down by the example of lifestyle. He challenges the Christians to follow his example and that of Jesus. He has a particular circumstance in mind when he says this. The Thessalonians were converted in the midst of affliction, and it is within such circumstances that they give witness to others. Those who are faithful amidst the tribulations of this life will be spared the final wrath of God. Paul is not painting a picture of doom; he is giving meaning to the hardships that the Christians are presently enduring.

A Pharisee, a lawyer or expert in the law, asks Jesus to identify which of the six hundred thirteen commandments is the most important, an issue that held considerable interest at the time. Jesus' answer is faithful to his own Jewish faith. He endorses the summons that constitutes the *Shema*, the most significant prayer of the Israelite religion (see Deuteronomy 6:5). He insists that the love of God must occupy one's entire being and not be simply a superficial allegiance. He then adds a second commandment, which is said to be like the first in importance. From this proclamation flows the responsibility to love God with one's entire being and to love one's neighbor as oneself.

In an article on "successful aging" (*New Theology Review*, November, 2010), Dr. Lawrence M. Lenoir proposes that the art of giving and receiving love is at the heart of growing old gracefully. Research shows that being in a loving relationship quiets the demons of depression and despair. So, if you want to be healthy, be loving. Jesus would agree.

The rabbis of Jesus' day argued about which was the greatest commandment of the six hundred thirteen in the Torah. When the Pharisees asked Jesus, he answered that what God wanted most from the chosen people who had been liberated from slavery and called to live in a covenantal relationship was a return of the love God showed to them. This love has two faces: loving God totally and loving one another as one loves oneself.

Loving is a contagious activity. If you are loved, you tend to be loving. Paul is sounding this note when he writes to the Thessalonians about how they became imitators of him and his fellow evangelizers Timothy and Silvanus, and of the Lord himself, receiving the word and living in faith, joy, and love for each other, because they believed in God's love for them, revealed in Christ.

Our love must flow outward in compassionate generosity. The Lord called on Israel to show its love by not oppressing aliens, not wronging weak orphans and defenseless widows, and not extorting the poor by demanding interest on loans. No less is asked of those who have received the Holy Spirit and live in community with the Father, Son, and Holy Spirit. That's us. Love one another.

❖ Consider/Discuss

- What do you think God wants most from you?
- Does anything prevent you from responding to God's love with all your heart, soul, and mind?
- Who is the neighbor who most needs your love at this time?

❖ Responding to the Word

It is difficult to love, especially when we have been hurt by others. Ask the Holy Spirit to bring you the "fire of God's love." Call on the Spirit to deepen your awareness of God's love for you, shown by giving us life and the gifts of faith, hope, and love.

October 30, 2011

THIRTY-FIRST SUNDAY IN ORDINARY TIME

Today's Focus: Be Good News

Both the prophet Malachi and Jesus are in agreement: good leadership means living the covenant. St. Paul is a model of being good news as well as preaching good news, of allowing the word of God to work in him. Authority bears fruit in selfless service and lifting burdens.

FIRST READING
Malachi 1:14b — 2:2b, 8–10

A great King am I, says the LORD of hosts,
    and my name will be feared among the nations.
And now, O priests, this commandment is for you:
    If you do not listen,
if you do not lay it to heart,
    to give glory to my name, says the LORD of hosts,
I will send a curse upon you
    and of your blessing I will make a curse.
You have turned aside from the way,
    and have caused many to falter by your instruction;
you have made void the covenant of Levi,
    says the LORD of hosts.
I, therefore, have made you contemptible
    and base before all the people,
since you do not keep my ways,
    but show partiality in your decisions.
Have we not all the one father?
    Has not the one God created us?
Why then do we break faith with one another,
    violating the covenant of our fathers?

PSALM RESPONSE
Psalm 131

In you, Lord, I have found my peace.

SECOND READING
1 Thessalonians 2:7b-9, 13

Brothers and sisters: We were gentle among you, as a nursing mother cares for her children. With such affection for you, we were determined to share with you not only the gospel of God, but our very selves as well, so dearly beloved had you become to us. You recall, brothers and sisters, our toil and drudgery. Working night and day in order not to burden any of you, we proclaimed to you the gospel of God.

And for this reason we too give thanks to God unceasingly, that, in receiving the word of God from hearing us, you received not a human word but, as it truly is, the word of God, which is now at work in you who believe.

GOSPEL
Matthew 23:1–12
Jesus spoke to the crowds and to his disciples, saying, "The scribes and the Pharisees have taken their seat on the chair of Moses. Therefore, do and observe all things whatsoever they tell you, but do not follow their example. For they preach but they do not practice. They tie up heavy burdens hard to carry and lay them on people's shoulders, but they will not lift a finger to move them. All their works are performed to be seen. They widen their phylacteries and lengthen their tassels. They love places of honor at banquets, seats of honor in synagogues, greetings in marketplaces, and the salutation 'Rabbi.' As for you, do not be called 'Rabbi.' You have but one teacher, and you are all brothers. Call no one on earth your father; you have but one Father in heaven. Do not be called 'Master'; you have but one master, the Christ. The greatest among you must be your servant. Whoever exalts himself will be humbled; but whoever humbles himself will be exalted."

❖ Understanding the Word

Malachi denounces the priests of Israel who have not only defiled their office but have also led the people astray with their faulty teaching. The honor given God's name by the nations is in sharp contrast with the dishonor accorded it by the priests. The command given the priests includes a threat of the punishment that will be exacted if is not followed. The reading does not tell us whether or not the priests took this condemnation to heart. For us it serves as a reminder that privileged positions within the community bring with them serious responsibilities. Failure to fulfill these responsibilities will meet with drastic consequences.

The metaphor of the nursing mother characterizes the deep affection Paul has for his converts. This image also effectively exemplifies apostolic self-giving. Both the mother and the missionary spend themselves with no thought of receiving anything in return other than the satisfaction of having given themselves out of love. Paul and his companions were within their rights to expect hospitality from their converts. However, they chose to forgo this prerogative. Instead, they proclaimed the gospel as they saw fit, asking for nothing in return. The recompense they receive for their ministry is the religious maturity of their converts, and for this they are grateful to God.

Jesus issues a scathing denunciation of the scribes and Pharisees. While he recognizes the authenticity of their office, he criticizes them for the obvious disparity between what they teach and how they live. He criticizes their method of interpreting the law and their love of praise. In their zeal to honor the law, they placed heavy burdens on the people, and they did nothing to alleviate their weight. Furthermore, they used outward displays of devotion to garner deferential treatment. Jesus insists that such pomposity has no place among his followers. He warns that those who exalt themselves now will experience ultimate humiliation; those who humble themselves now will enjoy ultimate exaltation.

A friend told me she had been the last in her family to stop going to Mass on Sundays. Her siblings had long since given it up. The reasons had a great deal to do with the quality of church leadership they experienced. Too much outward show of authority, too little indication of inner sanctity. Dispensing official teaching is not enough; living humbly and as a servant is the heart of ministry.

The harsh words of the prophet Malachi seem more relevant than ever in our day. When we priests fail to walk in the way of Christ, fail to give glory to God's name by what we do, we become unworthy of our calling to serve God's people. Of course, this kind of behavior is not limited to clergy. Jesus is speaking to the crowds and disciples about the Pharisees, the lay leaders who saw themselves as "separate" from the rest because of their outward signs of piety. He also calls them to authentic lives.

"The greatest among you must be your servant," Jesus says, a message he repeats again and again in the Gospels. His followers are as resistant to it now as they were then. But the faithful follower is not about titles, or ecclesiastical dress-up, or posturing in self-importance. Discipleship in the kingdom that Jesus came preaching is about being brothers and sisters who gather around Jesus Christ, the one Master, who humbled himself and waited for God to exalt him. May the same goal be ours.

✦ *Consider/Discuss*

- What is your experience of those called to shepherd God's people?
- Do you pray for your priests, your bishops, the Holy Father?
- Is humility a practical virtue in our world today?

✦ *Responding to the Word*

We pray for all who hold positions of leadership and authority in the Church, that they not only speak but embody the gospel in their lives. We can ask God to raise up more men and women who will instruct by example and words and who will walk humbly in the way of the Lord.

November 1, 2011

ALL SAINTS

Today's Focus: The Faces of Holiness

We remember all the holy women and men of every time and place and we thank God for them. God is the source of all holiness and has called to us, "Be holy as I am holy." We have heard this call to holiness and participate in it through Jesus, our Lord and Savior.

FIRST READING
Revelation 7:2–4, 9–14

I, John, saw another angel come up from the East, holding the seal of the living God. He cried out in a loud voice to the four angels who were given power to damage the land and the sea, "Do not damage the land or the sea or the trees until we put the seal on the foreheads of the servants of our God." I heard the number of those who had been marked with the seal, one hundred and forty-four thousand marked from every tribe of the Israelites.

After this I had a vision of a great multitude, which no one could count, from every nation, race, people, and tongue. They stood before the throne and before the Lamb, wearing white robes and holding palm branches in their hands. They cried out in a loud voice:
"Salvation comes from our God, who is seated on the throne,
and from the Lamb."
All the angels stood around the throne and around the elders and the four living creatures. They prostrated themselves before the throne, worshiped God, and exclaimed:
"Amen. Blessing and glory, wisdom and thanksgiving,
honor, power, and might
be to our God forever and ever. Amen."
Then one of the elders spoke up and said to me, "Who are these wearing white robes, and where did they come from?" I said to him, "My lord, you are the one who knows." He said to me,"These are the ones who have survived the time of great distress; they have washed their robes and made them white in the blood of the Lamb."

PSALM RESPONSE
Psalm 24:6

Lord, this is the people that longs to see your face.

SECOND READING
1 John 3:1–3

Beloved: See what love the Father has bestowed on us that we may be called the children of God. Yet so we are. The reason the world does not know us is that it did not know him. Beloved, we are God's children now; what we shall be has not yet been revealed. We do know that when it is revealed we shall be like him, for we shall see him as he is. Everyone who has this hope based on him makes himself pure, as he is pure.

GOSPEL
Matthew
5:1–12a

When Jesus saw the crowds, he went up the mountain, and after he had sat down, his disciples came to him. He began to teach them, saying:

"Blessed are the poor in spirit,
for theirs is the kingdom of heaven.
Blessed are they who mourn,
for they will be comforted.
Blessed are the meek,
for they will inherit the land.
Blessed are they who hunger and thirst for righteousness,
for they will be satisfied.
Blessed are the merciful,
for they will be shown mercy.
Blessed are the clean of heart,
for they will see God.
Blessed are the peacemakers,
for they will be called children of God.
Blessed are they who are persecuted for the sake
of righteousness,
for theirs is the kingdom of heaven.

"Blessed are you when they insult you and persecute you and utter every kind of evil against you falsely because of me. Rejoice and be glad, for your reward will be great in heaven."

❖ Understanding the Word

In John's vision, the sign-bearing angel comes from the east, the place of the rising of the sun and the direction from which salvation is expected. The destroying angels are told to cease their destructive actions so that the vast assembly can be sealed with the seal of God and, presumably, preserved from the suffering that these angels bring to the earth. The second scene takes place in the divine throne room in heaven, where a multitude from every nation, race, people, and tongue is gathered. This multitude consists of those who survived the distress of the end of time because they were purified through the blood of the sacrificial Lamb.

It is a generative love that the Letter of John describes; it is transforming; it makes all believers children of God. Everything that happens in the lives of believers is a consequence of their having been recreated as God's children. As children of God, they are new realities and, therefore, they are not accepted by the world, the old reality. Having been made children of God, they are promised an even fuller identification with God. They are also promised the ultimate vision of God, a vision that is denied believers "now" but is promised for "later."

The instruction known as the Sermon on the Mount was meant for Jesus' close followers, not for the broader crowds. All the teachings of Jesus are in some way directed toward the establishment of the reign of God. However, the values that he advocates in the Beatitudes are frequently the opposite of those promoted by society at large. Perhaps the way to interpret them is to look first at the blessings promised. We may then see that the values are indeed at odds with what society says will guarantee the blessings that we seek. It is clear that every Beatitude invites us to turn the standards of our world and our way of life upside down and inside out.

✣ Reflecting on the Word

In an interview, the Dalai Lama talked about the importance of recognizing one quality that all the world religions share as a common value—the virtue of compassion. This virtue is held up for imitation by all the major religious traditions: Buddhism, Christianity, Hinduism, Islam, and Judaism. It helps us to view each other with respect and appreciation.

Today's feast invites us to think about all the holy men and women who have opened their lives to God's grace and have embodied compassion in the world over the centuries. From the early days of the church the names of the martyrs were mentioned during Eucharist. Today we can remember all the holy ones who have touched our lives—men and women, family and friends, canonized and uncanonized saints over the centuries.

The last book of the Bible, Revelation, written at a time of persecution, offers us a symbolic vision of the end time when a multitude from every nation, race, people, and tongue will be gathered together. These are the ones who have been sealed as true servants of God and will sing an eternal song of salvation. We hope to be part of that jubilant chorus.

In the meantime, we are surrounded by this great cloud of witnesses who urge us on to complete our task of living as beloved children of God, to live out the plan of the kingdom Jesus preached in the Beatitudes, and to be a presence in the world of God's Spirit.

✣ Consider/Discuss

- Who are some of the saints who have touched your life over the years?
- Are there any "living saints" in your life now?
- Which of the Beatitudes best speaks to you as a way to holiness at this time?

✣ Responding to the Word

We may give thanks to God for the call to holiness we have heard in our own hearts and include the names of those who have shown us what it means to be holy. Ask the saints to continue to intercede for us so that we will be faithful in our efforts to bring about the kingdom of heaven.

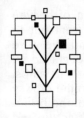

November 6, 2011

THIRTY-SECOND SUNDAY IN ORDINARY TIME

Today's Focus: Getting Prepped

Today's scriptures offer an incentive to be prepared for the return of the Lord, whenever that may occur. Being watchful is part of this preparation, because we do not know when or even how the Lord will come. If we wait watchfully, we wait worthily.

FIRST READING
Wisdom 6:12–16

Resplendent and unfading is wisdom,
    and she is readily perceived by those who love her,
    and found by those who seek her.
She hastens to make herself known in anticipation of their desire;
    whoever watches for her at dawn shall not be disappointed,
    for he shall find her sitting by his gate.
For taking thought of wisdom is the perfection of prudence,
    and whoever for her sake keeps vigil
    shall quickly be free from care;
because she makes her own rounds, seeking those worthy of her,
    and graciously appears to them in the ways,
    and meets them with all solicitude.

PSALM RESPONSE
Psalm 63:2b

My soul is thirsting for you, O Lord, my God.

In the shorter form of the reading, the passage in brackets is omitted.

SECOND READING
1 Thessalonians 4:13–18 or 4:13–14

We do not want you to be unaware, brothers and sisters, about those who have fallen asleep, so that you may not grieve like the rest, who have no hope. For if we believe that Jesus died and rose, so too will God, through Jesus, bring with him those who have fallen asleep. [Indeed, we tell you this, on the word of the Lord, that we who are alive, who are left until the coming of the Lord, will surely not precede those who have fallen asleep. For the Lord himself, with a word of command, with the voice of an archangel and with the trumpet of God, will come down from heaven, and the dead in Christ will rise first. Then we who are alive, who are left, will be caught up together with them in the clouds to meet the Lord in the air. Thus we shall always be with the Lord. Therefore, console one another with these words.]

195

Jesus told his disciples this parable: "The kingdom of heaven will be like ten virgins who took their lamps and went out to meet the bridegroom. Five of them were foolish and five were wise. The foolish ones, when taking their lamps, brought no oil with them, but the wise brought flasks of oil with their lamps. Since the bridegroom was long delayed, they all became drowsy and fell asleep. At midnight, there was a cry, 'Behold, the bridegroom! Come out to meet him!' Then all those virgins got up and trimmed their lamps. The foolish ones said to the wise, 'Give us some of your oil, for our lamps are going out.' But the wise ones replied, 'No, for there may not be enough for us and you. Go instead to the merchants and buy some for yourselves.' While they went off to buy it, the bridegroom came and those who were ready went into the wedding feast with him. Then the door was locked. Afterwards the other virgins came and said, 'Lord, Lord, open the door for us!' But he said in reply, 'Amen, I say to you, I do not know you.' Therefore, stay awake, for you know neither the day nor the hour."

✜ Understanding the Word

Israel's wisdom tradition is a compilation of the insights gleaned from reflection on life experience. The book of Wisdom makes a bold claim, namely, that Wisdom is perceived by those who love her, found by those who search for her. Actually, one's love of and search for Wisdom are evidence that one is already wise. It should be noted that while people search for Wisdom, Wisdom is also in search of them, moving through the highways and byways of life. Those who find Wisdom find peace and security, meaning and fulfillment. And once she has been found, one will be able to see her everywhere.

The concern of early Christians over the death of some of their number suggests that they believed that living the new life in Christ would exempt them from physical death. Thus they questioned both the authenticity of the faith of the deceased and the trustworthiness of this new life. Paul seeks to encourage those struggling with the death of a loved one and with questions of faith. He explains that those truly joined to Jesus are delivered from the power of death, for not even death can separate them from the love of Christ. Finally, at the end of time, all believers will be decisively joined with the Lord.

The parable of the ten virgins is told against the background of Palestinian wedding customs. Several features of the parable mark its end-of-time character. The most obvious are the banquet itself and the idea of waiting in darkness for an event to occur without knowing exactly when it will come to pass. The difference between the virgins is their preparedness. Half of them made provision for the possible delay of the bridegroom, the other half did not. This parable recounts the passage from the present age to the age of fulfillment. One is either ready to cross that threshold, or one is not. Jesus' exhortation is simple but strong: Be alert!

✢ *Reflecting on the Word*

At first hearing, there is a worrisome note in this parable Jesus tells near the end of Matthew's account of his ministry. We like to think of Jesus as the Lord of second chances, even third and fourth, and that we have plenty of time to get our act together and to gather the necessary "oil" to welcome him when he returns. But the bridegroom's final words are, "I do not know you."

Is Jesus indicating that a day will come when that opportunity to make up for what we have failed to do will not be given, that the time for springing into action will have come and gone? Could we find ourselves locked out of the party? Since most of us are sometimes foolish, sometimes wise, what form does foolishness take in our lives? What are we putting off doing?

Matthew uses this parable to fire up his community's desire for the return of the Lord, to call them to a more active hope in Jesus' return. It also serves to confront indifference and lethargy in our lives. That necessary oil can refer to doing those good works that allow the light to shine in the world, especially when darkness threatens.

Being wise means being prepared for a future with the Lord. Jesus is the Wisdom of God who gives us a share of this wisdom as a gift of the Spirit. Let us both seek wisdom and be prepared to welcome it when it comes to us.

✢ *Consider/Discuss*

- Do you identify with either the wise or foolish?
- How do you understand the call to "stay awake"?
- Do you consider yourself a person who seeks Wisdom?

✢ *Responding to the Word*

We pray for the gift of wisdom, to be seekers of wisdom, and that in our seeking, Wisdom will find us. We pray for the virtue of hope, which is grounded in the belief that Jesus will indeed come again, like a bridegroom, like a thief in the night, like the Son of Man in power and glory.

November 13, 2011

THIRTY-THIRD SUNDAY IN ORDINARY TIME

Today's Focus: How Are Your Investments Doing?

To whom much is given, much will be expected. We are to make a return from what has been entrusted to us. Using our time well means that we take what God has given to us, that precious possession of faith in Jesus Christ, and do something with it. Invest wisely!

FIRST READING
Proverbs 31:10–13, 19–20, 30–31

When one finds a worthy wife,
    her value is far beyond pearls.
Her husband, entrusting his heart to her,
    has an unfailing prize.
She brings him good, and not evil,
    all the days of her life.
She obtains wool and flax
    and works with loving hands.
She puts her hands to the distaff,
    and her fingers ply the spindle.
She reaches out her hands to the poor,
    and extends her arms to the needy.
Charm is deceptive and beauty fleeting;
    the woman who fears the LORD is to be praised.
Give her a reward for her labors,
    and let her works praise her at the city gates.

PSALM RESPONSE
Psalm 128:1a

Blessed are those who fear the Lord.

SECOND READING
1 Thessalonians 5:1–6

Concerning times and seasons, brothers and sisters, you have no need for anything to be written to you. For you yourselves know very well that the day of the Lord will come like a thief at night. When people are saying, "Peace and security," then sudden disaster comes upon them, like labor pains upon a pregnant woman, and they will not escape.

But you, brothers and sisters, are not in darkness, for that day to overtake you like a thief. For all of you are children of the light and children of the day. We are not of the night or of darkness. Therefore, let us not sleep as the rest do, but let us stay alert and sober.

In the shorter form of the reading, the passages in brackets are omitted.

GOSPEL
Matthew
25:14–30
or 25:14–15,
19–21

Jesus told his disciples this parable: "A man going on a journey called in his servants and entrusted his possessions to them. To one he gave five talents; to another, two; to a third, one—to each according to his ability. Then he went away. [Immediately the one who received five talents went and traded with them, and made another five. Likewise, the one who received two made another two. But the man who received one went off and dug a hole in the ground and buried his master's money.]

After a long time the master of those servants came back and settled accounts with them. The one who had received five talents came forward bringing the additional five. He said, 'Master, you gave me five talents. See, I have made five more.' His master said to him, 'Well done, my good and faithful servant. Since you were faithful in small matters, I will give you great responsibilities. Come, share your master's joy.' [Then the one who had received two talents also came forward and said, 'Master, you gave me two talents. See, I have made two more.' His master said to him, 'Well done, my good and faithful servant. Since you were faithful in small matters, I will give you great responsibilities. Come, share your master's joy.' Then the one who had received the one talent came forward and said, 'Master, I knew you were a demanding person, harvesting where you did not plant and gathering where you did not scatter; so out of fear I went off and buried your talent in the ground. Here it is back.' His master said to him in reply, 'You wicked, lazy servant! So you knew that I harvest where I did not plant and gather where I did not scatter? Should you not then have put my money in the bank so that I could have got it back with interest on my return? Now then! Take the talent from him and give it to the one with ten. For to everyone who has, more will be given and he will grow rich; but from the one who has not, even what he has will be taken away. And throw this useless servant into the darkness outside, where there will be wailing and grinding of teeth.' "]

❖ Understanding the Word

The woman in the poem from Proverbs is traditionally described as virtuous or worthy. However, the adjective in Hebrew has a much stronger sense. It denotes might or strength, the kind of valor found in armies. It is in this sense that the woman is worthy. This woman is extraordinary, not because valiant women cannot be found, but that among all valiant women this one is remarkable. She exemplifies virtues such as self-sufficiency, industry, versatility, trustworthiness, constancy, and general goodness. She is virtuous and successful because she possesses the wisdom that flows from fear of the Lord. Among all women, the one who fears the Lord is truly valiant.

The mysterious "day of the Lord" will be a day of rejoicing for the righteous, but one of sorrow for the wicked. Paul employs two powerful metaphors to describe this day. Its unexpected nature resembles a thief in the night; the suffering that accompanies it is referred to as "the birth pangs of the messiah." Paul uses the light-darkness, day-night dichotomies to describe both the situation in which the Thessalonians find themselves and the vigilance that this situation demands. As children of light and of the day, they must be alert, always on the watch so that when the day of the Lord comes, they are not found unprepared.

The parable in today's Gospel throws light on the meaning of preparedness. It is not a disposition of passive waiting or non-engagement because of the fear of possible failure. Rather, the preparedness rewarded here stems from the realization that one is a steward of the goods of another, and knowing the disposition of that other, one seeks to maximize the potential of those goods. The time of waiting is a period of opportunity, of active engagement, of creative growth. One's future salvation does not rest on the extent or quality of one's talent, but on how one utilizes that talent as one waits for the master to return.

❖ Reflecting on the Word

A song in the musical *Scottsboro Boys* observes that life is what we do while we're waiting to die. And this is how our life passes by. Today's parable calls for a more purposeful approach: life calls for investing what God has entrusted to you.

A "talent" was a year's wages. Jesus uses this parable to warn his followers that they are to spend their time wisely while waiting for him to return. They will do this by investing the treasure God has given them. Jesus was not talking here about natural talents, though that is a worthy enterprise. But a disciple of Jesus is to do something with the treasure of the gospel, the good news of the kingdom of God, the gift of faith in Jesus Christ.

God expects a return on this investment with us. We are to share the Good News with others, not keep it to ourselves. The gospel is the greatest treasure we have been given. We might feel we have only a limited understanding of our faith, but we are not to bury it in silence. Rather, plant the seed of God's word in the minds and hearts of others.

Our first reading about a "worthy wife" describes a person who invests in living life for others. She is also called the "capable wife" or the wife with a capacity for wisdom. The beginning of wisdom is fear of the Lord, honoring God by what we do in the world. Spend the time wisely while waiting for the Lord to return.

- How is Jesus like and unlike this master?
- What aspects of the gospel do you recognize as a treasure?
- How do you invest your understanding of the gospel in life?

❖ *Responding to the Word*

We pray for the wisdom to be children of the light, bringing the gospel to others, especially during times when darkness threatens and people act out of fear. We ask to be ready to welcome Jesus when he comes and asks us to render an account, so we might enter into his joy.

November 20, 2011

THIRTY-FOURTH SUNDAY IN ORDINARY TIME
THE SOLEMNITY OF OUR LORD JESUS CHRIST THE KING

Today's Focus: Dividing Day

The last Sunday of the liturgical year directs our attention to the last day, the end of time, when we will be held accountable for what we did and did not do. This is the day we acknowledge in the Creed: he will come again to judge the living and the dead.

FIRST READING
Ezekiel 34: 11–12, 15–17

Thus says the Lord GOD: I myself will look after and tend my sheep. As a shepherd tends his flock when he finds himself among his scattered sheep, so will I tend my sheep. I will rescue them from every place where they were scattered when it was cloudy and dark. I myself will pasture my sheep; I myself will give them rest, says the Lord GOD. The lost I will seek out, the strayed I will bring back, the injured I will bind up, the sick I will heal, but the sleek and the strong I will destroy, shepherding them rightly.

As for you, my sheep, says the Lord GOD, I will judge between one sheep and another, between rams and goats.

PSALM RESPONSE
Psalm 23:1

The Lord is my shepherd; there is nothing I shall want.

SECOND READING
1 Corinthians 15:20–26, 28

Brothers and sisters: Christ has been raised from the dead, the firstfruits of those who have fallen asleep. For since death came through man, the resurrection of the dead came also through man. For just as in Adam all die, so too in Christ shall all be brought to life, but each one in proper order: Christ the firstfruits; then, at his coming, those who belong to Christ; then comes the end, when he hands over the kingdom to his God and Father, when he has destroyed every sovereignty and every authority and power. For he must reign until he has put all his enemies under his feet. The last enemy to be destroyed is death. When everything is subjected to him, then the Son himself will also be subjected to the one who subjected everything to him, so that God may be all in all.

GOSPEL
Matthew
25:31–46

Jesus said to his disciples: "When the Son of Man comes in his glory, and all the angels with him, he will sit upon his glorious throne, and all the nations will be assembled before him. And he will separate them one from another, as a shepherd separates the sheep from the goats. He will place the sheep on his right and the goats on his left. Then the king will say to those on his right, 'Come, you who are blessed by my Father. Inherit the kingdom prepared for you from the foundation of the world. For I was hungry and you gave me food, I was thirsty and you gave me drink, a stranger and you welcomed me, naked and you clothed me, ill and you cared for me, in prison and you visited me.' Then the righteous will answer him and say, 'Lord, when did we see you hungry and feed you, or thirsty and give you drink? When did we see you a stranger and welcome you, or naked and clothe you? When did we see you ill or in prison, and visit you?' And the king will say to them in reply, 'Amen, I say to you, whatever you did for one of the least brothers of mine, you did for me.' Then he will say to those on his left, 'Depart from me, you accursed, into the eternal fire prepared for the devil and his angels. For I was hungry and you gave me no food, I was thirsty and you gave me no drink, a stranger and you gave me no welcome, naked and you gave me no clothing, ill and in prison, and you did not care for me.' Then they will answer and say, 'Lord, when did we see you hungry or thirsty or a stranger or naked or ill or in prison, and not minister to your needs?' He will answer them, 'Amen, I say to you, what you did not do for one of these least ones, you did not do for me.' And these will go off to eternal punishment, but the righteous to eternal life."

❖ Understanding the Word

The image of the good shepherd aptly characterizes God's concern and personal intervention in the shepherding of the flock. The first reading describes how God fulfills the role of shepherd primarily in two ways: by caring for the sheep and by separating the good from the bad. Those who were responsible for the sheep failed to carry out their responsibilities. They were not attentive to their charges and so the owner of the flock steps in to shepherd the flock personally. The rest of the oracle of salvation confirms this. The final scene is one of judgment, an appropriate theme for the last Sunday of the liturgical year.

Paul brings together several of his most treasured themes: the effectiveness of Christ's resurrection, human solidarity in Adam and in Christ, the sequence of events surrounding the end of time, the victory of Christ, and the ultimate reign of God. The reading carries us back through time to the primordial period of beginnings, and then forward to the end of time and the eschatological age of fulfillment. Every aspect of these events is grounded in the resurrection of Christ. At the final consummation, God will be all in all. All came from God; all returns to God. At the end, all purposes will be realized. All reality will have come home.

The scene of the Last Judgment as it unfolds before us today is both sobering and surprising. It is a scene of apocalyptic splendor and majesty, a scene of separation of the righteous from the unrighteous, a scene of reward and punishment. The image of the shepherd separating the sheep from goats would have been quite familiar to Jesus' original audience. What is surprising is the reason given for the judgment. It is not the accomplishment of some phenomenal feat. Rather, people are judged on whether or not they meet the very basic human needs of others. The scene is sobering because one gets the sense that there is no way of escaping it.

✤ Reflecting on the Word

Every so often when I am driving, I see that old bumper sticker calling us to commit random acts of kindness. Good advice in light of the story of the Last Judgment. Did you notice that the story makes no mention of many of the sins we usually worry about as the basis for the Last Judgment? This is not to say such things don't matter. But the emphasis here has to do with getting out there and responding to people really in need, basic needs relating to hunger, thirst, being a stranger—an unwelcome immigrant? (that one is certainly ripped from today's headlines!)—lacking clothes, needing health care (another relevant one), and being imprisoned.

While it is always interesting to watch other people being judged, it is not something most of us enjoy experiencing ourselves—especially when it comes to evaluating our moral lives. It is much easier to think of Jesus as the forgiving, compassionate, tender shepherd who is out there looking for us than as the one who comes in glory to judge and separate out the goats and the lambs. Who wants to be counted among the goats?

So, pick your area that will help you to be counted among the sheep. Food distribution, environmental concerns, immigration reform, clothing—include here those nets that can save lives threatened by various issues surrounding health care, or prison reform. Perhaps you thought this was one of those quaint stories Jesus tells that seem so long ago and far away. The last we hear from the Gospel of Matthew for this year invites your participation—*now*. The reason? When you do something for them, you do it for him.

✤ Consider/Discuss

- Have you had any experiences of being judged that proved helpful?
- Can you bring together images of Jesus as both shepherd and judge?
- Can you hear in today's Gospel an invitation to a fuller life?

✤ Responding to the Word

We pray with confidence to the Father to whom all things will be handed over by Christ, the new Adam, through whom we have become children of the kingdom. We ask the Spirit to teach us to recognize the freedom that comes from subjecting ourselves to God's rule and serving, as Christ served, those most in need.

Dianne Bergant, C.S.A., is Professor of Biblical Studies at Catholic Theological Union in Chicago. She holds master's and doctoral degrees in scripture studies from St. Louis University. She was president of the Catholic Biblical Association of America (2000–2001) and has been an active member of the Chicago Catholic/Jewish Scholars Dialogue for the past twenty years. For more than fifteen years, she was the Old Testament book reviewer of *The Bible Today*. Bergant was a member of the editorial board of that magazine for twenty-five years, five of those years as the magazine's general editor. She is now on the editorial board of *Biblical Theology Bulletin* and *Chicago Studies*. From 2002 through 2005, she wrote the weekly column "The Word" for *America* magazine.

James A. Wallace, C.Ss.R., is professor of homiletics at the Washington Theological Union, Washington, D.C. He is the author of *Preaching to the Hungers of the Heart* (Liturgical Press, 2002) and co-author of three books of homilies, *Lift Up Your Hearts: Homilies for the A, B, and C Cycles* (Paulist Press 2004, 2005, and 2006). He has served as president of the Academy of Homiletics, the Catholic Association of Teachers of Homiletics, and the Religious Speech Communication Association. His articles have appeared in various journals, and he has lectured on preaching in this country, Europe, and Asia.